Study Guide and Worki

for use with

Advanced Accounting

Seventh Edition

Joe B. Hoyle
University of Richmond

Thomas Schaefer
University of Notre Dame

Timothy Doupnik
University of South Carolina

Prepared by
Richard Rand
Tennessee Technological University

 Irwin

Boston   Burr Ridge, IL   Dubuque, IA   Madison, WI   New York   San Francisco   St. Louis
Bangkok   Bogotá   Caracas   Kuala Lumpur   Lisbon   London   Madrid   Mexico City
Milan   Montreal   New Delhi   Santiago   Seoul   Singapore   Sydney   Taipei   Toronto

Study Guide and Working Papers for use with
FUNDAMENTALS OF ADVANCED ACCOUNTING, SEVENTH EDITION
Hoyle, Schaefer, and Doupnik

Published by McGraw-Hill/Irwin, an imprint of The McGraw-Hill Companies, Inc., 1221 Avenue of the Americas, New York, NY 10020. Copyright © 2004, 2001, 1998, 1994, 1991, 1987, 1984 by The McGraw-Hill Companies, Inc. All rights reserved.

2 3 4 5 6 7 8 9 0 2QPD/2QPD 0 9 8 7 6 5 4

ISBN 0-07-283499-4

TABLE OF CONTENTS

Chapter 1

The Equity Method of Accounting for Investments
Chapter Outline

I. Reporting Investments in Corporate Equity Securities - The method used to account for a particular investment depends on the degree of influence the investor (stockholder) is able to exercise over the investee's operating and financial policies. This influence is indicated by the relative size of ownership.

A. The **fair value method** (*SFAS 115*, "*Accounting for Certain Investments in Debt and Equity Securities*," effective for fiscal years beginning after December 15, 1993), *SFAS 115* – which supersedes *SFAS 112* – does not apply to investments in equity securities accounted for under the equity method nor to investments in consolidated subsidiaries.

   1. *SFAS 115* is applied when the investor **lacks the ability** to significantly influence the investee's financial and operating policies. As a rule of thumb, this situation occurs when the investor owns **less than 20%** of a corporation's outstanding voting common stock.

   2. *SFAS 115* requires an enterprise to classify debt and equity securities into one of three categories *when significant influence is not present*: (1) trading securities, (2) available-for-sale securities, or (3) held-to-maturity securities. For all three categories of investments, dividend and interest income (including amortization of the premium or discount at acquisition) continue to be included in earnings.

      a. *Trading securities* — Investments in debt and equity securities that are purchased and held principally for the purpose of selling them in the near term are reported at fair value. Unrealized holding gains and losses are included in **earnings**.

      b. *Available-for-sale securities* — Debt and equity securities not assigned to another category are classified under this category. Such securities are reported at fair value, but unrealized holding gains and losses (net of income tax effects) are reported **as a separate component of stockholders' equity** until realized.

      c. *Held-to-maturity securities* — Debt securities meeting the requirements of this category are reported at amortized cost. Debt securities not included in this category and equity securities with readily determinable market values are classified as either trading or available-for-sale securities.

B. Consolidation of Financial Statements (*ARB 51*) – Consolidation is required when the investor controls another entity, usually through ownership of a majority (more than 50%) of the other entity's equity. When a parent/subsidiary relationship exists, the parent corporation must prepare *consolidated financial statements*.

C.   Equity method (*APB Opinion 18, FASB Interpretation 35* and *SFAS 142*) - The equity method is used when the investor's ownership interest gives it the ability to influence the investee's financial and operating policies. This is the lone parameter for mandating the equity method. Determining the investor's ability to exercise such influence is not always a clear-cut decision. Therefore, judgment is essential in appraising the status of each investment.

1.   To attain uniformity in application, the equity method is assumed to be appropriate if the investor owns 20% to 50% of the investee's outstanding voting stock. This assumption can be overcome by prevailing evidence to the contrary.

2.   An understanding of the equity method is best gained by initially examining the APB's treatment of two questions:

   a.   What parameters identify the area of ownership where the equity method is applicable?

   b.   How should the investor report this investment and the income generated by it to reflect the relationship between the two companies?

3.   *APB Opinion 18* furnishes direction to the accountant by listing several conditions that indicate the presence of the required degree of influence:

   a.   Investor representation on the board of directors of the investee.

   b.   Investor participation in the policy-making process of the investee.

   c.   Material intercompany transactions.

   d.   Interchange of managerial personnel.

   e.   Technological dependency.

   f.   Extent of ownership by the investor in relation to the size and concentration of other ownership interests in the investee.

4.   *Interpretation 35* states that the equity method is not appropriate for investments that manifest any of the following characteristics regardless of the investor's degree of ownership:

   a.   An agreement exists between investor and investee whereby the investor surrenders significant rights as a shareholder.

   b.   A concentration of ownership operates the investee without regard for the views of the investor.

   c.   The investor attempts but fails to obtain representation on the investee's board of directors.

II. Accounting for an Investment Using the Equity Method - In applying the equity method, the accounting objective is to report the investor's investment in a way that reflects the close relationship between the companies.

A. The investor maintains the following two accounts when using the equity method:

   1. Investment in S Company — balance sheet account

   2. Equity in Investee Income — income statement account

B. Once equity method application guidelines have been established, the process for recording the basic transactions is straightforward — the book value of the investment account is adjusted to reflect all changes in the book value of the investee's net assets.

   1. The investor accrues its percentage of the earnings reported by the investee each period by making the following entry:

Investment in S Company	XX	
Equity in Investee Income		XX

   2. Exceptions to the above entry — the investor's share of (a) extraordinary items and (b) prior-period adjustments, if material, should be disclosed separately in the income statement.

   3. Dividends received from the investee reduce the investment balance to reflect the decrease in the investee's book value, and the investor records the dividends received from the investee by making the following entry:

Cash	XX	
Investment in S Company		XX

C. The investor reports a change to the equity method when the ability to significantly influence an investee is achieved through a series of acquisitions. *APB Opinion 18* directs the investor to make a *retroactive* adjustment to convert all previously reported figures to the equity method at the time the equity method becomes applicable.

   1. This restatement establishes comparability between the financial statements of all years, as the investor makes the following entry:

Investment in S Company	XX	
Retained Earnings — Prior Period Adjustment		
— Equity in Investee Income..................		XX

   2. An adjustment must be made to remove the accounts required by *SFAS 115* that pertain to the investment prior to the obtaining of significant influence. The investor would make the following entry:

Unrealized Holding Gain — Shareholders' Equity...	XX	
Fair Value Adjustment (Available for Sale)......		XX

D. The parent's percentage of a loss incurred by the investee is recognized immediately by the investor with the carrying value of the investment account also being reduced.

   1. When a *permanent* decline in an equity method's value occurs, the investor must reduce the asset's balance to fair market value, but *APB Opinion 18* emphasizes that this loss must be permanent before such recognition is applied.

   2. At the point at which an investment account is reduced to zero by accumulated losses, the investor should stop using the equity method, rather than establish a negative balance.

E. If the investor sells all or part of its holdings in the investee, the equity method is applied until the transaction date, thus establishing an appropriate carrying value for the investment.

   1. The investor initially makes the following two journal entries to (1) record the investor's share of the investee's income for the period and (2) to record the receipt of dividends from the investee.

Investment in S Company	XX	
Equity in Investee Income		XX

Cash	XX	
Investment in S Company		XX

   2. The sale of the shares would be recorded with an entry such as the following:

Cash	XX	
Investment in S Company		XX
Gain on Sale of Investment		XX

   3. The credit to the investment account is based on the percentage of the investor's interest that is sold. For example, if the investor holds 40,000 shares of the investee's common voting shares, and subsequently sells 4,000 of those shares, then the investor would remove 10% (4,000 shares ÷ 40,000 shares) of the investment account.

   4. If the shares were sold at a loss, the account Loss on Sale of Investment would be debited rather than Gain on Sale of Investment being credited. If only part of the total shares were sold, the investor would continue to apply the equity method to the remainder of the investment as long as it could exercise significant influence over the investee.

III. Excess of Investment Cost over Book Value Acquired

    A.   The investor's purchase price (cost) seldom equals the underlying book value of the investee company's net assets, and the fair market value of the investee's net assets usually differ from their book value.

    B.   The cost of the acquisition of an interest in another company that achieves significant influence or control can be deconstructed into four basic components:

        1.   the investor's share of the book value of the investee's net assets at the acquisition date,

        2.   the investor's share of the excess of fair market value over book value of specific identifiable assets and liabilities, and

        3.   allocation of a portion of remaining excess over book value to identifiable, separable intangible assets not previously recorded. These intangible assets are representative of such things as name recognition, a loyal customer base, a well-trained work force, a valuable data base, or good labor/management relations.

        4.   Goodwill (excess of cost over fair market value of the investee's identifiable net assets and indentifiable and separable intangible assets not previously recorded) is an intangible asset that represents the previously unrecorded market value of the investee that is not separable.

    C.   It is important to realize that the investor does not show these individual amounts on its books. The fair market adjustments and other intangible assets are inferred from the Investment in Investee account. However, while these adjustments, other intangible assets and goodwill are not shown separately on the investor's books, the amounts must be tracked so that amortization amounts for the fair market value adjustments and the other intangible assets can be computed and recorded.

    D.   Except for land (which is never amortized or depreciated) and goodwill (which is not amortized in accordance with SFAS No. 142), amounts allocated to accounts having limited useful lives must be amortized by the investor.

        1.   If the investor is unable to relate the excess of cost over book value to the investee's specific accounts, the investor should then try to identify other separable intangible assets. These should be amortized over their expected useful lives.

        2.   Any remaining residual should be recorded as goodwill.

        3.   As mentioned earlier, the amortization process relates to assets held by the investee, the investor does not establish specific expense accounts. Therefore, the investor makes the following entry:

                Equity in Investee Income XX
                      Investment in S Company XX

IV. Elimination of Unrealized Gains in Inventory

    A.   Gains derived from intercompany transactions are not considered to be completely earned until the transferred goods are either consumed or resold to unrelated parties.}

    B.   *Downstream* sales of inventory relate to transfers made by the investor to the investee.

        1.   Any unrealized intercompany gain or loss resulting from the intercompany sale, and remaining on the books of the investor at the end of the period, is deferred at the end of the period. It is subsequently recognized as income at the time of the inventory's eventual disposal when applying the equity method.

        2.   The amount of the gain or loss to be deferred is equal to the investor's ownership percentage multiplied by the markup on the merchandise remaining at the end of the year.

            a.   An alternative five-step approach can also be used:

                i.   Compute the amount of intercompany gain present in the original transfer.

                ii.   Determine the percent of the transferred inventory that is still present as of the end of the period.

                iii.   Multiply Step 1 × Step 2 to determine the unrealized portion of the intercompany gain or loss.

                iv.   Determine the percentage of the investee owned by the investor.

                v.   Multiply Step 3 × Step 4 to determine the amount of the unrealized, intercompany gain that must be deferred.

        3.   At the end of the period of transfer, the following entry is made on the investor's books:

            Equity in Investee Income XX
                Investment in S Company XX

        4.   In the period when the remaining transferred inventory is sold to a third party, the remaining unrealized intercompany profit is recognized with the following entry:

            Investment in S Company XX
                Equity in Investee Income XX

    C.   *Upstream* sales of inventory relate to transfers made by the investee to the investor and are treated just the same as downstream sales.

Multiple Choice Questions

1. On January 1, 2003, Swanson Company buys 200,000 shares of Booker, Inc.'s common stock for $1,200,000, the book value of the shares. This purchase gave Swanson 40% ownership in Booker and the ability to significantly influence operating and financing decisions. During 2003, Booker reported net income of $400,000 and paid a $1.25 per share dividend. What is the balance in the Investment in Booker account in the records of Swanson Company at December 31, 2003?

   A. $1,160,000
   B. $1,420,000
   C. $1,110,000
   D. $1,350,000
   E. $1,200,000

2. Tara Company owns 20% of Hawkins, Inc. and applies the equity method. During the current year, Tara buys inventory costing $100,000 and sells it to Hawkins for $125,000. At the end of the year, only 25% of this merchandise (at the transfer price) is still being held by Hawkins. What amount of unrealized gain must be deferred by Tara in reporting on the equity method?

   A. $25,000
   B. $ 1,250
   C. $ 5,000
   D. $ 6,250
   E. $ 3,750

3. What is a downstream sale?

   A. A sale from an investor to its investee
   B. A sale from a producer to its outside supplier
   C. A sale from an investee to its investor
   D. A sale from one manufacturer to another
   E. A sale from a small company to a large one

4. TunaCo purchases 30% of Stanley, Inc. on January 1, 2003 for $1,000,000. This acquisition gives TunaCo the ability to apply significant influence to Stanley's operating and financing policies. Stanley reports assets on that date of $2,500,000 with liabilities of $300,000. One building with a 10-year remaining useful life has a book value of $400,000 and a fair market value of $550,000. During 2003, Stanley reports net income of $340,000 while paying dividends of $150,000. What is the Investment in Stanley account balance in TunaCo' accounting records at December 31, 2003?

   A. $1,000,000
   B. $ 947,500
   C. $ 952,000
   D. $1,185,500
   E. $1,052,500

5. Smith Company holds 20% of the outstanding shares of Leef Cards and appropriately applies the equity method of accounting. For 2004, Leef reports earnings of $100,000 and pays cash dividends of $22,000. During the year, Leef acquired inventory for $80,000, which was then sold to Smith for $100,000. At the end of 2001, Smith continues to hold merchandise with a transfer price of $40,000. Assuming no amortization expense related to this investment, what *Equity in Investee Income* should Smith report in 2004?

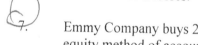

A. $18,400
B. $ -0-
C. $12,000
D. $14,000
E. $ 7,600

6. Norbin Company uses the equity method to account for its investment in Stice Company's common stock. After the acquisition date, the investment account reported on Norbin's balance sheet would

A. be increased by Norbin's share of Stice's earnings and decreased by Norbin's share of Stice's losses.
B. be increased by Norbin's share of Stice's earnings but not be affected by Norbin's share of Stice's losses.
C. not be affected by Norbin's share of Stice's earnings and losses.
D. not be affected by Norbin's share of Stice's earnings but be decreased by Norbin's share of Stice's losses.
E. be decreased by Norbin's share of Stice's earnings and increased by Norbin's share of Stice's losses.

7. Emmy Company buys 25% of Soupy, Inc's common stock on January 1, 2003 for $440,000. The equity method of accounting is to be used. Soupy's net assets on that date totaled $1,100,000. All of the excess of cost over book value is attributed to a copyright owned by Soupy, which is amortized over ten years. Soupy immediately begins selling inventory to Emmy as follows:

Year	Cost to Soupy	Transfer Price	Amount Held by Emmy at Year End (at Transfer Price)
2003	$ 50,000	$ 120,000	$ 24,000
2004	100,000	200,000	80,000

Inventory held at the end of one year is sold at the beginning of the next. Soupy reports net income of $110,000 in 2003 and $150,000 in 2004 while paying $50,000 in dividends each year. What is *Equity in Soupy's Income* to be reported by Emmy in 2004?

A. $27,500
B. $31,000
C. $11,000
D. $17.500
E. $14,500

8. Generally, what percentage of another company's stock must be owned to cause us to change our method of accounting for the investment from the Fair Value Method to the Equity Method?

   A. 10%
   B. 20%
   C. 25%
   D. 51%
   E. 100%

9. Which of the following is the best theoretical justification for consolidated financial statements?

   A. In form the companies are separate; in substance they are one entity.
   B. In form the companies are one entity; in substance they are separate.
   C. In form and substance the companies are one entity.
   D. In form and substance the companies are separate entities.
   E. Consolidation is required by federal law.

10. Which one of the following statements is **incorrect**?

    A. The equity method reflects the accrual basis of accounting.
    B. The concept of significant influence applies to the equity method but not to the cost method.
    C. If a company exercises significant influence over another company, consolidated financial statements are usually required.
    D. The equity method is a departure from the historical cost method.
    E. The concept of controlling interest applies to the equity method but not to the cost method.

Brief Essay Questions

1. How should amortization of the investor's share of the excess of cost over book value of the investee's net assets at the date of purchase be recorded in the investor's accounting records?

2. The equity method of accounting requires the investor to accrue income when it is earned by the investee. What are the theoretical problems that opponents of the equity method are quick to mention in regard to the recognition of equity income?

3. Under what conditions can a company hold 30% of another company's common voting stock and still not have significant influence?

4. Exactly what is Goodwill? When do we record it, and what does it represent?

Problems

1.   Pees Inc. purchased 80,000 shares of Q-Corp's 320,000 outstanding shares for $4.20 per share. As a result of this purchase, Pees was able to place one of its managers on the Q-Corp's board of directors. At the time of the acquisition on January 1, 2004, the book value of Q-Corp's net assets was $1,210,000, which approximated their fair market value. During 2004, Q-Corp earned $60,000 of net income and paid a $.15 per share dividend.

Required:

   A.   Provide the entry to be made by Pees to record its investment in Q-Corp.

   B.   Provide the entries which Pees should make to record the income resulting from its investment in Q-Corp and the dividends received from Q-Corp.

   C.   What should the appropriate year-end balance be in Pees' Investment in Q-Corp account?

2.   In January 2003, Clark Corporation acquired 40% of the outstanding common stock of Lois Company for $300,000. This investment provided Clark with the ability to exercise significant influence over Lois. The book value of Lois on the acquisition date was $500,000. Lois' primary asset was a patent having a book value of $200,000 and a fair market value of $400,000. The patent has a remaining useful life of ten years.

For the year ended December 31, 2003, Lois reported net income of $62,000 and paid cash dividends of $30,000 on its common stock.

Required:

What is the carrying value of Clark's investment in Lois at December 31, 2003?

3.   Oregon Corp. purchased a 30% interest in Maine Corp. on January 1, 2003. At the time, the book value of Maine Corp.'s net assets equaled the purchase price which Oregon Corp. paid. During 2003, Oregon Corp. sold inventory costing $40,000 to Maine Corp. for $60,000. At the end of 2003, Maine Corp. still had $15,000 of the inventory purchased from Oregon Corp. on hand. Maine Corp. reported net income of $72,000 for 2000 and paid no dividends.

Required:

   A.   What entries should be made on the books of Oregon Corp. by the end of 2003 as a result of the inventory sale to Maine Corp.?

   B.   What entry should also be made in 2004 as a result of the 2003 sale?

Advanced Accounting – 7/e

Solutions to Multiple Choice Questions

1. **C**
   Cost of purchase $1,200,000
   + Income accrual ($400,000 x 40%)   160,000
   - Dividend received (200,000 x $1.25)   (250,000)
   = Investment in Booker Company $1,110,000

   [handwritten: 200K, 16K, 155K]

2. **B**
   Inventory at year-end ($125,000 x .25) $ 31,250.00
   Gross profit markup ($25,000 ÷ $125,000)   × .20
   Unrealized gain $ 6,250.00
   Ownership share   × .20
   Intercompany unrealized gain — deferred $ 1,250.00

3. **A**

4. **E**

   Goodwill Computation

	%	BV		Useful Life	At 12/31/2003
TunaCo's Cost			1,000,000		
Stanley's Book Value	30.00%	2,200,000	660,000		
Difference			340,000		
Building	30.00%	150,000	45,000	10	4,500
Goodwill			295,000	N/A	-
Total Amortization					4,500

   Cost of purchase $1,000,000
   Income accrued ($340,000 x 30%)   102,000
   Annual amortization   (4,500)
   Dividend received ($150,000 x 30%)   (45,000)
   Investment in Stanley $1,052,500

5. **A**
   Remaining year-end inventory $ 40,000.00
   Gross profit markup ($20,000 ÷ $100,000)   × .20
   Profit in remaining inventory $ 8,000.00
   Ownership share   × 20%
   Unrealized intercompany gain $ 1,600.00

   Equity in income accrual ($100,000 x 20%) $ 20,000.00
   Unrealized intercompany gain (see above)   - (1,600.00)
   Equity in investee income $ 18,400.00

6. **A.**

7. **E**

Purchase price of Soupy stock	$ 440,000
Soupy's book value ($1,100,000 x 25%)	- (275,000)
Copyright	= 165,000
Life of copyright in years	÷ 10
Annual copyright amortization	$ 16,500

2003 % of Inventory on Hand = $24,000 ÷ $120,000 = 20%
2004 % of Inventory on Hand = $80,000 ÷ $200,000 = 40%

Income accrual ($150,000 x 25%)	$ 37,500
Annual copyright amortization	(16,500)
Recognition of 2003 unrealized gain ($70,000 x 20% x 25%)	3,500
Deferral of 2004 unrealized gain ($100,000 x 40% x 25%)	(10,000)
Equity income in Soupy Company	$ 14,500

8. **B**

9. **A**

10. **C**

Answers to Brief Essay Questions

1. The investor should report the amortization of the excess of cost over book value as an adjustment of its *Equity in Investee Income* account.

2. The equity method has been criticized because it allows the investor to recognize income that may or may not be received in any usable form during the foreseeable future. Income is accrued based on the investee's reported earnings and not the dividends received by the investor. Frequently, equity income will exceed the cash dividends received by the investor with no assurance that the difference will ever be forthcoming.

3. Several conditions can exist that would prevent "significant influence" from being present when 30% of the investee's stock is owned by the investor. First, the presence of a majority stockholder (50% or greater) would preclude any significant influence on the investor's part. Second, the oversight of government authority that exercises control or influence can negate any influence the investor might have.

4. Technically, goodwill is the excess of an investment's cost over the fair market value of the identifiable net assets acquired less any amount allocated to separable, identifiable intangible assets. The intangible assets can take many forms. Examples include, name recognition, a well-trained workforce, access to an exclusive market, and many others. In a larger sense, however, the concept of goodwill represents the recognition of intangible assets that have probably existed for some time, but cannot be identified with a separable asset. It is important to remember that goodwill can only be recorded following a purchase transaction, when a historical cost can be assigned.

Solutions to Problems

1. Analysis of the purchase price:

Price paid to acquire a 25% interest (80,000 x $4.20)	$ 336,000
Book value of the interest acquired ($1,210,000 x 25%)	(302,500)
Goodwill — excess of cost over fair market value	$ 33,500

A.
Investment in Q-Corp	336,000	
Cash		336,000
To record the investment in Q-Corp		

B.
Cash	12,000	
Investment in Q-Corp		12,000
To record the receipt of dividends of $.15 per share		

Investment in Q-Corp	15,000	
Equity in Q-Corp's Income		15,000
To recognize income		

C.
Cost	$ 336,000
Investment income ($60,000 x 25%)	15,000
Dividends received (80,000 x $.15)	(12,000)
Year-end balance in Investment in Q-Corp	$ 339,000

2. The ending balance in Clark's *Investment in Lois, Inc.*

Goodwill Computation

	%	BV			
Clark's Cost			300,000		
Q-Corp 's Book Value	40.00%	500,000	200,000		
				Useful	At
Difference			100,000	Life	########
Patent	40.00%	200,000	80,000	10	8,000
Goodwill			20,000	N/A	-
Total Amortization					8,000

The investment account is = $300,000 + ($62,000 × 40%) − ($30,000 × 40%) - $8,000
= $304,800

3.
Selling price of inventory	$ 60,000
Cost of inventory	(40,000)
Profit	$ 20,000

Year-end remaining inventory	$ 15,000
Profit element ($20,000 ÷ $60,000)	× 1/3
Profit in inventory	$ 5,000
Oregon Corp.'s ownership percentage	× 30%
Profit to be deferred	$ 1,500

Maine Corp.'s net income	$ 72,000
Oregon Corp.'s ownership percentage	× 30%
Oregon's share of Maine's net income	$ 21,600

A.
    Equity in Maine Income 1,500
        Investment in Maine Corp. 1,500
      To record deferred profit

    Investment in Maine Corp. 21,600
        Equity in Maine Income 21,600
      To record share of Maine income

B.
    Investment in Maine Corp. 1,500
        Equity in Maine Income 1,500
      To reverse profit deferral

Chapter 2

Consolidation of Financial Information

Chapter Outline

I. Expansion through Corporate Takeovers

The combining of two or more businesses into a single entity under common management and ownership control is a popular economic event.

    A.   Business combinations can be part of an overall managerial strategy to maximize shareholder value.

    B.   Many business combinations share one or more of the following characteristics that potentially enhance profitability:

        1.   Vertical integration of one firm's output and another firm's distribution or further processing.

        2.   Cost savings through elimination of duplicate facilities and staff.

        3.   Quick entry for new and existing products into domestic and foreign markets.

        4.   Economies of scale allowing greater efficiency and negotiating power.

        5.   The ability to access financing at more attractive rates. As firms grow in size, negotiating power with financial institutions can grow also.

        6.   Diversification of business risk.

    C.   The principal motivations for many business combinations can be traced to an increasingly competitive environment.

II. The Consolidation Process

    A.   SFAS 141 defines a business combination: "A business combination occurs when an enterprise acquires net assets that constitute a business or equity interests of one or more other enterprises and obtains control over that enterprise or enterprises."

        1.   Statutory Merger – Any business combination in which only one of the original companies continues to exist.

            a.   One company can obtain the assets of a second company. The second company then dissolves itself, ceasing to exist.

b. One company can acquire the capital stock of a second company. The second company's assets are transferred to the acquiring company, and the acquired company is then dissolved.

2. Statutory Consolidation – Two or more companies transfer either their assets or their capital stock to a newly formed corporation.

3. Acquisition of more than 50% of the Voting Stock – One company acquires enough equity interest in a second company to exercise effective control over it. (usually this is > 50%). The "controlled" company continues to exist.

B. Control Exercised through Variable Interest Entities (VIE).

1. Special Project Entities (SPE's) take the form of a trust, partnership, joint venture, or corporation.

   a. A sponsoring company sets up the SPE to engage in a limited, well-defined set of activities.

   b. Serves as an effective way to limit risk, since the risk of loss is usually restricted to the assets of the SPE.

   c. Control of an SPE is exercised through contractual arrangements with the sponsor, referred to as the "primary beneficiary".

   d. Control was not defined by owning a controlling equity interest in the SPE.

   e. Prior to FIN 46, an SPE could be excluded from consolidation when the sponsor owned less than a controlling equity interest, even though control was effectively achieved though other means.

2. FIN 46 requires the consolidation of any SPE whose control resides with a primary beneficiary. In this circumstance, the SPE is referred to as a *Variable Interest Entity* (VIE).

3. A controlling interest in a VIE exists when the following characteristics are present:

   a. The direct or indirect ability to make decisions about the entity's activities.

   b. The obligation to absorb the expected losses of the entity if they occur, or

   c. The right to receive the expected residual returns of the entity if they occur.

III.   Procedures for Consolidating Financial Information

A.   Any time one company acquires a controlling interest in another company, either through a cash purchase or through an exchange of common shares, we should apply the Purchase Method of accounting for the combination.

    1.   A *purchase* occurs whenever one company acquires control over another.

        a.   An acquisition price is determined based on the exchange transaction, and major characteristics of a purchase combination are:

            (1)   One company can be clearly identified as the acquiring (purchasing) party; the acquisition price includes any direct costs of creating the combination.

            (2)   Stock issuance costs are recorded as a reduction in paid-in capital; they are not a component of the acquisition price.

        b.   The acquired assets and liabilities are recorded at their market values because they are being purchased.

    2.   Several relationships may exist between the acquisition price and the fair market value of the acquired company's net assets.

        a.   Purchase price = fair market value of net assets acquired

            (1)   The entire purchase price is attributed to the share of book value attained and the share of any difference between market value and book value of specifically identifiable assets acquired or liabilities assumed.

        b.   Purchase price > fair market value of the net assets acquired.

            (1)   Goodwill is recognized for the amount of excess of purchase price in excess of fair market value of identifiable net assets of the acquired company and any other previously unrecorded, separable intangible assets.

            (2)   Goodwill is a permanent asset that is not amortized per SFAS No. 142.

        c.   Purchase price < than fair market value of the net assets acquired, which is known as a *bargain purchase*. Allocation of full market values to each asset and liability is not possible, so some reduction of market values must be made. The following rules apply in a bargain purchase situation:

            (1)   All (a) current assets, (b) liabilities, and (c) assets carried at market value are recorded at their fair market value.

            (2)   The fair market values of the noncurrent assets (**other than long-term investments in marketable securities**) are decreased

proportionately. If the total fair market value of the noncurrent assets is not great enough to absorb the entire reduction, **a deferred credit balance is established**, and is reported as an extraordinary gain in accordance with SFAS No. 141.

B. Purchase method where dissolution of the acquired company takes place.

    1. The assets and liabilities being acquired are recorded by the buyer at fair market value on the date of acquisition, and a consolidation entry is made directly in the financial records of the surviving company.

    2. Whenever the purchase price exceeds the total fair market value, all of the acquired company's assets and liabilities are consolidated at fair market value with the additional payment allocated to other intangible assets and to *goodwill*.

        a. Note that the assets and liabilities of the acquired company are actually added to the books of the acquiring company by means of a journal entry, just as in any other transaction where we are purchasing assets.

    3. If the purchase price is less than the total fair market value, a *bargain purchase* exists and is accounted for using the procedures described earlier.

C. Purchase method where separate incorporation of all parties is maintained.

    1. Basic consolidation procedures are the same as when dissolution takes place, and fair market values still serve as a basis for consolidating the subsidiary's net assets.

    2. Recognition of either goodwill or a deferred credit may be necessary, depending on the purchase price.

    3. Since dissolution does not occur, independent record-keeping continues to be maintained by each company.

    4. To facilitate the preparation of consolidated financial statements, a worksheet and consolidation entries are normally utilized to simulate the consolidation process so that financial statements can be produced periodically.

    5. The consolidation entries are made only on the worksheet and do not actually change the books of either the parent company or the subsidiary.

    6. A helpful set of steps is as follows:

        a. Enter the final adjusted trial balance amounts for the Parent company on the worksheet.

        b. Enter the final adjusted trial balance amounts for the Subsidiary company on the worksheet.

c. Make an entry on the worksheet to eliminate the *Investment in Subsidiary* account.

d. Make an entry on the worksheet to eliminate the subsidiary's equity balances as of the date of acquisition.

e. Make an entry on the worksheet to establish any amounts necessary to adjust the subsidiary's assets and liabilities to fair market value and to record any previously unrecorded, separable intangible assets identified during the acquisition period.

f. Make an entry on the worksheet to establish the *Goodwill* account.

IV. Intangibles

A. SFAS 141 requires that, in an acquisition, any access of purchase price in excess of fair market value be allocated between identifiable, separable intangible assets and goodwill.

B. Amounts assigned to goodwill should be those amounts that cannot be assigned to identifiable, separable intangible assets.

C. Examples of possible intangible assets to which excess cost can be allocated are:

1. Trademarks and tradenames.

2. Internet domain names

3. Noncompetition agreements

4. Customer lists

5. Books, magazines, other literary works.

6. Musical works such as compositions, song lyrics, and advertising jingles.

7. Pictures and Photographs

8. Licensing, royalty, standstill agreements

9. Operating and broadcast rights

10. Use rights such as landing, drilling, water, air, mineral, timber cutting, and route authorities.

11. Patented and unpatented technology

12. Computer software

13. Databases

14.	Trade secrets.

V.	Unconsolidated Subsidiaries

A.	Over the years, accountants have attempted to identify situations in which consolidated financial statements might not be appropriate for every subsidiary.

B.	The FASB addressed this issue in 1987 when it issued *Statement No. 94, "Consolidation of All Majority-Owned Subsidiaries."* This pronouncement required that all companies more than 50% owned must be consolidated with the exception of the following two cases:

1.	An investment where control is only temporary – *superceded by FASB 144.*

2.	An investment where control does not actually rest with the majority owners, such as when the subsidiary is in legal reorganization, is in bankruptcy, or when severe restrictions are imposed by foreign governments which limit or remove the power held by the owners.

C.	Before the issuance of *Statement No. 94,* business combinations were permitted to exclude subsidiaries from consolidation because of nonhomogeneity.

1.	The practice was criticized over the years as an excuse for removing large amounts of debt from an entity's balance sheet.

2.	The FASB eliminated nonhomogeneity as a reason for omitting a majority-owned subsidiary from consolidation.

VI.	The Pooling of Interests Method of Accounting for Business Combinations

A.	*APB Opinion 16* reasoned that one consolidation method alone could not appropriately account for all possible combinations, therefore both the *purchase method* and the *pooling of interests method* were designated as appropriate means of reporting business combinations.

B.	In theory, a *pooling* involves *the uniting of the ownership interests of two or more companies* by exchange of equity securities so that a continuity of ownership is maintained.

1.	The underlying concept is that nothing is changed by the combination except the composition of the reporting entity.

2.	The characteristics of a pooling are fundamentally different from those attributed to a purchase.

a.	Neither party can be truly viewed as an acquiring company.

b.	Precise cost figures stemming from the exchange of securities are difficult to ascertain.

    c.   The transaction affects the stockholders rather than the companies.

3.   Since a *fusion* of the companies occurs, rather than a *takeover*, no purchase price is calculated in a pooling of interests.

    a.   No allocation is needed, and no basis exists for either revaluing acquired assets and liabilities to fair market value or recognizing goodwill without a cost figure.

    b.   Book values are simply retained, and the book values of the two companies are merely brought together to form consolidated financial statements.

    c.   Revenues and expenses are combined on a retroactive basis *as if* the combination occurred on the first day of the accounting period; expenses incurred in bringing about the pooling of interests are expensed in the year in which they are incurred.

4.   The resulting equity of the pooled entity is equal to the sum of the equities of the two separate companies.

    a.   The sum of the two retained earnings accounts of the respective companies are not increased as a result of the pooling.

    b.   Problems associated with the pooling of interests method usually occur because the total par value of the issuer's stock differs from the total par value of the other company's stock, and the following three distinct relationships are possible.

        (1)   *Total Par Value of the Issuer's Stock = Total Par Value of the Other Company's Stock.* In this event, the total equity for the pooled company will be obtained by summing the balances in its common stock, additional paid-in capital, and retained earnings.

        (2)   *Total Par Value of the Issuer's Stock > Total Par Value of the Other Company's Stock.* In this event, the issuer records the issued stock at par and reduces its additional paid-in capital. If additional paid-in capital is not large enough to create the equality, then the issuer must reduce its retained earnings.

        (3)   *Total Par Value of the Issuer's Stock < Total Par Value of the Other Company's Stock.* In this event, the issuer must increase its additional paid-in capital to create the equality.

C.   Pooling of interests method where dissolution takes place.

1.   Because of the nature of a pooling, determination of an acquisition price is not relevant.

2.   Since no acquisition price is calculated, all direct costs of creating the combination are expensed immediately.

3.   Goodwill is never recognized in a pooling of interests and no valuation adjustments are recorded.

4.   The book values of the two companies are simply brought together to produce a set of consolidated financial records.

5.   The results of operations reported by both parties are combined on a retroactive basis as if the companies had always been together.

D.   A pooling of interests where separate incorporation is maintained also combines the book values of the companies as if they had always been together.

     A.   As with a purchase combination, a spreadsheet is often used as a tool to consolidate the two sets of numbers.

     B.   The following entries are made on the consolidation spreadsheet:

         1.   eliminate the Investment account balance.

         2.   eliminate the stockholders' equity accounts for the company that is the subject of the investment (usually the smaller company)

VII.   Pooling of Interests — the Controversy

Over the years, the legitimacy of the *pooling of interests method* has frequently been questioned. Preference for the method is based largely on the desirable impact on consolidated assets and liabilities. The controversial aspects of the *pooling of interests method* include the following:

A.   Any cost figures indicated by the exchange transaction that created the combination are ignored, and the number of shares exchanged has no impact on consolidated assets and liabilities. Thus, what is normally a significant event for both companies is simply omitted from any accounting consideration.

B.   Objective criteria for differentiating between a purchase and a pooling have always been difficult to identify.

C.   As an argument against pooling — many accountants believe that only one accounting approach should be applicable for all business combinations, and they contend that a purchaser and an acquisition price can be determined in virtually every case.

D.   Income balances previously reported are altered since operations are combined on a retroactive basis.

E.   Reported net income is usually higher in subsequent years than in a purchase since no goodwill or valuation adjustments are recognized that would require amortization.

VIII.   The FASB's Position

    A.   In SFAS No. 141, the FASB requires that all business combinations be accounted for using the purchase method, thereby eliminating the pooling method.

        1.   The pooling method provides users with less information than the purchase method.

        2.   The pooling method ignores the values exchanged in a business combination.

        3.   Under the pooling method, it is difficult to determine how much was invested in the combination by looking at the financial statements. Consequently, it is also difficult to track the performance of the investment.

        4.   Having two methods is confusing for investors.

        5.   The boost in earnings reported under the pooling method reflects artificial accounting differences.

        6.   Business combinations are, by their very nature, acquisitions and should be accounted for accordingly.

Multiple Choice Questions

1. Which of the following is not listed in the text as a motivation for business combinations?

    A.   Vertical integration.
    B.   Less competition.
    C.   Economies of scale.
    D.   Cost savings.
    E.   Quick access to new markets.

2. Which of the following costs incurred in bringing about a business combination accounted for as a purchase should enter into determining the net income of the combined company for the period in which the expenses are incurred?

	Finders' Fees	Stock Registration Fees	Brokers' Fees
A.	Yes	No	Yes
B.	Yes	No	No
C.	No	Yes	Yes
D.	Yes	Yes	Yes
E.	No	No	No

3. In accounting for a business combination as a purchase, a *bargain purchase* exists when

    A.   purchase price > book value.
    B.   fair market value > purchase price.
    C.   fair market value < book value.
    D.   fair market value > book value.
    E.   fair market value < purchase price.

4. In preparing the consolidation worksheet for a business combination accounted for as a purchase, which one of the following is the appropriate basis for valuing fixed assets of a wholly-owned subsidiary?

    A.   fair market value.
    B.   book value as shown on the books of the subsidiary.
    C.   book value plus any excess of purchase price over book value of the acquired assets and liabilities.
    D.   historical cost as shown on the books of the subsidiary.
    E.   current carrying value.

5.	In the event that the fair market value of the acquired company exceeds the purchase price, any amount in excess of the noncurrent asset balances is

	A.	Written off as a reduction of Paid-in Capital in Excess of Par.
	B.	Recorded as Negative Goodwill.
	C.	Recorded as an Extraordinary Gain.
	D.	Recorded as an Extraordinary Loss.
	E.	Recorded as an increase to Returned Earnings of the Parent company.

6.	Which of the following characteristics must be present to indicate a controlling interest in a variable interest entity?

		I.	The direct or indirect ability to make decisions about the entity's activities.
		II.	The obligation to absorb the expected losses of the entity if they occur.
		III.	The right to receive the expected residual returns of the entity if they occur.

	A.	I only.
	B.	II only.
	C.	III only.
	D.	Any one of the above is sufficient to indicate a controlling interest in a variable interest entity.
	E.	All of the above must be present to indicate a controlling interest in a variable interest entity.

7.	Shaw Company has the following account balances:

		FMV
Receivables	$ 100,000	100k
Inventory	150,000	150k
Land	100,000	200k
Building — net	250,000	300k
Liabilities	100,000	75k
Common stock	100,000	825k − 750k
Additional paid-in capital	150,000	= 75k. GW.
Retained earnings	250,000	

	Shaw's land has a fair market value of $200,000 while its building has a fair market value of $300,000. Shaw's liabilities have a fair market value of $75,000. Brooks Company obtains all of the outstanding shares of Shaw for $750,000 cash. In the financial statements prepared immediately after the business combination, what is the amount of goodwill?

	A.	$ 75,000
	B.	$100,000
	C.	$125,000
	D.	$250,000
	E.	$ 65,000

Items 8 and 9 are based on the following information.

On December 31, 2003, Sam Company was merged into Paul Company. In carrying out the business combination, Paul Company issued 60,000 shares of its $10 par value common stock, with a fair market value of $15 per share, for all of Sam Company's outstanding common stock. The stockholders' equity section of the two companies immediately before the business combination was:

	Paul Company	Sam Company
Common Stock	$ 500,000	$ 400,000
Additional Paid-in Capital	200,000	100,000
Retained Earnings	300,000	200,000

8.   In the December 31, 2003 consolidated balance sheet, the *Additional Paid-In Capital* account should be reported at

   A. $300,000.
   B. $200,000.
   C. $400,000.
   D. $500,000.
   E. $100,000.

9.   Under what circumstance can a subsidiary be excluded from consolidation?

   A.   If the relationship between the parent and the subsidiary is temporary.
   B.   If the control of the subsidiary actually rests with another party.
   C.   If the relationship between the parent and the subsidiary is temporary **and** the control of the subsidiary actually rests with another party.
   D.   If the subsidiary is located in a high risk area, such as a war zone.
   E.   All of the above are acceptable circumstances for excluding a subsidiary from consolidation.

10.   Direct combination costs and stock issuance costs are often incurred in the process of making a controlling investment in another company. How should those costs be accounted for in a purchase transaction?

	Direct Combination Costs	Stock Issuance Costs
A.	Increase Investment	Decrease Investment
B.	Increase Investment	Decrease Paid-In Capital
C.	Decrease Investment	Increase Expenses
D.	Decrease Paid-In Capital	Increase Investment
E.	Increase Expenses	Increase Expenses

Brief Essay Questions

1. What is a business combination? Distinguish between a statutory merger and a statutory consolidation.

2. What is the theoretical rationale for the *purchase method* of accounting for business combinations? Explain.

3. How is the amount of goodwill at the acquisition date determined? Explain.

4. What is the theoretical rationale for the *pooling of interests method* of accounting for business combinations? Explain.

Problems

1. On January 1, 2005, Chester Inc. acquires 100% of Festus Corp.'s outstanding common stock by exchanging 100,000 shares of Chester's $2 par value common voting stock. In addition, Chester paid $1,500,000 in cash. Chester also incurred direct combination costs of $350,000 and stock issuance costs of $650,000.

On January 1, 2005, Chester's voting common stock had a market value of $38.00 per share. Festus' voting common shares were selling for $12.50 per share. Festus' balances on the acquisition date, just prior to acquisition are listed below.

Cash	$ 530,000	$ 530,000
Receivables	610,000	650,000
Inventory	400,000	400,000
Land	600,000	700,000
Building (net)	500,000	580,000
Equipment (net)	375,000	300,000
Payables	(280,000)	(80,000)
Common Stock, $1 par value	(1,800,000)	(2,250,000)
Paid-In Capital	(660,000)	
R/E (12/31/04)	(275,000)	

(handwritten: Cash 1,500K / Stock 100K × 12.50 / Fees 350K)

Required:

A. Compute the value of Chester's investment account on the date of acquisition, January 1, 2005. *(handwritten: 1500K + 1250K + 350 = 3100K)*

B. Compute the value of the Goodwill account on the date of acquisition, January 1, 2005. *(handwritten: P. Price $ 3100K − 1800X 12.50 =)*

2. In a business combination occurring on April 1, 2004, Big Company issued 50,000 shares of its $10 par value common stock in exchange for all of the outstanding common stock of Bitty Company. On April 1, 2004, Big's Common stock had a market value of $18.75 per share. The following information was available concerning the two companies:

	Big Company	Bitty Company
Common stock, $10 par value	$ 1,000,000	
Common stock, $5 par value		$ 500,000
Additional paid-in capital	$ 30,000	$ 50,000
Retained Earnings	$ 170,000	$ 120,000

Required:

Determine the amount of the consolidated common stock, additional paid-in capital, and retained earnings immediately after the combination.

3. On October 1, 2004, X-Size Corp acquired 100% of Big Boys Inc. for $3,000,000 and 60,000 shares of X-Size $4-par common voting stock. X-Size's common voting stock had a market value of $22 on October 1, 2004, $26 on March 31, 2005, and $32 on March 31, 2006.

Big Boys had Land that was undervalued by $400,000, a building that was undervalued by $800,000 (Useful life = 8 years), and equipment was overvalued by $600,000 (Useful life = 5 years). Net Assets on October 1, 2004 was $3,100,000.

Big Boys' net income for the period April 1, 2004 to September 30, 2004 was $500,000. Net income for the year ending on March 31, 2005, was $1,800,000. Net income for the year ending on March 31, 2006, was $2,200,000. Big Boys paid the following dividends; $100,000 on June 1, 2004, $240,000 on November 15, 2004, $400,000 on April 20, 2005, and $630,000 on October 10, 2005.

Required:

A. Compute X-Size's Amortization Expense for the period ending March 31, 2006?

B. Compute the value of the X-Size's Investment in Big Boys account on March 31, 2006.

4. West Corp. acquires 100% of Barns Construction on July 1, 2003. The acquisition involves West issuing 75,000 shares of its $10 par value, voting common stock in exchange for all of Barns Construction's outstanding voting common stock.

There are $20,000 in direct combination costs and $45,000 in stock issuance costs. On the acquisition date, West's common shares are trading for $32.50 per share. The balances for West Corporation and Barns Construction just prior to the combination are as follows:

Account	West Corporation	Barns Construction BV	Barns Construction FMV
Cash	$ 260,000	$ 175,000	$ 175,000
Accounts Receivable	850,000	265,000	265,000
Inventory	625,000	300,000	325,000
Land	1,700,000	500,000	780,000
Buildings (net)	8,500,000	290,000	590,000
Equipment (net)	2,650,000	1,295,500	850,500
Accounts Payable	(215,000)	(275,000)	(275,000)
Notes Payable	(800,000)	(400,000)	(400,000)
Common Stock	(5,000,000)	(1,000,000)	
Paid-In-Capital	(7,300,000)	(250,000)	
Retained Earnings, 1/1/00	(950,000)	(900,500)	
Revenues	(13,300,000)		
Expenses	12,980,000		

Required: Prepare the consolidation worksheet for West and Barns as of July 1, 2003.

Solutions to Multiple Choice Questions

1. **B**

2. **E**

3. **B**

4. **C**

5. **C**

6. **D**

7. **A**

Purchase price of Shaw Company common stock	$ 750,000
Book value of Shaw Company	(500,000)
Cost in excess of book value	250,000
Excess assigned to:	
Undervalued land	(100,000)
Undervalued building	(50,000)
Overvalued liabilities	(25,000)
Goodwill	$ 75,000

8.   **D**   Sam Company's Paid-In Capital is eliminated in the consolidation process. Paul Company's Paid-In Capital account consists of the $200,000 in the account prior to the issuance of stock. The issuance of 60,000 shares at a fair market value $5 in excess of par value results in an additional $300,000 being added to the account.

9.   **B**

10. **B**

Answers to Brief Essay Questions

1.   A business combination occurs when two or more companies join together under common control. A business combination results in the creation of a single economic entity. The consolidation of financial information into a single set of financial records is required whenever one of the companies in the group directly or indirectly has a controlling financial in the other enterprises.

    In a statutory merger the acquired company is absorbed by the acquiring company so that only one company (the acquiring company) survives as a legally incorporated business. In a statutory consolidation, the net assets or capital stock of two or more companies are transferred to a newly formed corporation. Only the newly formed company exists as a legal entity after the business combination.

2.   In a business combination by *purchase*, an acquisition takes place. One of the parties can clearly be identified as the buyer and the other party as the seller. In a purchase situation, one group of owners (stockholders) is displaced by the owners of the purchasing company.

3.   Goodwill is defined as the excess of the purchase price over the fair market value of the net assets acquired plus other intangible assets not previously recorded

4.   In a *pooling of interests*, the transaction is regarded as a union of ownership interests of two or more companies by exchange of equity securities. In such transactions, the distinction between the acquiring and acquired company is not always evident and the price of the transaction may not be easily determined.

Solutions to Problems

1.   A.   Chester's Cost of the acquisition of Barns is computed as follows:

Cash Paid		$1,500,000
Shares of Common Stock Issued	100,000	
Market Value per Share	× $12.50	1,250,000
Direct Combination Costs		+ 350,000
Total Acquisition Cost		$3,100,000

B.   Chester's Goodwill computation is as follows:

Chester's Cost			3,100,000
Portion of Festus' Book Value Purchased by Chester	100%	2,735,000	2,735,000
Difference to be allocated			365,000
Inventory	100%	40,000	40,000
Land	100%	100,000	100,000
Building	100%	80,000	80,000
Equipment	100%	(75,000)	(75,000)
Goodwill			220,000

2.   Bitty's Common Stock, Additional Paid-in Capital, and Retained Earnings are all eliminated during the consolidation process. Big's Common Stock will increase for the number of shares issued x the par value. Big's Additional Paid-In Capital will increase by the number of shares issued x the excess of market value over par value. Big's Retained Earnings will not change.

Consolidated Equity Balances:

Common stock	$1,500,000
Additional paid-in capital	467,500
Retained earnings	170,000
Total	$2,137,500

3.   A.

Cost (3,000,000 + 60,000 x $22)			4,320,000		
BV	100%	3,100,000	3,100,000		
Diff			1,220,000		
Inventory	100%		-		-
Land	100%	400,000	400,000	0	-
Building	100%	800,000	800,000	8	50,000
Equipment	100%	(600,000)	(600,000)	5	(60,000)
Goodwill			620,000		-
					(10,000)

B.

Investment in Big Boys

Cost	4,320,000	240,000	Div
NI, 2005	1,300,000	400,000	Div
NI, 2006	2,200,000	630,000	Div
Amort, 2005	10,000		
Amort, 2006	10,000		
	6,570,000		

4. The Consolidation Spreadsheet for West and Barns appears as follows:

Account	West Corp.	Barns Construction	DR	CR	Consolidated Balance
Cash	$ 195,000	$ 175,000			$ 370,000
Accounts Rec.	850,000	265,000			1,115,000
Inventory	625,000	300,000	25,000		950,000
Land	1,700,000	500,000	280,000		2,480,000
Buildings (net)	8,500,000	290,000	300,000		9,090,000
Equipment (net)	2,650,000	1,295,500		445,000	3,500,500
Investment	2,457,500			2,457,500	-
Goodwill			147,000		147,000
Accounts Payable	(215,000)	(275,000)			(490,000)
Notes Payable	(800,000)	(400,000)			(1,200,000)
Common Stock	(5,750,000)	(1,000,000)	1,000,000		(5,750,000)
Paid-in-Capital	(8,942,500)	(250,000)	250,000		(8,942,500)
Retained Earnings	(950,000)	(900,500)	900,500		(950,000)
					-
Revenues	(13,300,000)				(13,300,000)
Expenses	12,980,000				12,980,000

The computation of Goodwill will is as follows:

West's Cost			2,457,500
Portion of Barn's Book Value Purchased by West	100%	2,150,500	2,150,500
Difference to be allocated			307,000
Inventory	100%	(25,000)	(25,000)
Land	100%	(280,000)	(280,000)
Buildings	100%	(300,000)	(300,000)
Equipment	100%	445,000	445,000
Goodwill			147,000

Chapter 3

Consolidations – Subsequent to the Date of Acquisition

Chapter Outline

I. Consolidation — the Effects Created by the Passage of Time

   A. This chapter examines the consolidation procedures that must be followed in subsequent periods whenever separate incorporation of the subsidiary is maintained.

   B. A worksheet and consolidation entries continue to provide structure for the rendering of a single set of financial statements for the combined entity.

   C. As time passes, additional complications are encountered.

      1. The parent must select and apply an accounting method to account for the relationship between the two companies. The investment balance recorded by the parent changes over time as a result of the method chosen, as does the income consequently recognized.

      2. The parent's investment balance is eliminated on the worksheet so that the subsidiary's actual assets and liabilities can be consolidated.

      3. Additionally, the income figure accrued by the parent is excluded each period so that the subsidiary's revenues and expenses can be included can be included when creating an income statement for the combined entity.

II. Investment Accounting by the Acquiring Company

   A. Consolidation of a subsidiary becomes necessary for external reporting whenever control exists; but, for internal record-keeping, the parent has a choice of three alternatives for monitoring the activities of its subsidiaries:

      1. the cost method

         a. Investment account always remains at cost.

         b. Dividends received are recorded as dividend revenue.

         c. Amortization of fair market value adjustments and intangible assets is not recorded.

      2. the equity method, or

         a. Investment account changes over time to recognize changes in the book value of the subsidiary.

         b. Dividends received are recorded as a reduction of the Investment balance.

         c. The parent recognizes a portion of the subsidiary's income on the parent's income statement in an account called Equity in Subsidiary Income. A corresponding entry is made to the Investment account. The portion recognized is equal to the parent's ownership percentage of the subsidiary.

      d.   Fair market value adjustments and intangible assets identified during the acquisition process are amortized. The amortization expense is charged to Equity in Subsidiary Income.

   3.   the partial equity method.

      a.   The Investment account is adjusted over time.

      b.   Dividends received are recognized as Dividend Revenue.

      c.   A portion of the subsidiary's income is accrued over time, just as with the Equity method.

      d.   No amortization of fair market value adjustments or intangivle assets is recognized.

  B.   Depending on the method applied, the acquiring company will record earnings from its ownership of the acquired company, and this total must be eliminated on the consolidated worksheet.

  C.   Under each one of these methods, the balance in the *Investment* account must be removed in producing consolidated financial statements.

III.   Subsequent Consolidations — Investment Recorded by the Equity Method

  A.   For a purchase combination consolidated after the acquisition date, certain "elimination" procedures are required to avoid double-counting of items related to the combination. and if the acquiring company has applied the equity method, the following process is appropriate.

   1.   For example, if the *Investment in Subsidiary* account remains on the consolidated balance sheet, it would imply that the Parent has an investment interest in itself! This simply would not make sense.

   2.   These "elimination" entries are posted ONLY to the consolidated worksheet, and do not impact the general ledger accounts of either the parent company or the subsidiary company.

   3.   Prior to posting any of the "elimination" entries to the consolidation worksheet, the Parent must remember to update its own records for the equity method adjustments to the investment account.

   4.   If the acquisition is made during the current fiscal period, the parent adjusts its *Investment* account to reflect the subsidiary's income and dividend receipts as well as any amortization expense relating to the purchase price allocations and goodwill.

  B.   Worksheet entries are used to establish consolidated figures for reporting purposes.

   1.   *Consolidation Entry S* "eliminates" the subsidiary's stockholders' equity accounts (as of the purchase date or the beginning of the period when this is a period other than the period of acquisition) from the consolidated balance sheet.

Consolidation Entry S

Common Stock (Subsidiary)	XX	
Additional Paid-In Capital (Subsidiary)	XX	
Retained Earnings, 1/1/0X (Subsidiary)	XX	
Investment in Subsidiary		XX

2. *Consolidation Entry A* effectively recognizes the unamortized portion of the fair market value adjustments associated with the subsidiary's assets (as determined at the acquisition date) and other intangible assets, and recognizes the goodwill, as of the beginning of the period (or the acquisition date if this is the period of acquisition).

Consolidation Entry A

Land (if undervalued on the Sub's books)...............	XX	
Buildings (if undervalued on the Sub's books)...........	XX	
Goodwill	XX	
Equipment (if overvalued on the Sub's books).......		XX
Investment in Subsidiary		XX

3. *Consolidation Entry I* eliminates the *Equity in Subsidiary Income* balance accrued by the parent.

Consolidation Entry I

Equity in Subsidiary Earnings	XX	
Investment in Subsidiary		XX

4. *Consolidation Entry D* removes intercompany dividend payments.

Consolidation Entry D

Investment in Subsidiary	XX	
Dividends Paid		XX

5. *Consolidation Entry E* records the current consolidated amortization expense on the purchase price allocations. (Remember that the fair market value difference associated with Land is NEVER amortized.)

Consolidation Entry E

Expenses	XX	
Equipment	XX	
Buildings		XX
Intangibles		XX

6. *Consolidation Entry P* eliminates any intercompany payable/receivable balances.

Consolidation Entry P

Liabilities	XX	
Current Assets		XX

C. If the purchase was made during a previous period, most of the consolidation entries described previously remain applicable regardless of the time that has elapsed since the combination was formed.

    1. The amount of the subsidiary's stockholders' equity to be removed in *Consolidation Entry S* will differ each period to reflect the balance as of the beginning of the current period.

    2. The allocations established by *Consolidation Entry A* will also change with each subsequent consolidation, and only the unamortized balances remaining as of the beginning of the current period are recognized in this entry.

IV. Subsequent Consolidations — Investment Recorded on Other than the Equity Method

    A. For a purchase combination where the parent has applied an accounting method other than the equity method, the consolidation procedures previously described are modified.

    B. The parent's use of the cost method is considered simpler than other methods.

        1. The parent company recognizes dividends received as *dividend income*, rather than as a reduction of the investment account, and therefore, does not change the *Investment in Subsidiary* account.

        2. If the parent applies the cost method, the intercompany income eliminated in *Consolidation Entry I* will consist only of the dividends transferred from the subsidiary.

        3. No separate *Consolidation Entry D* is needed (the intercompany dividends are eliminated in Entry I).

        4. In periods after the period of acquisition, the cost method recognizes neither *Equity in Subsidiary Income* nor *Amortization Expense*.

        5. Both *Equity in Subsidiary Income* (for all years prior to the current period) and accumulated amortization must be added directly to the consolidation worksheet. *Consolidation Entry *C* is used for this purpose, as it converts all prior amounts into equity method balances.

    C. The partial equity method is similar to the equity method with one important difference — the partial equity method does not adjust the subsidiary's reported income for any amortization associated with the acquisition.

        1. If the parent uses the partial equity method, the intercompany income to be removed in *Consolidation Entry I* is the equity accrual only; no amortization expense is included.

        2. Intercompany dividends are eliminated through *Consolidation Entry D*.

        3. During any time period after the year of purchase, the partial equity method does not recognize amortization expense, so that *Consolidation Entry *C* converts the appropriate account balances to the equity method by recognizing the expense that relates to all of the past years.

V.   Goodwill Impairment – SFAS No. 142

A.   When is goodwill impaired?

   1.   Goodwill is considered impaired when the fair value of its related reporting unit falls below its carrying value. Goodwill should **not** be amortized, but should be tested for impairment at the reporting unit level (operating segment or lower identifiable level).

   2.   Goodwill should be tested for impairment at least annually.

   3.   Interim impairment testing may be necessary in the presence of negative indicators such as an adverse change in the business climate or market, legal factors, regulatory action, an introduction of competition, or a loss of key personnel.

B.   How is goodwill tested for impairment?

   1.   All acquired goodwill should be assigned to reporting units. It would not be unusual for the total amount of acquired goodwill to be divided among a number of reporting units. Goodwill may be assigned to reporting units of the acquiring entity that are expected to benefit from the synergies of the combination even though other assets or liabilities of the acquired entity may not be assigned to that reporting unit.

   2.   Goodwill is tested for impairment a two-step approach.

      a.   Step 1 – Is the Market Value of a Reporting Unit Less Than Its Carrying Value?

         (1)   If the fair value of the reporting unit exceeds or equals its carrying amount, goodwill is not considered impaired and no further analysis is necessary.

         (2)   A previously determined fair value can continue to be used if:
         • The assets and liabilities that compose the reporting unit have not changed significantly since the most recent fair value determination.
         • The most recent fair-value determination resulted in an amount that exceeded the carrying amount of the reporting unit by a substantial margin.
         • Based on an analysis of events that have occurred and circumstances that have changed since the most recent fair-value determination, it is remote that a current fair-value determination would be less than the current carrying amount of the reporting unit.

b.   Step 2 – Is Goodwill's Implied Value Less Than Carrying Value?

    (1)   To determine the Implied Value of the Goodwill, use the most recently determined fair value of the reporting unit as a surrogate "cost".

    (2)   Compute Implied Goodwill just as you would if there had been an actual acquisition. An entity should allocate the fair value of the reporting unit to all of the assets and liabilities of that unit (including any unrecognized intangible assets), as if the reporting unit had been acquired in a business combination and the fair value of the reporting unit was the purchase price. The excess "purchase price" over the amounts assigned to assets and liabilities is the fair value of goodwill. This allocation is performed only for purposes of testing goodwill for impairment and does not require entities to record the "step-up" in net assets or any unrecognized intangible assets.

    (3)   If Implied Goodwill is less than carrying value, Goodwill must be written down. The write-down is recorded as a separate line item in the income statement as a Goodwill Impairment Loss.

C.   How is the impairment recognized in financial statements?

    1.   The aggregate amount of goodwill impairment losses should be presented as **a separate line item in the operating section of the income statement** unless a goodwill impairment loss is associated with a discontinued operation.

    2.   A goodwill impairment loss associated with a discontinued operation should be included (on a net-of-tax basis) within the results of discontinued operations.

VI.   Purchase Price — Contingent Consideration

A.   In a purchase, the final price paid by the acquiring company may ultimately depend on some future event such as the earnings of the subsidiary or the market value of any common stock issued.

B.   If additional assets must be conveyed by the parent at a later date, the original purchase price is recalculated.

C.   When additional assets are conveyed, Goodwill is increased in the consolidated financial statements or, if a bargain purchase has occurred, reductions in value are decreased or removed.

D.   If additional stock is issued at a later date, the new shares are recorded at fair market value but previously issued shares are adjusted to the same value.

VII. Subsequent Consolidations — Pooling of Interests

    A.   In consolidating a pooling of interests subsequent to the formation of the business combination, many worksheet procedures are identical to those used in a purchase combination.

    B.   The acquired company's stockholders' equity must still be removed on the worksheet along with various reciprocal balances: intercompany income, dividends, and receivable/payable accounts. However, some differences do exist.

    C.   Since all asset, liability, revenue, and expense accounts are consolidated at book value — neither *Consolidation Entry A* nor *Consolidation Entry E* are needed; no allocations or amortization are recorded.

VIII. Push-Down Accounting

    A.   A subsidiary acquired in a purchase may record any allocation directly into its own financial records rather than through the use of a worksheet, and subsequent amortization expense could also be recorded by the subsidiary.

    B.   Push-down accounting reports the assets and liabilities of the subsidiary at the amount the new owner paid, and it also assists the new owner in evaluating the profitability that the subsidiary is adding to the business combination.

    C.   Push-down accounting can also make the consolidation process easier since allocations and amortization need not be included as worksheet entries.

    D.   The SEC currently requires the use of push-down accounting for the separate financial statements of any subsidiary where no substantial outside ownership exists of the company's common stock, preferred stock, and publicly held debt.

    E.   The FASB has been studying push-down accounting and may issue more specific pronouncements concerning its application.

Multiple Choice Questions

Items 1 through 7 are based on the following information.

On January 1, 2005, Parkway Corporation purchases all of the outstanding common stock of Shaw Company for $440,000 cash. On that date, Shaw's net assets had a book value of $296,000. Equipment with an 8-year life was undervalued by $40,000 in Shaw's financial records. Goodwill resulting from this combination equals $104,000. Shaw reported net income of $50,000 in 2005 and $65,000 in 2006. Dividends of $5,000 were declared and paid in each of those two years.

Selected account balances as of December 31, 2007 for the two companies are as follows:

	Parkway	Shaw
Revenues	$ 500,000	$ 285,000
Expenses	350,000	200,000
Equipment (net)	250,000	120,000
Retained Earnings, 1/1/07	300,000	151,000
Dividends Paid	50,000	10,000

1. For each of the three methods discussed in the chapter, what should be the *Investment in Shaw Company* account balance in the records of Parkway Corporation at December 31, 2007?

	Equity Method	Partial Equity Method	Cost Method
A.	$573,800	$640,000	$296,000
B.	$605,000	$620,000	$440,000
C.	$620,000	$620,000	$440,000
D.	$610,000	$620,000	$296,000
E.	$605,000	$640,000	$440,000

2. What is *consolidated net income* for 2007 if the parent company uses the partial equity method?

   A. $230,000
   B. $250,000
   C. $220,000
   D. $235,000
   E. $225,000

3. What is *consolidated retained earnings* at January 1, 2007 if the parent company uses the equity method?

   A. $285,000
   B. $290,000
   C. $295,000
   D. $300,000
   E. $395,000

4. What is *consolidated retained earnings* at January 1, 2007 if the parent company uses the partial equity method?

   A. $285,000
   B. $290,000
   C. $295,000
   D. $300,000
   E. $395,000

5. What is *consolidated retained earnings* at January 1, 2007 if the parent company uses the cost method?

   A. $285,000
   B. $290,000
   C. $295,000
   D. $300,000
   E. $395,000

6. What is the total of 2007 *consolidated expenses*?

   A. $550,000
   B. $535,000
   C. $555,000
   D. $540,000
   E. $545,000

7. What is the December 31, 2007 *consolidated balance* for *Equipment*?

   A. $370,000
   B. $400,000
   C. $405,000
   D. $410,000
   E. $395,000

8. According to SFAS 141, for purposes of testing goodwill for impairment, the appropriate level of testing is at the

   A. Consolidated entity level
   B. Parent company level
   C. Operating unit level
   D. Subsidiary company level
   E. Reporting unit level

9. Powell Company buys all of the outstanding common shares of South Bay Company on January 1, 2005 for $1,500,000 cash. This price resulted in goodwill of $300,000. Because the subsidiary earned especially high profits over the next two years, Powell was required to pay South Bay's previous owners an additional $450,000 cash on January 1, 2007. How should Powell report this additional payment?

    A.   A retroactive adjustment is made record the $450,000 as additional goodwill, as if the payment had been made on January 1, 2007.
    B.   The $450,000 is expensed in 2007.
    C.   The extra $450,000 payment is applied as a reduction of consolidated retained earnings.
    D.   The additional $450,000 payment is reported as an increase in consolidated retained earnings at January 1, 2007.
    E.   The $450,000 payment is applied as a decrease in consolidated stockholders' equity.

10. Greenberg Company purchases Andrews Company on January 1, 2005 by issuing 20,000 shares of $5 par value common stock having a $60 per share market price. The business combination resulted in $450,000 of goodwill. Greenberg agrees to guarantee the value of the stock issued to the former owners of Andrews. Greenberg agrees to issue additional shares if the price of the stock drops during a two-year period. Subsequently, the market price of the Greenberg stock drops from $60 to $50 per share. On January 1, 2007, Greenberg was required to issue an additional 4,000 shares of its stock to the former shareholders of Andrews. How should Greenberg report the issuance of the additional 4,000 shares?

    A.   All of the subsidiary's asset and liability accounts must be revalued based on their fair market values at January 1, 2007.
    B.   The fair market value of the new shares will increase the Goodwill balance.
    C.   The new shares are recorded at the earlier market value and then a retroactive adjustment is made for the difference.
    D.   The recorded value of the earlier shares is reduced to the current market value while the new shares are also recorded at this same market value.
    E.   A retroactive adjustment is made to record the $200,000 market value of the new shares as if they were issued at January 1, 2005.

Brief Essay Questions

1. On January 1, 2005, Patrick Company purchases 100 percent of the outstanding common shares of Sportswear Inc. for $1,500,000. On that date, Patrick reported retained earnings of $150,000 while Sportswear reported an $80,000 balance. Patrick reported net income of $75,000 in 2005 and $90,000 in 2006, and paid $25,000 in dividends each year. Sportswear reported net income of $50,000 in 2005 and $65,000 in 2006, and paid $5,000 in dividends each year. Annual amortization of $7,000 results from the combination. If Patrick applies the equity method, calculate the *Investment in Sportswear Inc.* account balance on December 31, 2006. How would your answer differ if Patrick uses the partial equity method?

2. What is the SEC's rationale for requiring the use of push-down accounting for the separate financial statements of any subsidiary where no substantial outside ownership exists of the company's common stock, preferred stock, and publicly held debt.

Problems

1. On January 1, 2005, Giant Inc. purchased all of the outstanding common shares of Tiny Co. for $3,600,000 cash. On that date, Tiny's equity accounts had the following balances: *Common Stock* — $500,000; *Additional Paid-In Capital* — $1,800,000; and *Retained Earnings* — $700,000. All of Tiny's assets were fairly stated except for equipment having a book value of $180,000 and a fair market value of $270,000, and a building having a book value of $600,000 and a fair market value of $800,000. The equipment is estimated to have a remaining useful life of five years, and the building has a ten-year remaining useful life. Tiny also had a copyright with a fair market value of $310,000 and an expected useful life of 5 years on 1/1/05.

    During 2005, Tiny reported net income of $1,325,000 and paid dividends of $850,000.

    During 2006 Tiny reported net income of $900,000 and paid dividends of $1,100,000.

    Required:

    A. Analyze the purchase price by preparing an *Allocation of Purchase Price* and an *Amortization Schedule*.

    B. Assume that Giant uses the equity method to account for its investment in Tiny. Prepare all entries to be made on the books of Giant for 2005 regarding its investment in Tiny.

    C. Prepare the consolidation worksheet entries for the year ended December 31, 2005 assuming Giant uses the equity method of accounting.

2. *Required:*

    Assuming that Giant Inc. uses the equity method to account for its investment in Tiny Co., prepare the consolidation worksheet entries for the year ended December 31, 2006.

3. *Required:*

    Assuming that Giant Inc. uses the partial equity method to account for its investment in Tiny Co., prepare the consolidation worksheet entries for the year ended December 31, 2005.

4. *Required:*

    Assuming that Giant Inc. uses the cost method to account for its investment in Tiny Co., prepare the consolidation worksheet entries for the year ended December 31, 2005.

5. On January 1, 2005, Old Guy Shoes acquired 100% of a sport shoe company, Viagrunners, for $820,000 cash. At that date, the book value of Viagrunners was $630,000. Viagrunner was carrying land on January 1, 2005 that had a book value of $15,000 and a market value of $40,000. All other assets were carried at fair value.

The following balances existed for Old Guy Shoes and its wholly-owned sport shoe subsidiary, Viagrunners, at December 31, 2005:

Account	Old Guy Shoes BV	Viagrunners BV	Viagrunners FMV
Cash	$ 860,000	$ 70,000	$ 70,000
Accts Receivable	460,000	120,000	110,000
Inventory	725,000	195,000	125,000
Investment in Viagrunner	640,000		
Land	400,000	15,000	55,000
Building (net)	900,000	90,000	120,000
Equipment (net)	1,200,000	210,000	150,000
Acct. Pay.	(235,000)	(250,000)	(110,000)
Common Stock	(600,000)	(100,000)	
PIC	(3,900,000)	(350,000)	
R/E - 1/1/05	(680,000)	(180,000)	
Dividends	250,000		
Revenues	(6,800,000)	(1,500,000)	
Expenses	6,600,000	1,680,000	
Equity in Viagrunner NI	180,000		

The fair market value of Old Guy's investment in Viagrunners has dropped to $540,000 as of December 31, 2005.

Required:

Is Goodwill related to Old Guy's investment in Viagrunners impaired at December 31, 2005?

Solutions to Multiple Choice Questions

1. **B** Allocation of Purchase Price at January 1, 2005:

Purchase price	$ 440,000
Book value of Shaw	(296,000)
Excess of cost over book value	144,000
Allocation to Equipment based on fair market value	(40,000)
Goodwill	$ 104,000

Annual amortization expense:	
Equipment ($40,000 ÷ 8 years)	$ 5,000
Total	$ 5,000

Equity method:

Investment in Shaw Company — initial cost	$ 440,000
Income accrual — 2005	50,000
Amortization — 2005	(5,000)
Dividends received — 2005	(5,000)
Income accrual — 2006	65,000
Amortization — 2006	(5,000)
Dividends received — 2006	(5,000)
Income accrual — 2007	85,000
Amortization — 2007	(5,000)
Dividends received — 2007	(10,000)
Investment in Shaw Company — 12/31/07	$ 605,000

Partial equity method:

Investment in Shaw Company — initial cost	$ 440,000
Income accrual — 2005	50,000
Dividends received — 2005	(5,000)
Income accrual — 2006	65,000
Dividends received — 2006	(5,000)
Income accrual — 2007	85,000
Dividends received — 2007	(10,000)
Investment in Shaw Company — 12/31/07	$ 620,000

Cost method:

Investment in Shaw Company — 12/31/07	$ 440,000

2. **A** Consolidated net income:

Revenues (add book values)	$ 785,000
Expenses (add book values and include amortization)	(555,000)
Consolidated net income	$ 230,000

3. **D** If Parkway Corporation uses the equity method, its retained earnings balance at January 1, 2007 will reflect the consolidated total. Thus, Parkway's balance of $300,000 also represents consolidated retained earnings.

4.   B   If Parkway Corporation uses the partial equity method, its retained earnings balance at January 1, 2007 will be correct except for the omission of amortization.

Parkway Corporation's retained earnings at 1/1/07	$ 300,000
Amortization for 2005-2006 ($5,000 x 2 years)	(10,000)
Consolidated retained earnings at 1/1/07	$ 290,000

5.   E

Parkway Corporation's retained earnings at 1/1/07	$ 300,000
Additional equity accrual — 2005 ($50,000 – $5,000)	45,000
Additional equity accrual — 2006 ($65,000 – $5,000)	60,000
Amortization for 2005-2006 ($5,000 x 2 years)	(10,000)
Consolidated retained earnings at 1/1/07	$ 395,000

6.   C

Book value of Parkway Corporation's 2007 expenses	$ 350,000
Book value of Shaw Company's 2007 expenses	200,000
Amortization for 2007	5,000
Consolidated expenses for 2007	$ 555,000

7.   E

Book value of Parkway Corporation's Equipment	$ 250,000
Book value of Shaw Company's Equipment	120,000
Allocation to Equipment based on fair market value	40,000
Amortization for 2005-2007 ($5,000 x 3 years)	(15,000)
Consolidated Equipment at 12/31/07	$ 395,000

8.   E

9.   A   This question involves contingent consideration based on the subsidiary's future earnings. If a subsequent payment is made because of a specified amount of income is earned, consolidated goodwill is increased.

10. D

Answers to Brief Essay Questions

1.   If Patrick Company uses the equity method, the *Investment in Sportswear Inc.* account balance on December 31, 2006 is calculated to be $1,591,000.

Initial cost at January 1, 2005	$ 1,500,000
Sportswear net income — 2005	50,000
Sportswear net income — 2006	65,000
Dividends paid by Sportswear ($5,000 x 2)	(10,000)
Amortization — 2005-2006 ($7,000 x 2)	(14,000)
Investment in Sportswear Inc. at December 31, 2006	$ 1,591,000

If Patrick Company uses the partial equity method, the *Investment in Sportswear Inc.* account balance on December 31, 2006 is calculated to be $1,605,000.

Initial cost at January 1, 2005	$ 1,500,000
Sportswear net income — 2005	50,000
Sportswear net income — 2006	65,000
Dividends paid by Sportswear ($5,000 x 2)	(10,000)
Investment in Sportswear Inc. at December 31, 2006	$ 1,605,000

2. The SEC's rationale for requiring push-down accounting is based on the notion that when the form of ownership is within the control of the parent company, the accounting basis should be the same whether the entity continues to exist or is merged into the parent's operations. Consequently, the SEC believes that a change in ownership justifies a new basis of accounting for the subsidiary's assets and liabilities.

Solutions to Problems

1. A. Giant Inc.
   Allocation of Purchase Price
   January 1, 2005

					Amortization
Giant's Cost			$ 3,600,000		
Portion of Tiny's Book Value Purchased by Giant	100%	3,000,000	3,000,000		
Difference to be allocated			600,000		
Equipment	100%	90,000	90,000 ÷ 5 =		18,000
Buildings	100%	200,000	200,000 ÷ 10 =		20,000
Copyright			310,000 ÷ 5 =		62,000
Total			$ -		100,000

(This analysis of purchase price is independent of the method that the parent will use to account for its investment; that is, the results are the same for all methods.)

B. Entries on the books of Giant Inc.:

Date	Accounts	Debit	Credit
1/1/05	Investment in Tiny	3,600,000	
	Cash		3,600,000
	to record investment in Tiny		
12/31/05	Investment in Tiny	1,325,000	
	Equity in Tiny Income		1,325,000
	to record Giant's share of Tiny's Income		
12/31/05	Cash	850,000	
	Investment in Tiny		850,000
	to record receipt of dividends from Tiny		
12/31/05	Equity in Tiny Income	100,000	
	Investment in Tiny		100,000
	to reocrd amortization expense		

C. Consolidation worksheet entries for the year ended December 31, 2005 (**Hint** — use the mnemonic device *SAIDE*):

Date	Accounts	Debit	Credit
12/31/05	**ENTRY S**		
	Common Stock - Tiny	500,000	
	Paid-In Capital - Tiny	1,800,000	
	Retained Earnings - 1/1/05	700,000	
	Investment in Tiny		3,000,000
12/31/05	**ENTRY A**		
	Equipment	90,000	
	Building	200,000	
	Copyright	310,000	
	Investment in Tiny		600,000
12/31/05	**ENTRY I**		
	Equity in Tiny Income	1,325,000	
	Investment in Tiny		1,325,000
12/31/05	**ENTRY D**		
	Investment in Tiny	850,000	
	Dividends		850,000
12/31/05	**ENTRY E**		
	Amortization Expense	100,000	
	Equipment		18,000
	Building		20,000
	Copyright		62,000

2. Consolidation worksheet entries for the year ended December 31, 2006 — using the equity method:

Date	Accounts	Debit	Credit
12/31/06	**ENTRY S**		
	Common Stock - Tiny	500,000	
	Paid-In Capital - Tiny	1,800,000	
	Retained Earnings - 1/1/06	1,175,000	
	Investment in Tiny		2,475,000
12/31/06	**ENTRY A**		
	Equipment	72,000	
	Building	180,000	
	Copyright	248,000	
	Investment in Tiny		500,000
12/31/06	**ENTRY I**		
	Equity in Tiny Income	900,000	
	Investment in Tiny		900,000
12/31/06	**ENTRY D**		
	Investment in Tiny	1,100,000	
	Dividends		1,100,000
13/31/06	**ENTRY E**		
	Amortization Expense	100,000	
	Equipment		18,000
	Building		20,000
	Copyright		62,000

3. Consolidation worksheet entries for the year ended December 31, 2005 — using the partial equity method:

Date	Accounts	Debit	Credit
12/31/05	**ENTRY *C**		
	Retained Earnings	850,000	
	Investment in Tiny		850,000
	to adjust the balances to what they would have been if Giant had used the equity method.		
12/31/05	**ENTRY S**		
	Common Stock - Tiny	500,000	
	Paid-In Capital - Tiny	1,800,000	
	Retained Earnings - 1/1/05	700,000	
	Investment in Tiny		3,000,000
12/31/05	**ENTRY A**		
	Equipment	90,000	
	Building	200,000	
	Copyright	310,000	
	Investment in Tiny		600,000
12/31/05	**ENTRY I**		
	Equity in Tiny Income	1,325,000	
	Investment in Tiny		1,325,000
12/31/05	**ENTRY D**		
	Investment in Tiny	850,000	
	Dividends		850,000
12/31/05	**ENTRY E**		
	Amortization Expense	100,000	
	Equipment		18,000
	Building		20,000
	Copyright		62,000

4. Consolidation worksheet entries for the year ended December 31, 2005 — using the cost method:

Date	Accounts	Debit	Credit
12/31/05	**ENTRY S**		
	Common Stock - Tiny	500,000	
	Paid-In Capital - Tiny	1,800,000	
	Retained Earnings - 1/1/05	700,000	
	Investment in Tiny		3,000,000
12/31/05	**ENTRY A**		
	Equipment	90,000	
	Building	200,000	
	Copyright	310,000	
	Investment in Tiny		600,000
12/31/05	**ENTRY I**		
	Dividend Income	850,000	
	Dividends		850,000
12/31/05	**ENTRY D**		
	Not applicable in the Cost Method		
12/31/05	**ENTRY E**		
	Amortization Expense	100,000	
	Equipment		18,000
	Building		20,000
	Copyright		62,000

5. **Step 1: Is FMV of the investment < Carrying amount of the investment?**

In this case, the FMV of the investment is $540,000. The book value of the investment is $640,000. Therefore since $540,000 < $640,000, we must go to Step #2.

Step 2: Is the Implied Goodwill < the carrying amount for Goodwill?

To determine this, we must first know the carrying amount for Goodwill. In the original acquisition, Old Guy paid $820,000 for 100% of Viagrunner.

Purchase Price	$ 820,000
Book Value of Viagrunner	630,000
Cost in Excess of BV	$ 190,000
Fair market value adjustment for Land	25,000
Goodwill	$ 165,000

Next we must compare the "implied" goodwill to the carrying amount for goodwill ($165,000). In our problem, we know that the current value of the investment is $540,000.

Current Fair Value	$ 540,000
Fair Value of Viagrunner's Net Assets	520,000
Implied Goodwill	$ 20,000

Now, compare "implied" goodwill to the carrying amount for goodwill:

$20,000 (implied goodwill) < $165,000 (carrying amount for goodwill)

Therefore, we conclude that goodwill is impaired and must be adjusted downward by $145,000.

Chapter 4

Consolidated Financial Statement and Outside Ownership

Chapter Outline

I.   Consolidations Involving a Noncontrolling Interest

    A.   In regard to any combination in which a noncontrolling interest remains, a theoretical controversy is created as to

        1.   The appropriate consolidation values that should be assigned to the subsidiary's accounts and

        2.   The method of disclosing the presence of the other owners.

    B.   Virtually nothing in official accounting pronouncements has ever addressed the issue of valuation theory in combinations involving less than 100 percent ownership.

        1.   The FASB recently started examining this issue which may lead to the issuance of a statement requiring one theory to be used.

        2.   Companies are currently free to apply any one of several approaches in reporting the accounts of a subsidiary.

    C.   Under the **economic unit concept**, accounting emphasis on preparing consolidated financial statements is placed on the entire entity that results from the business combination.

        1.   Valuation of subsidiary accounts is based on the implied value of the company as a whole — as determined by the purchase price.

        2.   Specific subsidiary assets and liabilities are consolidated at their fair market values.

        3.   A noncontrolling interest balance is also calculated from the implied value of the company and is reported as a component of stockholders' equity.

    D.   The **proportionate consolidation concept** presumes that the ultimate objective of consolidated financial statements is to serve as a report to stockholders of the parent company.

        1.   Valuation of subsidiary accounts is based on the parent company's cost and specific subsidiary assets and liabilities are consolidated at the ownership percentage of their fair market values.

2. The noncontrolling interest is not represented in any manner within the consolidation process.

E. The **parent company concept** is a hybrid approach derived from concepts of both the *economic unit concept* and the *proportionate consolidation concept*.

    1. The book value of each subsidiary asset and liability account is consolidated in total while any difference between cost and fair market value is included based on the parent's ownership percentage.

    2. Noncontrolling interest is calculated from the subsidiary's book value and is most frequently shown between the liability and stockholders' equity sections of the consolidated balance sheet.

II. Consolidations Involving a Noncontrolling Interest — Subsequent to Acquisition

A. According to the *parent company concept*, all noncontrolling interest amounts are calculated in reference to the book value of the subsidiary company.

B. Only four noncontrolling interest figures are determined for reporting purposes:

    1. Noncontrolling interest in the subsidiary as of the beginning of the current year.

    2. Noncontrolling interest in the subsidiary's current year income.

    3. Noncontrolling interest in the subsidiary's dividend payments.

    4. Noncontrolling interest as of the end of the year — found by combining the three balances above.

C. Noncontrolling interest balances are accumulated in a separate column in the consolidation worksheet.

    1. The beginning of the year figure is recorded on the worksheet as a component of *Consolidation Entry S*.

    2. The noncontrolling interest's share of the subsidiary's income is established by a columnar entry that simultaneously reports the balance in both the consolidated income statement and the noncontrolling interest column.

    3. Dividends paid to these outside owners are reflected by extending the subsidiary's *Dividends Paid* balance (after eliminating intercompany transfers) into the noncontrolling interest column as a reduction.

    4. The end-of-year noncontrolling interest total is the summation of the three items above and is reported between consolidated liabilities and stockholders' equity.

III.   Step Acquisitions

    A.   An acquiring company may make several different purchases of a subsidiary's stock in order to gain control.

    B.   In step acquisitions, each individual investment is accounted for separately with its own allocations and amortization.

IV.   Preacquisition Income

    A.   For comparison purposes, all operational figures (revenues and expenses) of the subsidiary are consolidated as if the acquisition had taken place on the first day of the current year.

    B.   A **Preacquisition Income** figure is then deducted on the consolidated income statement to remove the earnings of the subsidiary relating to the ownership for the time period prior to the purchase.

V.   Sales of Subsidiary Stock

    A.   The proper book value must be established within the parent's *Investment* account so that the sales transaction can be correctly recorded.

    B.   The investment balance is adjusted as if the equity method had been applied during the entire period of ownership.

    C.   If only a portion of the shares are being sold, the book value of the Investment account must be reduced based on either a FIFO or a weighted average cost flow assumption.

    D.   Any interest retained by the parent company should be accounted for by consolidation, the equity method, or the market-value method.

Multiple Choice Questions

1. Which of the following conceptual approaches reports the noncontrolling interest on the balance sheet as an equity and in the statement of retained earnings as a reduction?

    A. Economic Unit Concept
    B. Proportionate Consolidation Concept
    C. Parent Company Concept
    D. Proportionate Unit Concept
    E. Economic Parent Concept

2. A basic proposition of the *economic unit concept* is that the

    A. ultimate objective of consolidated financial statements is to serve as a report to the stockholders of the parent company.
    B. subsidiary's book value and the purchase price paid by the parent are viewed as separate elements that can be accounted for individually within the consolidation process.
    C. subsidiary's individual accounts cannot be divided along ownership lines.
    D. values utilized for consolidation reflect the parent's payment attributed to each subsidiary asset and liability.
    E. controlled company must always be consolidated in phases depending on the parent's level of ownership.

Questions 3 through 5 are based on the following information.

On January 1, 2006, Cobb Enterprises acquired 80% of Bob's Bricks Inc.'s outstanding common shares. In acquiring this interest, Cobb paid a total of $3,000,000. Bob's Bricks' net assets had a book value of $2,600,000 at the time. A building with a ten-year life and a book value of $200,000 was worth $350,000. Any other excess amount was attributed to goodwill. Cobb reports net income for 2006 of $700,000 (without regard for its ownership in Bob's Bricks), while Bob's Bricks has $350,000 in earnings.

3. For each of the three following concepts, what is the amount of goodwill?

	Economic Unit Concept	Proportionate Consolidation Concept	Parent Company Concept
A.	$1,030,000	$ 770,000	$1,000,000
B.	$1,000,000	$ 800,000	$ 800,000
C.	$1,550,000	$ 770,000	$ 770,000
D.	$ 800,000	$ 800,000	$1,030,000
E.	$1,000,000	$ 250,000	$ 800,000

4.   For each of the following three concepts, what is the amount of consolidated net income?

	Economic Unit Concept	Proportionate Consolidation Concept	Parent Company Concept
A.	$1,050,000	$ 968,000	$1,038,000
B.	$ 978,000	$ 978,000	$ 978,000
C.	$ 993,000	$ 978,000	$ 968,000
D.	$ 978,000	$ 968,000	$ 968,000
E.	$1,035,000	$1,038,000	$1,038,000

5.   For each of the following three concepts, what value should be attributed to the building in a consolidated balance sheet at the date of the business combination?

	Economic Unit Concept	Proportionate Consolidation Concept	Parent Company Concept
A.	$350,000	$310,000	$350,000
B.	$320,000	$280,000	$310,000
C.	$310,000	$160,000	$320,000
D.	$320,000	$310,000	$350,000
E.	$350,000	$280,000	$320,000

Items 6 and 7 are based on the following information:

On January 1, 2005, Ashley Inc. acquires 60% of Marea Co.'s outstanding common stock in a purchase transaction. Marea reported common stock on that date of $150,000 with retained earnings of $80,000. Equipment, which had a ten-year remaining life, was undervalued in Marea's financial records by $20,000. Franchise agreements valued at $50,000 are to be amortized over 20 years.

Marea earns income and pays cash dividends as follows:

	Net Income	Dividends Paid
2005	$ 40,000	$ 15,000
2006	$ 65,000	$ 20,000
2007	$ 90,000	$ 30,000

6.   What is noncontrolling interest in Marea's 2007 income?

A. $24,000
B. $54,000
C. $60,000
D. $36,000
E. $44,000

7.   What is *noncontrolling interest* in Marea Co. at the end of 2007?

    A. $144,000
    B. $216,000
    C. $170,000
    D. $255,000
    E. $196,000

8.   On October 1, 2004, Pearson Inc. acquired 80% of the outstanding common stock of Slade Co. for $480,000. Both the book value and the fair market value of the subsidiary's net assets on that date were equal to $600,000. During 2004, Slade reports revenues of $125,000 and expenses of $50,000, both of which occur evenly throughout the year. On a consolidated income statement for the year ended December 31, 2004, what should be reported as the *noncontrolling interest* in Slade's net income and as preacquisition income?

    A. $56,250 and $18,750
    B. $15,000 and $11,250
    C. $56,250 and $ 3,750
    D. $15,000 and $ 5,000
    E. $11,250 and $56,250

9.   On January 1, 2005, Hawkeye Inc.'s net assets have a book value of $1,200,000, although equipment (with a six-year remaining useful life) having a book value of $180,000 has a fair market value of $240,000. On January 1, 2005, U.S.Eyes Corporation paid $980,000 cash for 55% of Hawkeye's outstanding common stock. On December 31, 2008, Hawkeye reports a balance in the *Equipment* account of $230,000 while U.S.Eyes reports an *Equipment* account balance of $625,000. What is the consolidated balance of the *Equipment* account on December 31, 2008, assuming U.S. Eyes uses the equity method?

    A. $855,000
    B. $888,000
    C. $882,500
    D. $875,000
    E. $866,000

10.   On January 1, 2005, Pierce Inc. acquired 80% of the outstanding common stock of Sloan Co. for $540,000. Sloan's net assets had a book value of $600,000 on that date although equipment (with a ten-year life) having a book value of $10,000 had a fair market value of $30,000. Any remaining allocation is to go to goodwill. On December 31, 2005, Sloan reports revenues of $125,000 and expenses of $50,000 while Pierce reports operating revenues of $400,000 and expenses of $250,000. What is consolidated net income for 2005?

    A. $225,000
    B. $228,800
    C. $223,400
    D. $346,200
    E. $255,300

Brief Essay Questions

1. Why does a purchase consolidation become more complex when a *noncontrolling interest* is present?

2. How does the presence of a *noncontrolling interest* affect the consolidation elimination entries at the date of acquisition and subsequent to the date of acquisition?

3. If a parent acquires several blocks of a subsidiary's common stock over a period of time before gaining control, how are the several purchases handled in the consolidation process?

Problems

1. Sockeye Co. has net assets of $2,350,000. Sockeye has land that was bought originally for $320,000 is now worth $680,000. Bream Inc. pays $2,400,000 for 75% of Sockeye's outstanding common stock.

   Required:

   Determine the amount that should be attributed to goodwill.

2. On April 1, 2006, Tiger Inc. acquires 60% of Stripes & Spots Co.'s (S&S) outstanding common stock by issuing 45,000 shares of its $1 par value common stock. Tiger's stock has a $42 per share market value. Consolidation costs of $210,000 were also paid. S&S has equipment (with a 8-year remaining useful life) undervalued on its books by $400,000. Land on S&S's books is undervalued by $500,000 S&S has franchise contracts valued at $600,000. The contracts are to be amortized over 5 years. Prior to the business combination, the financial records of the two companies show the following account balances:

	Tiger	S&S
Current Assets	$ 500,000	$ 400,000
Fixed Assets	400,000	200,000
Liabilities	100,000	200,000
Common Stock	400,000	200,000
Additional Paid-In Capital	100,000	100,000
Retained Earnings	300,000	100,000

   Required:

   Determine the consolidated balance sheet figures immediately after the business combination.

3. On January 1, 2006, Arkansas Inc. purchased 60% of Alabama Co.'s 10,000 outstanding shares of $5 par value common stock for $400,000. At that time, Alabama Co. had $100,000 of *Contributed Capital in Excess of Par* and $180,000 in *Retained Earnings*. All assets and liabilities were fairly valued except for one building which had a $150,000 fair *market value* and a $90,000 *book value,* and a previously unrecorded database with a value of $200,000. The remainder is to be allocated to goodwill.

Required:

A. Provide an analysis of the purchase price.

B. Provide the consolidation worksheet entries that would be necessary to prepare a consolidated balance sheet at the date of acquisition.

4. At the end of 2006, Alabama Co. (refer to **Question 3** above) reported $80,000 of net income, and during the year paid cash dividends of $10,000. Arkansas Inc. believes that the building has a ten-year remaining useful life. The database is to be written off over three years.

Required:

Assuming that Arkansas Inc. accounts for its investment in Alabama Co. by the equity method, provide the consolidation worksheet entries that would be required on December 31, 2006.

5. On January 1, 2005 Big Moose Entertainment bought a 60% interest in National Television Network. Big Moose paid for the transaction with $55,000 cash and 5,000 shares of Big Moose common stock (par value $2.00 per share). On January 1, Big Moose stock had a market value of $24.50 per share. On January 1, NTN's land is undervalued by $17,000. In addition, NTN buildings were undervalued by $20,000 (10 year life), equipment was overvalued by $12,000 (6 year life), and notes payable were overvalued by $4, (6 year life). The remainder is allocated to goodwill. Big Moose and NTN had the following balances on December 31, 2005.

Account	Big Moose	NTN
Current Assets	$ 429,600	$ 98,825
Investment in NTN	184,600	
Land	67,000	15,000
Buildings	193,000	69,375
Equipment	282,000	115,500
A/P	(19,620)	(7,250)
Long-term N/P	(125,000)	(56,700)
CStk ($1 par)	(310,000)	(90,000)
PIC	(639,500)	(110,000)
R/E - 1/1/05	(11,880)	(22,250)
Dividends Paid	28,000	6,000
Revenues	(2,962,500)	(671,000)
Expenses	2,895,000	652,500
Equity in NTN's Net Income	(10,700)	

Required:

A. Analyze Big Moose's *Investment in National Television Network* account at 12/31/05.

B. Provide the consolidation worksheet entries assuming that Big Moose Entertainment uses the equity method to account for its investment in National Television Network.

C. Prepare the consolidation worksheet for the consolidation of Big Moose Entertainment and National Television Network on 12/31/05.

Solutions to Multiple Choice Questions

1. **A**

2. **C**

3. **B**   Basic information derived from this item follows:

Book value of Bob's Bricks = $2,600,000
Fair market value of Bob's Bricks' net assets* = $2,750,000
Implied value of Bob's Bricks ($2,000,000 ÷ 80%) = $3,750,000
*includes the adjustment for the buildings.

Economic entity concept – valuation of subsidiary accounts:

Implied Value of Bob's Bricks			$ 3,750,000			
BV of Bob Bricks' net assets	100%	2,600,000	2,600,000			
Difference to be allocated			1,150,000			
Allocated to Buildings	100%	150,000	150,000	÷	10 =	15,000
Goodwill			$ 1,000,000			
Total Amortization Expense						15,000

Proportional consolidation concept — purchase price allocation:

Purchase Price			$ 3,000,000			
BV of Bob's Bricks' net assets	80%	2,600,000	2,080,000			
Difference to be allocated			920,000			
Allocated to Buildings	80%	150,000	120,000	÷	10 =	12,000
Goodwill			$ 800,000			
Total Amortization Expense						12,000

Parent Company Concept – Purchase Price Allocation:

Purchase Price			$ 3,000,000			
BV of Bob's Bricks' net assets	80%	2,600,000	2,080,000			
Difference to be allocated			920,000			
Allocated to Buildings	80%	150,000	120,000	÷	10 =	12,000
Goodwill			$ 800,000			
Total Amortization Expense						12,000

4.   D   Basic information derived from this item and the above solution follows:

Economic entity concept — consolidated net income:

Cobb Enterprises Net Income			$ 700,000
Bob's Bricks Inc. Net Income	100%	350,000	350,000
Amortization Expense			(15,000)
Total Net Income			1,035,000
Noncontrolling Interest in Bob's Bricks, Inc. Net Income*	20%	285,000	$ (57,000)
Consolidated Net Income			978,000

*Remember that the Economic Unit Concept presumes that the amortization relates to the subsidiary's assets. Therefore, it is deducted from the subsidiary's net income when computing Noncontrolling Interest in Subsidiary Net Income.

Proportional Consolidation Concept – Consolidated Net Income

Cobb Enterprises Net Income			$ 700,000
Bob's Bricks Inc. Net Income	80%	350,000	280,000
Amortization Expense*			(12,000)
Total Net Income			968,000

*Under both the Proportionate Consolidation Concept and the Parent Company Concept, amortization is based on the percentage of the fair market value adjustments that are owned by the parent. Remember that with the Economic Unit Concept, amortization is based on 100% of the fair market value adjustment and the implied value of the subsidiary, regardless of the percentage owned.

Parent Company Concept – Consolidated Net Income

Cobb Enterprises Net Income			$ 700,000
Bob's Bricks Inc. Net Income	100%	350,000	350,000
Amortization Expense			(12,000)
Total Net Income			1,038,000
Noncontrolling Interest in Bob's Brick's, Inc. Net Income	20%	$ 350,000	$ (70,000)
Consolidated Net Income			968,000

5.	E		Economic Unit Concept	Proportionate Consolidation Concept	Parent Company Concept
		Book value of building	$200,000	$160,000	$200,000
		Allocation based on FMV	150,000	120,000	120,000
		Consolidated Value	$350,000	$280,000	$320,000

6. **D**   Noncontrolling interest in Marea Co.'s 2007 income ($90,000 × 40%) <u>$36,000</u>

7. **A**   To calculate the noncontrolling interest in Marea Co. at the end of 2007, start with the noncontrolling interest in Marea's book value at the acquisition date, add the noncontrolling interest share of Marea's income for each year subsequent to acquisition, and then subtract the dividends paid to outside owners.

Marea Co.'s book value at the acquisition date — January 1, 2005:

Common stock	$ 150,000	
Retained earnings	80,000	$ 230,000

Increase in book value — 2005:

Net income	$ 40,000	
Dividends paid	(15,000)	25,000

Increase in book value — 2006:

Net income	$ 65,000	
Dividends paid	(20,000)	45,000

Increase in book value — 2007:

Net income	$ 90,000	
Dividends paid	(30,000)	60,000
Marea Co.'s book value at 12/31/07		$ 360,000
Outside ownership percentage		× 40%
Noncontrolling interest in Marea at 12/31/07		**$ 144,000**

8. **B**

Revenues — Slade Co.	$ 125,000
Expenses — Slade Co.	(50,000)
Net income — Slade Co.	$ 75,000
Outside ownership % at 12/31/04	× 20%
Noncontrolling interest in Slade Co's Net Income	**$ 15,000**

Preacquisition income ($75,000 x 20% x 9/12 year)   **$ 11,250**

9. **E**   Undervaluation of equipment ($240,000 – $180,000) $ 60,000
            Ownership percentage   ×   55%
            Initial allocation to equipment on 1/1/05 $ 33,000
            Useful life of equipment   ÷   6
            Annual amortization   **$ 5,500**

            Book value of Hawkeye Inc.'s equipment $ 625,000
            Book value of U.S.Eyes Co.'s equipment   230,000
            Initial allocation to equipment on 1/1/05   33,000
            Four years of amortization ($5,500 x 4 years)   (22,000)
            Consolidated balance on 12/31/08   **$ 866,000**

10. **C**

Purchase Price			$ 540,000		
BV of Sloan Co.'s net assets	80%	600,000	480,000		
Difference to be allocated			60,000		
Allocated to equipment	80%	20,000	16,000	÷ 10 =	1,600
Goodwill			$ 44,000		
Total Amortization Expense					$ 1,600

            Income of Pierce $ 150,000
            Income of Sloan   75,000
            Less: Amortization Expense   (1,600)
            Consolidated Net Income $ 223,400

Answers to Brief Essay Questions

1.   A purchase consolidation becomes more complex when a noncontrolling interest is present because the accountant must decide which theoretical approach will be used to value the subsidiary's assets and liabilities in the financial statements of the business combination. Three theoretical approaches are available: (1) the *economic entity concept*, (2) the *proportionate consolidation concept*, and (3) the *parent company concept*.

2.   At the date of acquisition:

If consolidated financial statements are prepared on the date of acquisition and there is a noncontrolling interest, *Consolidation Entry S* will reflect the allocation of the subsidiary's equity accounts at book value between the noncontrolling interest and the parent's investment. For example, the following entry would be made (numbers assumed).

Date	Accounts	Debit	Credit
	ENTRY S		
	Common Stock	100,000	
	Additional Paid-In Capital	200,000	
	Retained Earnings	150,000	
	Investment in Subsidiary (80%)		360,000
	Noncontrolling Interest in Subsidiary (20%)		90,000

Consolidation Entry A would not be affected by the existence of a noncontrolling interest. Only the parent's share of the difference between the book value and the fair market value is recognized.

Subsequent to the date of acquisition:

Only one of the SAIDE consolidation entries is affected by the existence of a noncontrolling interest, and that is *Consolidation Entry S*. However, the noncontrolling interest recognized in *Consolidation Entry S* is based on the **beginning of the year balances** in the subsidiary's *Retained Earnings* account. Since the noncontrolling interest will share in the income and dividends paid by the subsidiary, the consolidated worksheet should reflect the allocation of net income and dividends and the year-end balance for the noncontrolling interest should be reflected in the consolidated balance sheet.

3.   In a step-by-step acquisition, no single purchase price exists for the acquired firm. Instead, there must be an *analysis of purchase price* schedule and separate *amortization schedule* prepared for each purchase. The consolidated worksheet entries may then either be repeated for each single purchase or combined on a separate schedule and entered in totals. The key to a successful consolidation where an acquisition has occurred is to (a) take your time, (b) analyze each transaction separately, and (c) create a separate *amortization schedule* for each purchase. Then, if desired, you may prepare a combined schedule which shows the effect of all the separate purchases.

Solutions to Problems

1. Computation of Goodwill:

Purchase Price			$ 2,400,000
BV of net assets	75%	2,350,000	1,762,500
Difference to be allocated			637,500
Allocated to land	75%	360,000	270,000
Goodwill			$ 367,500

2. Computation of Goodwill:

Purchase Price ((45,000 shares x $42/share) + $210,000)			$ 2,100,000
Book Value of net assets	60%	2,000,000	1,200,000
Difference to be allocated			900,000
Allocated to land	60%	500,000	300,000
Allocated to equipment	60%	400,000	240,000
Allocated to franchise contracts	60%	600,000	360,000
Total to goodwill			-

CONSOLIDATION WORKSHEET - Tiger Inc. and Stripes and Spots Co.
Date of Acquisition - 1/1/06

Account	Tiger Inc.	Stripes & Spots Co.	Consolidation Entries DR	Consolidation Entries CR	Noncontrolling Interest	Consolidated Balance
Current assets	6,642,000	3,150,000				9,792,000
Fixed Assets	12,600,000	7,800,000	(A) 540,000			20,940,000
Investment in Spring Co.	2,100,000			(S) 1,200,000		-
				(A) 900,000		
Franchise Contracts			(A) 360000			360,000
Total Assets	21,342,000	10,950,000				31,092,000
Liabilities	(7,360,000)	(8,950,000)				(16,310,000)
Noncontrolling Interest				(S) 800,000	(800,000)	(800,000)
Common Stock	(2,045,000)	(600,000)	(S) 600,000			(2,045,000)
Additional Paid-in Capital	(9,357,000)	(1,300,000)	(S) 1,300,000			(9,357,000)
Retained Earnings	(2,580,000)	(100,000)	(S) 100,000			(2,580,000)
Total Liabilities & Stockholders' Equity	(21,342,000)	(10,950,000)				(31,092,000)

3.   A.   Arkansas Inc.
Analysis of Purchase Price Paid
For a 60% Ownership Interest in Alabama Co.

Purchase Price			$ 400,000
Book Value of net assets*	60%	330,000	198,000
Difference to be allocated			202,000
Allocated to Building	60%	60,000	36,000
Allocated to Database	60%	200,000	120,000
Total allocated to goodwill			46,000

*Book Value:

Common Stock	$ 50,000
Contributed Capital	100,000
Retained Earnings	180,000
Total Book Value	$ 330,000

B.   Consolidation Entries

Date	Accounts	Debit	Credit
	ENTRY S		
	Common Stock	50,000	
	Additional Paid-In Capital	100,000	
	Retained Earnings	180,000	
	Investment in Alabama Co. (60%)		198,000
	Noncontrolling Interest in Alabama Co.(40%)		132,000
	ENTRY A		
	Building	36,000	
	Database	120,000	
	Goodwill	46,000	
	Investment in Alabama Co.		202,000

4. *Consolidation Entry S* and *Consolidation Entry A* would be the same as shown in the solution for
    Item 3 and are therefore not repeated in this solution.

Date	Accounts	Debit	Credit
	ENTRY I		
	Equity in Alabama Income	4,400	
	Investment in Alabama Co.		4,400

Alabama Co.'s net income	$ 80,000
Arkansas' Ownership %	60%
Arkansas Inc.'s share of Alabama Co.'s net incor	48,000
Less:	
Amortization of fair market value difference related to the building ($36,000/10)	(3,600)
Amortization of database ($120,000/3)	(40,000)
Equity in Alabama's net income	$ 4,400

Date	Accounts	Debit	Credit
	ENTRY D		
	Investment in Alabama Co.	6,000	
	Dividends		6,000
	ENTRY E		
	Amortization Expense	43,600	
	Building		3,600
	Database		40,000

5. Big Moose Entertainment and National Television Network

    A. Analysis of Investment in NTN account:

Purchase Price			$ 177,500
+ BME's share of NTN's Net Income	60%	18,500	11,100
- Dividends Received from NTN			(3,600)
- Amortization of fair market differences			(400)
Investment at 12/31/05			$ 184,600

B.   Consolidation Entries

Date	Accounts	Debit	Credit
12/31/05	**ENTRY S**		
	Common Stock - NTN	90,000	
	Paid-In Capital - NTN	110,000	
	Retained Earnings - 1/1/05	22,250	
	Investment in NTN		133,350
	Noncontrolling Interest in NTN		88,900
12/31/05	**ENTRY A**		
	Land	10,200	
	Buildings	12,000	
	Notes Payable	2,400	
	Goodwill	26,750	
	Equipment		7,200
	Investment in Tiny		44,150
12/31/05	**ENTRY I**		
	Equity in Tiny Income	10,700	
	Investment in Tiny		10,700
12/31/05	**ENTRY D**		
	Investment in Tiny	3,600	
	Dividends		3,600
12/31/05	**ENTRY E**		
	Amortization Expense	400	
	Equipment	1,200	
	Notes Payable		400
	Building		1,200

BME's Purchase Price			$ 177,500			
BV of NTN's net assets	60%	222,250	133,350			
Difference to be allocated			44,150			
Allocated to land	60%	17,000	10,200			
Allocated to buildings	60%	20,000	12,000	÷	10 =	1,200
Allocated to equipment	60%	(12,000)	(7,200)	÷	6 =	(1,200)
Allocated to notes payable	60%	4,000	2,400	÷	6 =	400
Goodwill			$ 26,750			
Total Amortization Expense						400

CONSOLIDATION WORKSHEET - Big Moose Entertainment and National Television Network
Date of Consolidation = 12/31/05

Account	BME	NTN	Consolidation Entries		Noncontrolling Interest	Consolidated Balance
			DR	CR		
Revenues	(2,962,500)	(671,000)				(3,633,500)
Expenses	2,895,000	652,500	(E) 400			3,547,900
Equity in NTN's Net Income	(10,700)		(I) 10,700			-
Noncontrolling Interest in NTN's Net Income					7,400	7,400
Net Income	(78,200)	(18,500)				(78,200)
R/E - 1/1/05	(11,880)	(22,250)	(S) 22,250			(11,880)
Net Income	(78,200)	(18,500)				(78,200)
Dividends	28,000	6,000		(D) 3,600	2,400	28,000
R/E - 12/31/05	(62,080)	(34,750)				(62,080)
Current Assets	429,600	98,825				528,425
Land	67,000	15,000	(A) 10,200			92,200
Buildings	193,000	69,375	(A) 12,000	(E) 1,200		273,175
Equipment	282,000	115,500	(E) 1,200	(A) 7,200		391,500
Investment in NTN	184,600		(D) 3,600	(S) 133,350		-
				(A) 44,150		
				(I) 10,700		
Goodwill			(A) 26,750			26,750
Total Assets	1,156,200	298,700				1,312,050
Accounts Payable	(19,620)	(7,250)				(26,870)
Notes Payable	(125,000)	(56,700)	(A) 2,400	(E) 400		(179,700)
Noncontrolling Interest				(S) 88,900	(88,900)	(93,900)
Common Stock	(310,000)	(90,000)	(S) 90,000			(310,000)
Additional Paid-in Capital	(639,500)	(110,000)	(S) 110,000			(639,500)
Retained Earnings	(62,080)	(34,750)				(62,080)
Total Liabilities & Stockholders' Equity	(1,156,200)	(298,700)				(1,312,050)

Chapter 5

Consolidated Financial Statements – Intercompany Asset Transactions

Chapter Outline

I.   Intercompany Inventory Transactions

    A.   The transfer of assets between the companies involved in a business combination is a common practice.

    B.   The opportunity for such direct acquisitions (especially of inventory) is often a major motive for the combination.

    C.   Intercompany transfer of assets are commonplace in companies that are constructed as a vertically integrated chain of organizations; these entities seek to reduce their costs by developing affiliations in which one operation furnishes products to another.

    D.   Since consolidated financial statements report on the consolidated entity as if it were a single company, the effects of intercompany asset transfers must be eliminated because the transactions do not occur with an unrelated outside party.

    E.   Intercompany asset transfers complicate the consolidation process in terms of asset valuation, revenue recognition, and expense recognition.

    F.   Asset valuation and revenue/expense recognition issues arise in consolidation when assets are transferred at an amount other than book value.

        1.   The selling company's books will include a gain or loss which has not been verified by an arm's length transaction with an external third party.

            a.   From the perspective of the consolidated entity, the income is not correctly stated in the year of the sale due to the intercompany gain/loss. The gain/loss must be eliminated from consolidated income in the period of transfer.

            b.   In subsequent periods, the gain/loss will reside in the selling company's retained earnings and must be eliminated in each of those periods as long as the asset is still held by the consolidated entity.

            c.   The buying company will record the asset at its acquisition cost.

            d.   On the books of the buyer, if the asset acquired is depreciable, the depreciation expense for each year that the asset is held will need to be adjusted on the consolidated worksheet to account for the difference between the original "COST" and the new consolidated "CARRYING VALUE" of the asset.

        2.   If the asset is inventory, unrealized intercompany gains/losses must be eliminated as long as the inventory remains unsold to an outside third party.

        3.   Intercompany inventory sales/purchases are among the most frequently encountered intercompany transactions; the individual accounting systems of the two companies will record the transfer as a sale by one party and as a purchase by the other.

4. Because the transaction did not involve an unrelated outside party, the sales and purchases balances created by the transfer must be eliminated in the consolidation process (*Entry TI*).

5. Any transferred inventory that is held at the end of the year is recorded at its transfer price which will often include an unrealized gain.

6. For consolidation purposes, the unrealized intercompany gain remaining in unsold inventory must be deferred by eliminating the amount from the *Inventory* account on the *balance sheet* and from the ending inventory figure in *Cost of Goods Sold* (*Entry G*) on the *income statement*.

7. Since the effects of the transfer carry over to the subsequent fiscal period, the unrealized gain must be removed a second time — from the *beginning inventory component of Cost of Goods Sold* and from the *beginning Retained Earnings balance* (*Entry *G*).

8. The retained earnings figure being adjusted is that of the original seller.

9. If the equity method has been applied and the transfer was downstream, the *beginning Retained Earnings balance* will be correct; therefore, in this particular situation, the adjustment is to the *Investment* account.

10. The consolidation process is designed to shift the gain from the period of transfer into the time period in which the goods are actually sold to unrelated parties or consumed.

F. *Entry *C* was introduced in Chapter 3 as an initial consolidation adjustment required whenever the equity method is not applied by the parent company, and it converts the parent's beginning retained earnings to a consolidated total.

G. *ARB 15* indicates that alternative approaches are available in calculating the noncontrolling interest's share of a subsidiary's net income; recognition of outside ownership *may or may not* be affected by unrealized gains resulting from intercompany transfers.

1. In the text, noncontrolling interest balances are adjusted only on upstream sales from the subsidiary to the parent.

2. Downstream sales are made by the parent and are therefore viewed as having no effect on the outside interest.

3. Giving effect to upstream transfers but not to downstream transfers is merely an attempt to select the most logical approach from among several acceptable alternatives.

II. Intercompany Land Transfers

A. Intercompany land transfers are probably the least complicated of the intercompany transactions.

B. Logically, one of three situations will occur:

1. The land is sold at cost and, in this situation, the historical cost concept is maintained in the consolidation entry.

2. The land is sold at an amount greater than cost and, in this situation, the seller records a gain in the year the land is sold.

a. From a consolidated perspective, *income* in the year of the sale and *retained earnings* in subsequent years will be overstated and the *Land* account of the buyer will be overstated.

b. When a gain occurs, *Entry TL* will be needed in the year of the sale.

c. *Entry *GL* will be made in subsequent years until the land is sold or otherwise disposed of to an outside third party.

3. The land is sold at an amount less than cost.

   a. In this situation, the seller sells the land at a loss.

   b. From a consolidated viewpoint, *income* in the year of the sale and *retained earnings* in subsequent years will be understated and the *Land* account of the buyer will be understated.

C. Any gain created by intercompany land transfers is unrealized and will remain so until the land is sold or otherwise disposed of to an outside third party.

D. For each subsequent consolidation, the recorded value of the *Land* account must be reduced to the original cost with the unrealized gain that was recorded by the seller also being eliminated.

   1. In the year of the transfer, an actual gain account exists in the accounting records of the seller and must be removed.

   2. In all later periods, since the unrealized gain has become an element of the seller's *beginning Retained Earnings balance*, the reduction is made to this equity account.

   3. It the land is ever sold to an outside party, the intercompany gain is realized and must be recognized in that time period.

III.   Intercompany Transfers of Depreciable Assets

A. As with other intercompany transfers, the unrealized gain must be deferred for consolidation purposes to establish the appropriate historical cost balances.

B. The difference between the transfer-based accounting value and the historical cost of the asset will change each year due to the effects of depreciation.

   1. The unrealized gain amount in *retained earnings* will also be reduced annually since excess *depreciation expense* is recognized (and closed to *retained earnings*) based on the inflated transfer price.

   2. Consequently, elimination of the unrealized gain (in *retained earnings*) and the reduction of the asset value to historical cost will differ from one year to the next.

   3. Within the consolidation process, the recorded *depreciation expense* must be decreased every period to an amount appropriately based on the asset's original acquisition price.

C. The following *consolidation worksheet elimination entries* must be made:

   1. *Entry TA* (year of transfer) removes the unrealized gain and returns the asset account to a balance based on the original historical cost.

2. *Entry ED* (year of transfer) eliminates the current year overstatement of *depreciation expense* caused by the inflated transfer price; this entry must be repeated each year over the economic life of the depreciable asset.

3. *Entry *TA* (year following transfer) eliminates the remaining effect of the prior year's transfer so that consolidated account balances are based on the original historical cost figures.

Summary of Worksheet Elimination Entries
For Intercompany Asset Transactions

CODE	ENTRY	PURPOSE
TI	Sales Cost of Goods Sold	To eliminate intercompany sales & purchases balances in the year the sale occurs
G	Cost of Goods Sold Inventory	To remove unrealized gain created by an intercompany sale in the year the sale occurs
*G	Retained Earnings Cost of Goods Sold	To remove the unrealized gain from beginning figures so it can be recognized in the current period. Used when the sale is UPSTREAM.
*G	Investment in Subsidiary Retained Earnings	To remove the unrealized gain from beginning figures so it can be recognized in the current period. Used when the sale is DOWNSTREAM.
*C	Investment in Subsidiary Retained Earnings	To recognize an increase in the book value of the subsidiary and amortization related to the investment in the subsidiary.
TL	Gain on Sale of Land Land	To eliminate the effects of an intercompany transfer of land, in the year that the transfer occurs.
*GL	Retained Earnings Land	To eliminate the effects of an intercompany transfer of land that occurred in a previous year. Make this entry every year until the land is sold to a third party.
TA	Gain on Sale of Equipment Equipment (*or other asset*) Accumulated Depreciation	To remove the unrealized gain created by an intercompany sale of a fixed asset in the year the sale occurs, and to return fixed asset balances to historical cost basis.
*TA	Retained Earnings Equipment (*or other asset*) Accumulated Depreciation	To remove the unrealized gain created by an intercompany sale of a fixed asset in a previous period, and to return fixed asset balances to historical cost basis.
ED	Accumulated Depreciation Depreciation Expense	To eliminate overstatement of depreciation expense caused by an inflated transfer price.

Multiple Choice Questions

1. Red Inc. owns 70% of White Co.'s outstanding common stock. Price Inc. reports *cost of goods sold* in 2004 of $850,000 while White Co. reports $520,000. During 2004, Red Inc. sells inventory costing $100,000 to White Co. for $125,000. 40% of these goods are not resold by White Co. until the following year. What is *consolidated cost of goods sold*?

    A. $1,395,000
    B. $1,255,000
    C. $1,360,000
    D. $1,235,000
    E. $1,345,000

2. Maust Inc. owns 70% of Light Co.'s common stock. On January 2, 2003, Maust sold Light some equipment for $90,000. The equipment had a carrying amount of $60,000. Light is depreciating the acquired equipment over a fifteen-year remaining useful life by the straight-line method. The net adjustments to calculate 2003 and 2004 *consolidated net income* would be an increase (decrease) of

	2003	2004
A.	$ (28,000)	$ 2,000
B.	$ 2,000	$ -0-
C.	$(24,000)	$ –0–
D.	$(6,000)	$ 24,000
E.	$ (14,000)	$ (500)

Items 3 through 7 are based on the following information.

Presented below are several figures reported for Post Inc. and Mitchell Co. as of December 31, 2004.

	Post Inc.	Mitchell Co.
Inventory	$ 400,000	$ 200,000
Sales	900,000	500,000
Cost of Goods Sold	300,000	180,000
Expenses	180,000	140,000

Post Inc. acquired 80% of Mitchell Co.'s outstanding common stock on January 1, 2003. Land use rights valued at $281,250 were owned by Mitchell Co. and should be amortized over twenty years. During 2003, Mitchell sold Post inventory costing $80,000 for $100,000. 30% of this inventory was not sold to external parties until 2004. During 2004, Mitchell sold inventory costing $100,000 to Post for $150,000. Of this inventory, 25 % remained unsold on December 31, 2004.

3. What is the 2004 *consolidated sales* figure?

    A. $1,400,000
    B. $1,550,000
    C. $1,050,000
    D. $1,350,000
    E. $1,250,000

4. What is the 2004 consolidated cost of goods sold figure?

    A. $480,000
    B. $336,500
    C. $337,000
    D. $330,500
    E. $370,000

5. What is the *consolidated inventory* on December 31, 2004?

    A. $603,500
    B. $593,500
    C. $619,500
    D. $587,500
    E. $546,500

6. What is the 2004 *consolidated expenses* figure?

    A. $320,000
    B. $308,750
    C. $328,250
    D. $322,750
    E. $331,250

7. What is the noncontrolling interest's share of Mitchell Co.'s 2004 net income?

    A. $37,200
    B. $34,700
    C. $39,200
    D. $35,700
    E. $36,700

8. On January 1, 2004, Rogers Inc. sold equipment costing $2,800,000 with accumulated depreciation of $1,680,000 to Cooper Corp., a wholly owned subsidiary, for $1,500,000. Rogers had owned the equipment for six years and was depreciating the equipment using the straight-line method over ten years with no salvage value. Cooper will continue to use the straight-line method over the remaining four years of the equipment's economic life. In consolidated statements at December 31, 2004, the cost and accumulated depreciation, respectively, should be.

    A. $2,800,000 and $1,680,000
    B. $2,800,000 and $2,055,000
    C. $1,500,000 and $ 375,000
    D. $2,800,000 and $1,960,000
    E. $1,500,000 and $1,680,000

9. In 2002, Ennis Inc. purchased land from its 70%-owned subsidiary for $125,000. The subsidiary originally paid $80,000 for the land several years earlier. In 2004, Ennis Inc. needed to raise some cash and sold the land to an unrelated third party for $115,000. What amount of gain or loss on the sale of the land should be reported in the *consolidated income statement* in 2002 and 2004?

	2002	2004
A.	$ 45,000 gain	$ 35,000 gain
B.	$ –0–	$ 10,000 loss
C.	$ 45,000 gain	$ 10,000 loss
D.	$ –0–	$ 35,000 gain
E.	$ –0–	$ 45,000 gain

10. Marco Towers Inc. owns 80% of Flatbush Condos Co. On January 1, 1998, Park Inc. acquired equipment with a twenty-year life for $3,600,000. No salvage value was anticipated and the equipment was to be depreciated on the straight-line basis. On January 1, 2003, Marco Towers sold the equipment to Flatbush Condos for $3,000,000. At that time, the equipment had a remaining useful life of fifteen years, but still had no expected salvage value. In preparing financial statements for 2004, how does this transfer affect the calculation of *consolidated net income*?

   A. Consolidated net income must be decreased by $20,000.
   B. Consolidated net income must be decreased by $16,000.
   C. Consolidated net income must be increased by $20,000.
   D. Consolidated net income must be increased by $16,000.
   E. Consolidated net income must be decreased by $480,000.

Brief Essay Questions

1. How does the consolidation process for the intercompany transfer of a depreciable asset differ from that for inventory and land, assuming the depreciable asset is transferred at a gain?

2. On December 4, 2004, Bazley Inc. sold some of its heavy equipment to Cleave Co., its subsidiary. When will the gain on this sale be earned?

Problems

1. Packwell Manufacturing Inc. owns 70% of the outstanding common stock of Silvertone Co. Silvertone reports net income for 2004 of $220,000. Since being acquired, Silvertone has regularly supplied inventory to Packwell. Inventory costing $300,000 was sold to Packwell for $350,000 in 2003. In 2004, Silvertone sold inventory costing $260,000 for $318,000. 15% of the inventory that Packwell purchases from Silvertone during any one year is not used until the following year.

    ### Required:
    A. What is the noncontrolling interest's share of Silvertone's income in 2004?

    B. Prepare the 2004 consolidation entries that would be required by the above intercompany inventory transfers.

2. Pumpian Inc. has an 80% interest in Sizemore Co. On January 1, 2003, land having an historical cost of $40,000 is sold in an intercompany transaction for $50,000.

    ### Required:

    A. If Pumpian sold the land to Sizemore, what would be the appropriate consolidation worksheet entries at the end of 2003 and 2004 as a result of the transaction?

    B. If Sizemore sold the land to Pumpian, what would be the appropriate consolidation worksheet entries at the end of 2003 and 2004 as a result of the transaction?

3. Portland Inc. owns 60% interest in Sherman Co. On January 1, 2003, equipment having a historical cost of $100,000 and a book value of $70,000 is sold in an intercompany transfer for $80,000. The equipment has a remaining useful life of four years. Sherman Co. reports *net income* of $140,000 in 2003 and $160,000 in 2004.

    ### Required:

    A. If Portland Inc. sold the equipment to Sherman Company, what would be the appropriate consolidation worksheet entries for 2003 and 2004?

    B. What effect, if any, would the transaction in part A have on the valuation of the noncontrolling interest?

    C. If Sherman sold the equipment to Portland, what would be the appropriate consolidation worksheet entries for 2003 and 2004?

    D. What effect, if any, would the transaction in part C have on the valuation of the noncontrolling interest?

Advanced Accounting – 7/e

4. Porter Inc. holds a 70% interest in Stevenson Co. During 2003, Porter sold inventory costing $30,000 to Stevenson for $40,000. During 2003, Stevenson reports *net income* of $120,000 and during 2004 the reported *net income* is $140,000.

Required:

A. Prepare the consolidation worksheet entries required in 2003 and 2004 if forty percent of the intercompany inventory is still on hand at the end of 2003.

B. What is the noncontrolling interest in income for 2003 and 2004?

C. Prepare the required consolidation worksheet entries if Stevenson had sold the inventory to Porter.

Solutions to Multiple Choice Questions

1. **B**
Intercompany gain ($125,000 – $100,000)	$ 25,000
Inventory remaining at year-end	× 40%
Unrealized intercompany gain at December 31, 2004	$ 10,000

Cost of goods sold – Red, Inc.	$ 850,000
Cost of goods sold — Green Co.	520,000
Remove intercompany transfer	(125,000)
Defer unrealized gain	+ 10,000
Consolidated cost of goods sold	$1,255,000

2. **A**   Individual records after transfer:

   2003
   Equipment — $90,000
   Gain — $30,000
   Depreciation expense — $6,000 ($90,000 ÷ 15 years)
   Income effect (net) — $24,000 ($30,000 gain – $6,000 depreciation expense)

   2004
   Depreciation expense — $6,000

   Consolidated figures — based on historical cost:

   2003
   Equipment at 1/2/03 — $60,000
   Depreciation expense — $4,000 ($60,000 ÷ 15 years)

   2004
   Depreciation expense — $4,000

   Adjustment for consolidation purposes:
   2003 — $24,000 income is reduced to a $4,000 expense. Thus, income is reduced by **$28,000** ($24,000 + $4,000).

   2004 — $6,000 expense is reduced to a $4,000 expense. Thus, income is reduced by **$2,000** ($6,000 – $4,000).

3. **E**
Post Inc.'s reported sales	$ 900,000
Mitchell Co.'s reported sales	500,000
Elimination of intercompany sales	(150,000)
Consolidated sales	$1,250,000

4. **B**
Cost of goods sold — Post Inc.	$ 300,000
Cost of goods sold — Mitchell Co.	180,000
Elimination of 2004 intercompany purchases	(150,000)
Deferral of 2004 unrealized gain ($50,000 x 25%)	12,500
Recognition of 2003 unrealized gain ($20,000 x 30%)	(6,000)
Consolidated cost of goods sold for 2004	$ 336,500

5. **D**
Inventory — Post Inc.	$ 400,000
Inventory — Mitchell Co.	200,000
2004 unrealized gain	(12,500)
Consolidated inventory	$ 587,500

6.	E	Expenses — Post Inc. Expenses — Mitchell Co. 2004 amortization of land use rights ([$281,250 x 80%] ÷ 20 years) Consolidated expenses	$ 180,000 140,000 (11,250) $ 331,250

7.	B	Mitchell Co.'s reported income for 2004 Unrealized gain deferred in 2003 Unrealized gain deferred in 2003 Realized income of Mitchell Co. Noncontrolling interest percentage Noncontrolling interest's share of Mitchell Co. income	$ 180,000 6,000 (12,500) 173,500 × 20% $ 34,700

8.   D   Historical cost of the equipment $ 2,800,000
Accumulated depreciation at 12/31/04 ($1,680,000 + $280,000) = $1,960,000

9.   D   In 2002, no sale to an unrelated third party occurred. Thus, no gain is recognized in the 2002 *consolidated income statement*.

In 2004, a sale to an unrelated third party occurred. For the Consolidated entity, the historical cost of the land is $80,000. Since Jones Inc. sold the land for $115,000, a **$35,000 gain** ($115,000 – $80,000) is reported on the 2004 *consolidated income statement*.

10.   C   The equipment was not sold to an unrelated third party. Thus, from the point of view of the consolidated entity, depreciation expense must be based on the original historical cost of the equipment. Since the parent sold the equipment to the subsidiary at a gain, the subsidiary will record excess depreciation expense that must be eliminated in consolidation. The elimination of excess depreciation has the effect of increasing *consolidated net income*. Excess depreciation is calculated below:

Annual depreciation based on transfer price ($3,000,000 ÷ 15 years)	$ 200,000
Annual depreciation based on original cost ($3,600,000 ÷ 20 years)	(180,000)
Excess depreciation	20,000

Answers to Brief Essay Questions

1.   Like other intercompany inventory and land transfers, unrealized gains created by intercompany transfers of depreciable assets must be eliminated along with the overstatement of the asset. However, because of subsequent depreciation, these adjustments systematically change from period to period. Following the transfer of the depreciable asset, depreciation expense is calculated by the buyer based on the new inflated transfer price. Thus, expense is recorded that reduces the carrying value of the asset at a rate in excess of appropriate depreciation; book value moves closer to the historical cost figure each time that depreciation is recorded. Additionally, since the excess depreciation is closed annually to retained earnings, the overstatement of the equity account resulting from the unrealized gain is constantly reduced. To produce consolidated figures at any point in time, the remaining inflation in these figures (as well as in the current depreciation expense) must be determined and removed.

2.   The gain is earned over time as Blaze Co. uses the equipment or sells it to an outside party.

Solutions to Problems

1. A.

Reported 2004 income of Silvertone Co.	$ 220,000
2003 intercompany gain realized in 2001 ($50,000 x 15%)	7,500
2004 intercompany gain to be realized in 2002 ($58,000 x 15%)	(8,700)
Realized 2004 income of Silvertone Co.	218,800
Outside ownership percentage	× 20%
Noncontrolling interest's share of Silvertone Co.'s income	$ 43,760

   B. Consolidation entries for 2004 are as follows:

Consolidation Entry *G
Retained Earnings 1/1/01 (Silvertone Co.)   7,500
    Cost of Goods Sold   7,500
To remove intercompany gain from balances carried over from 2000 so that it can be recognized.

Consolidation Entry TI
Sales   318,000
    Cost of Goods Sold (purchases)   318,000
To eliminate effects of intercompany transfer of inventory.

Consolidation Entry G
Cost of Goods Sold   8,700
    Inventory   8,700
To remove intercompany gain from 2004 so that it can be appropriately recognized in 2005.

2. A.

Consolidation Entry TL — 2003
Gain on Sale of Land   10,000
    Land   10,000
To eliminate effects of intercompany land sale.

Consolidation Entry *GL — 2004
Retained Earnings (Pumpian Inc.)   10,000
    Land   10,000
To eliminate the effects of intercompany land sale in a previous year.

   B.

Consolidation Entry TL — 2003
Gain on Sale of Land   10,000
    Land   10,000
To eliminate effects of intercompany land sale.

Consolidation Entry *GL — 2004
Retained Earnings (Sizemore Co.)   10,000
    Land   10,000
To eliminate the effects of intercompany land sale in a previous year.

3.   A.   Consolidation Entry TA — 2003
Gain on Sale of Equipment 10,000
Equipment 20,000
     Accumulated Depreciation — Equipment 30,000
To remove unrealized gain and restore historical cost balances.

Consolidation Entry ED — 2003
Accumulated Depreciation — Equipment 2,500
     Depreciation Expense 2,500
To eliminate the overstatement of depreciation expense caused by a price in excess of historical cost.

Consolidation Entry *TA — 2004
Retained Earnings 7,500
Equipment 20,000
     Accumulated Depreciation — Equipment 27,500
To eliminate the effects of the 2003 intercompany sale of assets.

Consolidation Entry ED — 2004
Accumulated Depreciation — Equipment 2,500
     Depreciation Expense 2,500
To eliminate the overstatement of depreciation expense caused by a price in excess of historical cost.

B.   Because the sale is downstream, the minority interest is unaffected by the gain.

C.   The *consolidation worksheet entries* TA, ED, and *TA will be the same as in Solution A. Note that the direction of the sale does not affect these entries.

D.   The minority interest valuation is affected by these entries because only realized income is allocated.

Allocation of Noncontrolling Interest — 2003
Income reported by Sherman Co.	$ 140,000
Less unrealized gain	(10,000)
Realized income	130,000
Noncontrolling Interest percentage	× 40%
Income allocated to Noncontrolling Interest	$ 52,000

Allocation to Noncontrolling Interest — 2004
Consolidation Entry *TA will debit *Retained Earnings* of the seller for $7,500. Thus Consolidation Entry S will then eliminate shareholders' equity and recognize the allocation of that equity to the parent and the Noncontrolling Interest based on the realized amounts.

4.   A.   *Consolidation Entry TI — 2003*
Sales.. 40,000
      Cost of Goods Sold (purchases) 40,000
To eliminate effects of intercompany transfer of inventory.

Consolidation Entry G — 2003
Cost of Goods Sold (ending inventory component) 4,000
      Inventory (balance sheet account) 4,000
To eliminate unrealized gain on intercompany inventory sale. Note: profit = 10,000 x 40% = $4,000 in unsold state.

Consolidation Entry *G — 2004
Retained Earnings (Porter Inc.) 4,000
      Cost of Goods Sold (beginning inventory component) ... 4,000
To remove unrealized gain from cost of goods sold so that it may be realized in the current period.

B.   Because the inventory sale is downstream, the Noncontrolling Interest is unaffected by the sale.

2003 income	$ 120,000
Noncontrolling interest percent	× 30%
Noncontrolling interest in 2003 income	$ 36,000
2004 income	$ 140,000
Noncontrolling interest percent	× 30%
Noncontrolling interest in 2004 income	$ 42,000

C.   Consolidation worksheet entries would be the same as in Solution A except that the $4,000 in Consolidation Entry *G would be associated with the Retained Earnings of Stevenson Co.

Chapter 6

Variable Interest Entities, Intercompany Debt, Consolidated Cash Flows, and Other Issues

Chapter Outline

I.   Special Purpose Entities and Variable Interest Entities

     A.   An SPE

          1.   can be a trust, partnership, joint venture, or corporation

          2.   typically has neither independent management nor employees

          3.   usually established for a defined purpose

          4.   often has a "sponsor" company.

     B.   The "sponsor" company often does not exercise equity control over the SPE. Control is often achieved through other means.

     C.   An SPE that rewards its "sponsor" on bases other than the level of equity interest, is referred to a "Variable Interest Entity".

     D.   FASB Interpretation No. 46

          1.   If a "business enterprise has a controlling financial interest in a variable interest entity, assets, liabilities, and results of the activities of the variable interest entity should be included with those of the business enterprise."

          2.   An SPE will qualify as a VIE if it meets one of the following conditions

               a.   The total equity at risk is not sufficient to permit the entity to finance its activities without additional subordinated financial support from other parties. Generally, this threshold is reached if equity at risk < 10%.

               b.   The equity investors in the VIE lack one of the following three characteristics:

                    (1)   The direct or indirect ability to make decisions about an entity's activities through voting rights or similar rights.

                    (2)   The obligation to absorb the expected losses of the entity if they occur.

                    (3)   The right to receive the expected residual returns of the entity.

3. Characteristics of "primary beneficiary"

    a. The direct of indirect ability to make decisions about the entity's activities.

    b. The obligation to absorb the expected losses of the entity if they occur, or

    c. The right to receive the expected residual returns of the entity if they occur.

4. Since there is no cost associated with acquiring the controlling interest in the VIE, an "implied value" must be determined.

5. Determining the consolidation amount for a VIE. Use the sum of

    a. Consideration paid by the primary beneficiary, and

    b. The fair value of the newly consolidated liabilities and noncontrolling interests.

6. Disclosure requirements of FIN 46

    a. For primary beneficiaries that must consolidate a VIE

        (1) The nature, purpose, size, and activities of the VIE

        (2) The carrying amount and classification of consolidated assets that are collateral for the VIE's obligations.

        (3) Lack of recourse if creditors of a consolidated VIE have no recourse to the general credit of the primary beneficiary.

    b. For companies holding a "significant" interest in a VIE, but not qualifying as a primary beneficiary.

        (1) The nature of its involvement with the VIE and when that involvement began.

        (2) The nature, purpose, size, and activities of the VIE.

        (3) The enterprise's maximum exposure to loss as a result of its involvement with the VIE.

II. Intercompany Debt Transactions

    A. No real consolidation problem is created when one member of a business combination loans money to another. The resulting receivable/payable accounts as well as the interest income/expense balances are identical and can be directly offset in the consolidation process.

    B. The acquisition of an affiliate's debt instrument from an outside party does require special handling so that consolidated financial statements can be produced.

        1. Since the acquisition price will usually differ from the book value of the liability, a gain or loss has been created which is not recorded within the individual

records of either company.

2.   Because of the amortization of any associated discounts and/or premiums, the interest income being reported by the buyer will not correspond with the interest expense of the debtor.

3.   In the consolidation process, all balances must be adjusted to reflect the effective retirement of the debt.

C.   In the year of acquisition, all intercompany accounts (the liability, the receivable, interest income, and interest expense) are eliminated during the consolidation process while the gain or loss (which produced all of the discrepancies) is recognized.

1.   Although several alternatives exist, the textbook assigns all income effects resulting from the retirement to the parent company, the party ultimately responsible for the decision to reacquire the debt.

2.   Any noncontrolling interest is, therefore, not affected by the adjustments utilized to consolidate intercompany debt.

D.   Even after the year of retirement, all intercompany accounts must be eliminated again in each subsequent consolidation; however, the beginning retained earnings of the parent company is adjusted rather than a gain or loss account.

1.   The change in retained earnings is needed because a gain or loss was created in a prior year by the retirement of the debt, but only interest income and interest expense were recognized by the two parties.

2.   The amount of the change made to retained earnings at any point in time is the original gain or loss adjusted for the subsequent amortization of discounts or premiums.

III.   Subsidiary Preferred Stock

A.   The specific nature of a subsidiary's preferred stock has a significant impact on the procedures to be applied during the consolidation process.

1.   Preferred stocks that have a set call value and no rights other than a cumulative dividend are viewed as being equivalent to debt instruments.

2.   Preferred stocks that have voting and/or participation rights are considered ownership (or equity) interests.

B.   Subsidiary preferred stock may be viewed as a debt instrument.

1.   The cost of the parent's acquisition is simply eliminated on the worksheet against the *Preferred Stock* account as if the shares had been retired.

2.   Any difference between the par value and the acquisition price of these shares is adjusted in the consolidation process through *additional paid-in capital* or *retained earnings*.

3.   Any outside ownership retained in this preferred stock is valued based on the call value of the stock and reported as a noncontrolling interest in the consolidated financial statements.

C.   Subsidiary preferred stock may be viewed as an equity instrument.

    1.   The total book value of the subsidiary must be allocated between the preferred shares and the common shares based on the rights specifically granted to the preferred stock.

    2.   Once the book value has been allocated between the two classes of stock, the preferred stock acquisition is handled in a manner that parallels an investment in common stock.

    3.   Any excess purchase price is attributed to specific accounts based on fair market values and to other previously unrecorded intangible assets identified during the acquisition period with any residual payment assigned to goodwill.

IV.   Consolidated Statement of Cash Flows

A.   The statement is produced from the *consolidated balance sheet and income statement* and not from the separate cash flow statements of the component companies.

B.   Intercompany cash transfers are omitted from this statement because they do not occur with an outside unrelated third party.

C.   The *Noncontrolling Interest's Share of the Subsidiary's Income* is not included as a cash flow although any dividends paid to these outside owners are reported as a financing activity.

V.   Consolidated Earnings Per Share

A.   This calculation normally follows the pattern described in intermediate accounting textbooks.

    1.   *Consolidated net income* is divided by the *weighted-average number of parent shares outstanding*.

    2.   If convertibles (such as bonds or warrants) exist for the parent shares, their weight must be included — but only if earnings per share is reduced.

B.   However, if the subsidiary has dilutive equity convertibles, a different approach must be taken.

    1.   The subsidiary's *earnings per share* (both *primary* and *fully diluted*) are calculated first to arrive at

        a.   an *earnings figure* and

        b.   a *shares figure*.

    2.   The portion of the *shares figure* belonging to the parent is calculated.

    3.   That percentage of the *subsidiary's earnings* is then added to the *parent's income* in order to complete the *earnings per share calculation*.

VI.   Subsidiary Stock Transactions

    A.   If the subsidiary issues new shares of stock or reacquires its own shares as treasury stock, a change is created in the book value underlying the parent's *Investment* account, the increase or decrease should be reflected by the parent as an adjustment to this balance.

    B.   The book value of the subsidiary that corresponds to the parent's ownership is measured before and after the transaction with any alteration recorded directly to the *Investment* account.

    C.   The parent's *Additional Paid-In Capital* (or *Retained Earnings*) account is normally adjusted, although tile recognition of a gain or loss is allowed.

    D.   Treasury stock acquired by the subsidiary may also necessitate a similar adjustment to the parent's investment account, and any subsidiary treasury stock is eliminated during the consolidation process.

Multiple Choice Questions

1. Mitchell Inc. owns 100% of Bright Co. For 2004, Mitchell reports net income (without consideration of its investment in Bright) of $60,000, while Bright reported net income of $45,000. The parent had an 8% bond payable outstanding on January 1, 2004 with a book value of $126,000, and a face amount of $120,000. The subsidiary acquired the bond on that date for $122,000 from the bond market. During 2004, Bright reported interest income from the Mitchell bonds in the amount of $9,600. What is *consolidated income for 2004*?

    A. $105,000
    B. $ 95,400
    C. $114,600
    D. $ 98,400
    E. $ 93,400

2. On January 1, 2004, Points Inc. acquired a $100,000 bond originally issued by its subsidiary. The bond, which pays $9,000 interest every December 31, was originally issued by the subsidiary to earn an 8% effective interest rate. The bond had a book value of $104,000 on January 1, 2004. Points pays $95,000 indicating an effective interest rate of 10%. What amount of interest expense should be eliminated?

    A. $10,000
    B. $ 8,320
    C. $ 9,500
    D. $10,400
    E. $ 9,560

3. Hoyle Greeting Cards has the following *stockholders' equity* accounts:

6% cumulative preferred stock	$ 400,000
Common stock	3,600,000
Additional paid-in capital	5,500,000
Retained earnings	2,500,000

    The preferred stock is participating and, therefore, is considered an equity instrument. Parkway Inc. buys 80% of the common stock for $10,000,000 and 60% of the preferred stock for $1,300,000. Assuming all assets are carried at fair market value, and no identifiable intangible assets are discovered during the consolidation, what amount is attributed to goodwill on the date of the transaction?

    A. $1,360,000
    B. $1,700,000
    C. $1,940,000
    D. $2,660,000
    E. $ 640,000

Items 4 through 6 are based on the following information.

Parkview Inc. owns 80% of Skyline Co.'s 20,000 shares of outstanding common stock. The *Investment in Skyline Co.* account on the Parkview's books shows a balance of $480,000. In addition, Skyline has a book value of $30 per share.

4.   Assume that Skyline sells 5,000 previously unissued shares of its common stock to third parties for $40 per share. How does this transaction affect the *Investment in Skyline Co.* account on the Parkview's books?

    A.   The account must be increased by $32,000.
    B.   The account must be increased by $160,000.
    C.   The account is not affected since the shares were sold to outside parties.
    D.   The account must be decreased by $160,000.
    E.   The account must be decreased by $32,000.

5.   Assume that Skyline sells 5,000 previously unissued shares of its common stock to third parties for $20 per share. How does this transaction affect the *Investment in Skyline Co.* account?

    A.   The account must be increased by $32,000.
    B.   The account must be increased by $160,000.
    C.   The account is not affected since the shares were sold to outside parties.
    D.   The account must be decreased by $160,000.
    E.   The account must be decreased by $32,000.

6.   Assume that Skyline sells 5,000 previously unissued shares of its common stock solely to Parkview Inc. for $40 per share. How does this transaction affect the *Investment in Skyline Co.* account?

    A.   The account must be increased by $160,000.
    B.   The account must be increased by $18,000.
    C.   The account must be increased by $32,000.
    D.   The account must be increased by $70,000.
    E.   The account is not affected since the shares were sold to outside parties.

7.   Parry Inc. owns all of Sally Co.'s outstanding common stock. For 2004, Parry reports income (exclusive of any investment income) of $600,000. Parry has 100,000 shares of common stock outstanding. Parry also has 10,000 shares of preferred stock outstanding that receives a dividend of $25,000 per year. Sally reports net income of $400,000 for 2004 with 100,000 shares of common stock outstanding. Sally also has a thousand $1,000 bonds outstanding that pay annual interest of $90 per bond. Each of these bonds can be converted into four shares of common stock. Parry owns none of these bonds which are common stock equivalents. Assume an income tax rate of thirty percent. Rounding percentage calculations to the nearest whole percent, the consolidated *primary earnings per share* for 2004 is calculated to be

    A. $ 7.63.
    B. $10.00.
    C. $ 9.59.
    D. $ 6.00.
    E. $ 8.29.

8.   Shelton Co. has the following stockholders' equity accounts:

5% cumulative preferred stock	$ 400,000
Common stock	700,000
Additional paid-in capital	500,000
Retained earnings	300,000

The preferred stock is nonparticipating, nonvoting, and callable at 108. It therefore is considered as a debt instrument. Parkway Inc. buys 80% of Shelton's common stock for $1,700,000 and 70% of Shelton's preferred stock for $180,000. At the date of acquisition, the amount to be reported as *Noncontrolling Interest* in Shelton Co. is

A. $129,600.
B. $309,600.
C. $301,280.
D. $318,080.
E. $447,680.

9.   Portview Inc. owns 100% of Stacy Co.'s outstanding common stock. Portview reported sales of $600,000 during 2004 while Stacy reported $400,000. During 2004, Stacy transferred inventory to Portview costing $40,000 for $60,000. At the end of the year, Portview was still holding $15,000 of this inventory. Total receivables on the *consolidated balance sheet* were $100,000 at the beginning of 2000 and $125,000 at year-end. No intercompany debt existed at the beginning or end of 2004. Using the *direct approach*, the *amount of cash generated from sales* during 2004 is calculated to be

A. $940,000.
B. $975,000.
C. $965,000.
D. $915,000.
E. $949,000.

10.   Pence Inc. owns all of Slater Co.'s outstanding common stock. Slater reports sales of $500,000 during 2004 while Pence reported $800,000. During the year, Pence transferred inventory to Slater costing $80,000 for $100,000. 40% of this inventory was still in Slater's inventory at the end of 2004. Total receivables on the *consolidated balance sheet* were $100,000 at the beginning of 2004 and $180,000 at year-end. No intercompany debt transactions existed at the beginning or end of the year. Using the *direct approach*, the *amount of cash generated by sales* is calculated to be

A. $1,120,000.
B. $1,200,000.
C. $1,300,000.
D. $1,280,000.
E. $1,225,000.

11.   Which of the following is NOT a characteristic of Special Purpose Entities?

A.   An SPE can be a trust, a partnership, a joint venture, or a corporation.
B.   An SPE usually has a narrowly defined purpose.
C.   An SPE usually has a "sponsor" company that controls decision-making for the SPE
D.   Generally, in most cases, SPE's can be excluded from the consolidation process of the "sponsor" company.
E.   FIN 46 outlines the conditions that would require the consolidation of an SPE as a Variable Interest Entity.

12. A company holding a "significant" interest in a Variable Interest Entity, must disclose all of the following, except

   A. The nature of the variable interest entity.
   B. The purpose of the variable interest entity.
   C. The names of the officers of the variable interest entity
   D. The size of the variable interest entity.
   E. The primary activities of the variable interest entity

13. Big Dan Fabrics recently acquired $6,000,000 of the bonds of Karen's Remnant Rack, Inc., one of its subsidiaries, paying more than the carrying value of the bonds. To whom would the loss probably be attributed?

   A. To Karen's Remnant Rack because the bonds were issued by Karen's Remnant Rack.
   B. The loss should be amortized over the life of the bonds and need not be attributed to either party.
   C. The loss should be deferred until it can be determined to whom the attribution can be made.
   D. To Big Dan because Big Dan is the controlling party in the business combination.
   E. The loss should be allocated between Big Dan and Karen's Remnant Rack based on the purchase price and the original face value of the debt.

14. Which of the following is NOT identified by FASB FIN 46 as a characteristic of a "primary beneficiary" of an SPE?

   A. Ownership of a controlling equity interest in the SPE.
   B. The ability to make decisions about the SPE's activities.
   C. The obligation to absorb expected losses of the SPE.
   D. The right to receive expected residual returns from the SPE.
   E. All of the above are characteristics of a "primary beneficiary".

15. In a variable interest entity with an implied value that exceeds the fair market value of its net assets, how is the difference treated?

   A. The difference is treated as Goodwill and must be recorded on the consolidated balance sheet.
   B. The difference is treated as an intangible asset and must be recorded and amortized over a period no less that 5 years.
   C. The difference is ignored. Since the VIE really has no "cost" associated with it, and Goodwill is only recorded when it is purchased, we would ignore the difference.
   D. The difference is written off as an extraordinary loss by the VIE.
   E. The difference is written off as an extraordinary loss by the primary beneficiary.

Brief Essay Questions

1. A parent company purchases bonds from a third party that had been issued originally by one of its subsidiaries. From a consolidation perspective, what accounting issues arise as a result of the purchase?

2. A parent company acquires the outstanding bonds of a subsidiary from a third party. Explain how the parent company calculates the gain or loss on the acquisition.

3.	CableCo has developed the technology to offer high-speed broadband internet service to its customers over a wireless broadcast system. The system was recently tested during an outdoor music concert attended by over 1,000,000 people. However, the commercial market simply does not exist. It may take up to 5 years to develop the market to the point where the service is profitable. CableCo sets up an SPE to for the sole purpose of developing the market for the new wireless broadband service. CableCo sells the technology to the SPE for $100 million. The SPE obtains funding from a local bank. However, the local bank requires CableCo to guarantee the loan to the SPE. CableCo puts up it own stock as collateral against the loan.

In this circumstance, is CableCo a "primary beneficiary"? Is the SPE a variable interest entity?

4.	Parker Inc. controls Screen Co. Screen's stockholders' equity accounts are shown below:

9% cumulative, participating preferred stock, $100 par value, 12,000 shares outstanding	$ 1,000,000
Common stock, $50 par value, 40,000 shares outstanding	2,000,000
Retained earnings	3,000,000
Total stockholders' equity	$ 6,000,000

Should Screen's preferred stock be viewed as debt or equity interests? If Screen's preferred stock is viewed as debt, how is the consolidation process affected? If Screen's preferred stock is viewed as an equity interest, how is the consolidation process affected?

Problems

1.	Palmer Inc. obtained controlling interest in Stewart Co. on January 1, 2005 for a total consideration of $5,000,000. At that time, Stewart had the following equity accounts:

8% cumulative, participating preferred stock, $100 par value, 5,000 shares outstanding	$ 500,000
Common stock, $1 par value, 2,000,000 shares outstanding	2,000,000
Retained earnings	4,000,000

There were no dividends in arrears on the preferred stock. Palmer purchased 30% of the outstanding shares of preferred stock for $450,000. The remainder of the $5,000,000 acquisition was for 80% of the common stock. All assets and liabilities were fairly valued on Stewart's books at the date of acquisition except for one building which was undervalued by $200,000. During 2005, Stewart reported net income of $1,600,000 and paid dividends of $280,000. The building has a remaining useful life of ten years.

Required:

A.	Provide an analysis of purchase price in good form.

B.	Provide the *consolidation worksheet entries* for 2005 assuming that Palmer uses the *cost method* to account for its investment in Stewart.

2. The following data applies to Parker Inc. and its subsidiary Stansbury Co. The basic data apply to each of the requirements. Round any percentage calculations to the nearest whole percent.

Stansbury Co.:
    Shares outstanding   100,000 shares
    Book value of company $ 1,200,000

Parker Inc.:
    Shares of Stansbury owned   80,000 shares
    Book value of shares owned $ 960,000

Required:

A. Determine the entry to be made on Parker's books if Stansbury issues 10,000 shares of common stock to a third party for $10 per share.

B. Determine the entry to be made on Parker's books if Stansbury issues 10,000 shares of common stock to a third party for $15 per share.

C. Determine the entry to be made on Parker's books if Stansbury purchases 10,000 shares of its common stock from a third party at $14 per share.

Solutions to Multiple Choice Questions

1.   **D**

Mitchell's reported income	$ 60,000
Bright's reported income	45,000
Eliminate interest expense - intercompany	(9,600)
Recognize gain on retirement of debt	
($125,000 - $122,000)	3,000
Consolidated Net Income	$ 98,400

2.   **B**   Interest expense to be eliminated ($104,000 x 8%) $ 8,320

3.   **C**

Par Value:

Common Stock	$ 3,600,000	90%
Preferred Stock	400,000	10%
Totals	$ 4,000,000	100%

	Common	Preferred	Total
Book Value of Stacy Co.	$ 12,000,000	$ 12,000,000	
Portion assigned to each	90%	10%	
Book value assigned to each	$ 10,800,000	$ 1,200,000	
Purchase Price	$ 10,000,000	$ 1,300,000	
80% of Book Value	(8,640,000)		
60% of Book Value		(720,000)	
Goodwill	$ 1,360,000	$ 580,000	$ 1,940,000

4.   **A**   The additional shares are sold at a price greater than Skyline's book value. Because of this transaction, Parkview no longer has an 80% interest in a subsidiary having a $600,000 net book value. Instead, the parent now holds 64% (16,000 shares ÷ 25,000 shares) of a company with a book value of $800,000 ($600,000 + $200,000). The underlying book value equivalency of Parkview's investment has risen from $480,000 to $512,000 (64% of $800,000). This increase has been created by Skyline's ability to sell shares of stock at $10 more than the book value. The $32,000 increase is entered into Parkview's financial records as an adjustment in both the *Investment* account (since the underlying book value of the subsidiary has increased) as well as *Additional Paid-In Capital*. The calculations are shown below:

Book value of Skyline prior to selling new	
shares to outside parties (20,000 x $30)	$ 600,000
Parkview's prior ownership percentage	× 80%
Book value equivalency of Parkview's ownership	$ 480,000

Adjusted book value of Skyline	
after issuing new shares	
to outsiders ($600,000 + 5,000 shares at $40)	$ 800,000
Parkview's adjusted ownership % (16,000 ÷ 25,000)	× 64%
Adjusted book value equivalency of Parkview's ownership	512,000
Book value equivalency of Parkview's ownership	(480,000)
Required increase in *Investment in Skyline Co.* account	$ 32,000

5.   **E**   Skyline is selling the new shares to outsiders less than book value (i.e., at a discount). This necessitates a reduction in the recorded value of the *consolidated additional paid-in capital*. Parkview's ownership interest is being diluted, thus creating a decrease in the underlying book value of Parkview's investment. This reduction is calculated below:

Adjusted book value of Skyline ($600,000 + $100,000)	$ 700,000
Parkview's adjusted ownership (16,000 ÷ 25,000)	× 64%
Book value equivalency of Parkview's ownership	(448,000)
Parkview's current book value of investment	480,000
Required decrease in *Investment in Skyline Co.* account	$ 32,000

6.   **B**   Parkview purchased the 5,000 shares at a price greater than the book value of Skyline. Because Parkview made the acquisition. The transaction is handled differently than a subsidiary's sale of stock to outsiders. The acquisition causes Parkview's *Investment* account to exceed Skyline's underlying book value by $18,000. Since Parkview paid a price greater than Skyline's book value, the excess is attributed to goodwill (unless the amount can be traced to specific asset or liability accounts). As in any purchase combination, Parkview would record the entire $210,000 payment as an investment and then use *Consolidation Entry A* on the consolidation worksheet to report the allocation.

Adjusted book value of Skyline ($600,000 + $200,000)	$ 800,000
Parkview's ownership % after purchase (21,000 ÷ 25,000)	× 84%
Book value equivalency of Parkview's ownership	(672,000)
Current book value of *Investment in Skyline Co.*	
account ($480,000 + $210,000)	690,000
Difference in Skyline's book value and investment	
book value after Parkview's purchase of	
the additional 5,000 shares)	$ 18,000

7.   **C**   Figures for Sally's Primary Earnings Per Share:

Earnings:	
Net income	$ 400,000
Interest expense saved if bonds are converted	90,000
Income tax on saved interest expense at 30%	(27,000)
Earnings for *primary earnings per share*	$ 463,000

Shares:	
Outstanding	100,000
Assumed conversion of bonds	20,000
Shares for *primary earnings per share* calculation	120,000

Earnings for *primary earnings per share*	$ 463,000
Parry Inc.'s ownership interest (100,000 ÷ 120,000)	× 83%
Income from Sally to be included in *consolidated*	
primary earnings per share	$ 384,290

Calculation of Consolidated Earnings Per Share:
Earnings:

Net income	$ 600,000
Dividends paid on Parry Inc.'s preferred stock	(625,000)
Income from Sally to be included	384,290
Earnings for *consolidated earnings per share*	$ 959,290
Shares outstanding	÷ 100,000 shares
Consolidated earnings per share	
($959,290 ÷ 100,000)	$ 9.59

8.   **E**   Book Value Assigned to Preferred Stock:

Purchase price of 70% interest	$ 180,000
Call value of remaining 30% interest ($120,000 x 108%)	129,600
Book value assigned to preferred stock	$ 309,600

Book Value Assigned to Common Stock:

Total book value of subsidiary	$ 1,900,000
Book value assigned to noncontrolling interest	(309,600)
Total book value assigned to common stock	1,590,400
Outside ownership percentage	× 20%
Noncontrolling interest in common stock	$ 318,080

Total Noncontrolling Interest in Shelton Co.:

Call value of preferred stock	$ 129,600
Noncontrolling interest in common stock	318,080
Total noncontrolling interest	$ 447,680

9.   **D**

Portview's reported sales	$ 600,000
Stacy's reported sales	400,000
Intercompany inventory transfers	(60,000)
Outside sales	940,000
Elimination of increase in receivables	(25,000)
Cash generated by sales	$ 915,000

10.   **A**

Pence's reported sales	$ 800,000
Slater's reported sales	500,000
Intercompany inventory transfers	(100,000)
Outside sales	1,200,000
Elimination of increase in receivables	(80,000)
Cash generated by sales	$1,120,000

11.   **D**

12.   **C**

13.   **E**

14.   **A**

15.   **E**

Answers to Brief Essay Questions

1.   Since the bonds were purchased from an outside party, the acquisition price is likely to differ from the book value of the bonds as found in the subsidiary's records. The difference creates accounting problems in handling the intercompany transaction. From a consolidated perspective, the bonds have been retired; a gain or loss should be reported with no further interest being recorded. In reality, each company will continue to maintain these bonds in their individual financial records. Also, since discounts or premiums are likely to be present, both of these account balances, as well as the interest income or expense will change from period to period because of amortization. For reporting purposes, all individual accounts must be eliminated with the gain or loss being reported so that the events are shown from the point of view of the consolidated entity.

2.   The gain or loss to be reported is the difference between the price paid and the book value of the debt on he date of acquisition.

3.   CableCo will be considered a primary beneficiary, because it has the obligation to absorb the expected losses of the SPE. If the broadband service does not generate sufficient cash to pay off the loan, then the lender will seek recourse against CableCo. CableCo's stock will be sold to pay off the debt. Furthermore, CableCo's stock value will likely suffer due to the failure of the SPE, resulting in the necessity of selling even more stock than originally anticipated due to the depressed value.

    The SPE will qualify as a variable interest entity, because it has less than 10% of its equity at risk. In this case, the SPE has effectively none of its equity at risk. The risk is actually born 100% by the primary beneficiary.

4.   Screen's preferred stock should be viewed as equity security because of its participation rights. Preferred shares with a participation right resemble common stock.

    A subsidiary's preferred stock that is viewed as an equity interest is accounted for in the same manner as a common stock purchase. Any excess acquisition paid for the preferred stock is assigned to specific accounts based on fair market value and then to goodwill. These allocations are subsequently amortized.

    If Screen's preferred stock was viewed as debt security, shares acquired by Parker are eliminated on the consolidation worksheet as if the stock had been retired. Because preferred stock is legally an equity, its retirement cannot result in the reporting of a gain or loss to the consolidated entity. Instead, the difference between the stock's par value and the acquisition price paid by the parent must be recorded as an adjustment to *Additional Paid-In Capital* (or to *Retained Earnings* if a reduction is required and the *Additional Paid-In Capital* account is not of sufficient size). When preferred stock is viewed as debt, shares that are held by outside parties are assigned a balance equal to the call value of the securities (plus any dividends in arrears).

Solutions to Problems

1.   A.   Step One: Preferred stock is determined to have the characteristics of equity.

                    Step Two: Allocate book value between the two classes of stock. In this instance where the preferred is cumulative and fully participating, use of the par values is appropriate.

	Par Value	%	Retained Earnings
Preferred stock	$ 500,000	20%	$ 800,000
Common stock	2,000,000	80%	3,200,000
Totals	$ 2,500,000	100%	$ 4,000,000

PALMER INC. AND STEWART CO.

Allocation of Preferred and Common Stock Purchase Prices

Preferred Stock

Purchase price paid for preferred stock	450,000
Preferred stock book value equivalent to Palmer's ownership (($500,000 + $800,000) x 30%	(390,000)
Cost in excess of book value	60,000
Allocation to specific accounts:	
Building ($200,000 x 20% x 30%)	(12,000)
Goodwill	$ 48,000

Common Stock

Purchase price paid for common stock ($5,000,000 -	$ 4,550,000
Common stock book value equivalent to Palmer's ownership (($2,000,000 + $3,200,000) x 80%)	(4,160,000)
Cost in excess of book value	390,000
Allocation to specific accounts:	
Building ($200,000 x 80% x 80%)	(128,000)
Goodwill	$ 262,000

B.   Consolidation Entries

Date	Accounts	Debit	Credit
12/31/2005	**ENTRY S**		
	Preferred Stock	500,000	
	Common Stock	2,000,000	
	Retained Earnings	4,000,000	
	Investment in Stewart Co. Preferred Stock		390,000
	Investment in Stewart Co. Common Stock		4,160,000
	Noncontrolling Interest in NTN		1,950,000
12/31/2005	**ENTRY A**		
	Buildings	140,000	
	Goodwill	310,000	
	Investment in Stewart Co. Preferred Stock		60,000
	Investment in Stewart Co. Common Stock		390,000
12/31/2005	**ENTRY I**		
	Dividend Income	196,000	
	Dividends Paid		196,000
12/31/2005	**ENTRY E**		
	Amortization Expense	14,000	
	Buildings		14,000

2.   A.   Analysis:

Adjusted book value ($1,200,000 + $100,000)	$ 1,300,000
Current parent ownership % (80,000 ÷ 110,000)	73%
Book value equivalency of ownership	$ (949,000)
Current book value of investment	960,000
Required investment reduction	$ 11,000

Date	Accounts	Debit	Credit
	REQUIRED ENTRY		
	Additional Paid-In Capital - Parker Inc.	11,000	
	Investment in Stansbury Co.		11,000

B.   Analysis

Adjusted book value ($1,200,000 + $150,000)	$ 1,350,000
Current parent ownership % (80,000 ÷ 110,000)	73%
Book value equivalency of ownership	$ (985,500)
Current book value of investment	960,000
Required investment reduction	$ (25,500)

Date	Accounts	Debit	Credit
	REQUIRED ENTRY		
	Investment in Stansbury Co.	25,500	
	Additional Paid-In Capital - Parker Inc.		25,500

C.   Analysis:

Adjusted book value ($1,200,000 - $140,000)	$	1,060,000
Current parent ownership % (80,000 ÷ 90,000)		89%
Book value equivalency of ownership	$	(943,400)
Current book value of investment		960,000
Required investment reduction	$	16,600

Date	Accounts	Debit	Credit
	REQUIRED ENTRY		
	Additional Paid-In Capital - Parker Inc.	16,600	
	Investment in Stansbury Co.		16,600

Chapter 7

Consolidated Financial Statements - Ownership Patterns and Income Taxes

Chapter Outline

I.   Indirect Subsidiary Control

      A.   Control of subsidiary companies within a business combination is often of an indirect nature; one subsidiary possesses the stock of another rather than the parent having direct ownership.

           1.   These ownership patterns may be developed specifically to enhance control or for organizational purposes.

           2.   Such ownership patterns may also result from the parent company's acquisition of a company that already possesses subsidiaries.

      B.   One of the most common corporate structures is the father-son-grandson configuration where each subsidiary in turn owns one or more subsidiaries.

      C.   The consolidation process is altered somewhat when indirect control is present.

           1.   The worksheet entries are effectively doubled by each corporate ownership layer but the concepts underlying the consolidation process are not changed.

           2.   The calculation of the realized income of a subsidiary company is an important step in an indirect ownership structure.

               a.   The determination of realized income figures is needed for equity income accruals as well as for the calculation of noncontrolling interest balances.

               b.   Any company within the business combination that is in both a parent and a subsidiary position must recognize the equity income accruing from its subsidiary before calculating its own realized income.

II.   Indirect Subsidiary Control — Connecting Affiliation

      A.   A connecting affiliation exists whenever two or more companies within a business combination hold an equity interest in another member of that organization.

      B.   Despite this variation in the standard ownership pattern, the consolidation process is essentially the same for a connecting affiliation as for a father-son-grandson organization.

      C.   Once again, any company in both a parent and a subsidiary position must recognize an appropriate equity accrual as a prerequisite for computing its own realized income.

III.   Mutual Ownership

    A.   A mutual affiliation exists whenever a subsidiary owns shares of its parent company.

    B.   Parent shares being held by a subsidiary can be accounted for by the treasury stock approach.

        1.   The cost paid to acquire the parent's stock is reclassified during the consolidation process to a treasury stock account and no income is accrued.

        2.   The treasury stock approach is popular in practice because of its simplicity.

    C.   Parent shares being held by a subsidiary can also he accounted for by the conventional approach.

        1.   The subsidiary's ownership is reported in a manner that parallels the parent's accounting for investments in the members of a business combination.

        2.   The subsidiary must record any income accruing from its ownership of the parent based upon use of the equity method.

        3.   Because of the mutual ownership pattern, realized income figures for either party can only be determined by solving two simultaneous equations.

IV.   Income Tax Accounting for a Business Combination

    A.   A consolidated tax return can be prepared to cover all companies comprising an affiliated group.

        1.   Any other companies within the business combination must file separate tax returns.

        2.   A domestic corporation may be included in an affiliated group it the parent company (either directly or indirectly) owns at least eighty percent of the voting stock of the subsidiary as well as eighty percent of each class of its nonvoting stock.

        3.   The filing of a consolidated tax return provides several potential advantages to the members of an affiliated group.

            a.   Intercompany profits are not taxed until realized.

            b.   Intercompany dividends are not taxed, although these distributions are nontaxable for all members of an affiliated group whether a consolidated return or a separate return is filed.

            c.   Losses of one affiliate can be used to reduce the taxable income earned by other members of the group.

4.   If a consolidated tax return is filed, an allocation of the total expense must be made to each of the component companies to arrive at the realized income figures that serve as a basis for noncontrolling interest calculations.

5.   Income tax expense is frequently assigned to each subsidiary based on the amounts that would have been paid on separate returns.

B.   Members of a business combination that are foreign companies or that do not meet the eighty percent ownership rule, as previously described, must file separate income tax returns.

1.   Companies that are members of an affiliated group can still elect to file separate tax returns.

2.   Deferred income taxes must often be recognized when separate returns are filed because of temporary differences stemming from unrealized gains and losses as well as intercompany dividends.

C.   The tax basis of a subsidiary's assets and liabilities may differ from their consolidated values, which are based on the fair market values on the date the combination is created.

1.   If additional taxes will result in future years (for example — if the tax basis of an asset is lower than its consolidated value so that future depreciation expense for tax purposes will be less), a deferred tax liability is created by a combination.

2.   The deferred tax liability is then written off, creating a reduction in income tax expense in future years so that the net expense recognized matches the combination's book income (a lower number because of the extra depreciation on the consolidated value).

D.   Net operating losses recognized by a company can be used to reduce taxable income from the previous three years (a *carryback*) or for the future fifteen years (a *carryforward*).

1.   If one company in a newly created combination has an *operating loss carryforward*, the future income tax benefits are recognized as a *deferred income tax asset*.

2.   A *valuation allowance* must also be recorded to reduce the deferred tax asset to the amount that is more likely than not to be realized.

Multiple Choice Questions

1.   Perview Inc. owns 70% of Software Co. Software Co. owns 80% of Bronston Co. Operating income figures for 2004 are presented below, which contain no investment income. Included in both Software's and Bronston's income is a $120,000 *unrealized gain on intercompany transfers* to Perview.

	Perview Inc.	Software Co.	Bronston Co.
Operating Income	$1,250,000	$720,000	$400,000

What is Perview Inc.'s realized income for 2004?

A. $1,978,000
B. $1,826,800
C. $2,194,000
D. $1,910,800
E. $2,074,000

2.   Palmroy Inc. owns 70% of Sport Co. which, in turn, owns 60% of Frank Co. Operating income figures (without investment income) as well as unrealized gains that are included within the income for the year are presented below.

	Palmroy Inc.	Sport Co.	Frank Co.
Operating Income	$870,000	$600,000	$420,000
Unrealized Gains	$ 60,000	$100,000	$ 75,000

On the *consolidated income statement* for the year, what balance is reported for the noncontrolling interest in the subsidiaries' income?

A. $316,000
B. $254,000
C. $138,000
D. $350,100
E. $212,100

3.   Patchner Inc. owns 80% of Spring Co. while Spring Co. owns 20% of the outstanding shares of Patchner Inc. No goodwill or any other allocations came from either of these acquisitions. Patchner reports *operational income* of $250,000 for 2004 while Spring earned $100,000 during the same year. Assuming the conventional approach is being used, the amount reported on a *consolidated income statement* for the *noncontrolling interest* in Spring's income is

A. $78,571
B. $15,714
C. $42,857
D. $35,714
E. $43,257

Advanced Accounting – 7/e

4.   For companies that comprise an affiliated group, which of the following is a benefit associated with the filing of a consolidated tax return?

A.   Intercompany profits are taxed before they are realized.
B.   Intercompany dividends are taxed at a lower rate that applies to all dividends between members of an affiliated group, regardless of whether a consolidated return is filed.
C.   Intercompany profits are never taxed, even when they are realized.
D.   Intercompany profits may be taxed twice in certain cases.
E.   Losses incurred by one affiliated company can be used to reduce taxable income earned by other members of that group.

5.   Which one of the following statements is true?

A.   The amortization of goodwill affects the calculation of income taxes on a consolidated return only if the goodwill is amortized over a thirty-year period.
B.   *SFAS 109* requires the recording of a deferred income tax asset for any NOL carryforward.
C.   Goodwill is deductible for income tax purposes as long as a company exports a significant amount of its domestic production.
D.   Net operating losses may he carried back for fifteen years and applied as a reduction to taxable income figures previously reported.
E.   When a consolidated income tax return is filed, separate returns must always be filed by all of the component corporations.

6.   Alton Inc. owns 80% of the voting stock of Edinburg Co. The purchase price exceeded the underlying book value of Edinburg Co.'s assets and liabilities by $30,000. At the same time, Edinburg holds a 30% interest in the outstanding common stock of Alton. The Alton stock was purchased at a price which exceeds the underlying book value by $20,000. Each company uses the cost method to account for its investment in the other. During 2005, the following information was obtained:

	Operating Income	Dividend Income	Total Income
Alton Inc.	$160,000	$ 32,000	$192,000
Edinburg Co.	$ 60,000	$ 30,000	$ 90,000

All dividend income recognized by the two companies is due to investment in the other company. If the *treasury stock method* is used, what amount would be recorded in the *consolidated financial statements* as the *noncontrolling interest* in Edinburg's income?

A. $ 6,400
B. $18,000
C. $ 6,000
D. $12,000
E. $10,600

7.	If a subsidiary owns shares of its parent, a mutual affiliation is said to exist. Which one of the following statements is true?

A.	This investment is not considered to be intercompany in nature; therefore, it does not have to be eliminated for consolidation purposes.
B.	The amount of the investment eliminated and the income allocated to the subsidiary can only be calculated by using the treasury stock approach.
C.	The treasury stock approach reclassifies the cost of the shares as treasury stock with an equity accrual being recorded.
D.	This investment is intercompany in nature and therefore must be eliminated for consolidation purposes. The amount to be eliminated and the income allocated to the subsidiary can be calculated in two different ways.
E.	The amount of the investment eliminated and the income allocated to the subsidiary can only be calculated by using the conventional approach.

8.	On January 3, 2004, Packer Inc. purchases all of Silver River Co.'s outstanding common stock for $360,000 in cash. On that date, the subsidiary has net assets with a $350,000 fair market value, but with a $300,000 income tax basis. The income tax rate is 30%. Neither company has reported any *deferred income tax assets* or *deferred income tax liabilities*. What amount of goodwill should be recognized on the date of the business combination?

A.	$ –0–
B.	$40,000
C.	$10,000
D.	$19,000
E.	$25,000

Items 9 and 10 are based on the following information.

The following figures are reported by Payne Inc. and its 80% owned subsidiary, Shelley Co., for the year ended December 31, 2003. Shelley paid dividends of $25,000 during 2003.

	Payne Inc.	Shelley Co.
Sales	$ 400,000	$ 300,000
Cost of Goods Sold	(200,000)	(200,000)
Operating Expenses	(100,000)	(50,000)
Dividend Income	20,000	-
Net Income	$ 120,000	$ 50,000

Amortization expense relating to Payne's takeover of Shelley is $5,000 per year, and is related to a database owned by Shelley. In 2002, unrealized gains of $20,000 on upstream transfers were deferred to 2003. In 2003, unrealized gains of $10,000 on upstream sales were deferred to 2004

9. Assuming a 30% income tax rate, what *income tax expense* should be shown in the *consolidated income statement* if a *consolidated income tax return* is filed in 2003

    A. $48,000
    B. $44,400
    C. $42,900
    D. $51,600
    E. $46,500

10. Assuming a 30% income tax rate, what is the amount of income tax currently payable in 2003

    A. $51,600
    B. $46,500
    C. $48,000
    D. $44,400
    E. $42,900

Brief Essay Questions

1. According to current income tax laws, a business combination may elect to file a consolidated income tax return encompassing all companies that comprise an affiliated group. What are the essential criteria for including a subsidiary within an affiliated group?

2. What are the advantages of a business combination filing a consolidated income tax return?

3. In accounting for a mutual ownership, what unique conceptual issues are raised?

Problems

1. Dakota Inc. purchased 80% of the outstanding stock of Tennessee Co. on January 1, 2004 for $800,000. Tennessee Co. purchased 70% of Knoxville Co. on January 1, 2004 for $500,000. All assets and liabilities were fairly valued on Tennessee Co.'s books and on Knoxville Co.'s books. Each of the parent companies used the cost method to account for its subsidiary and no dividends were paid by either Knoxville or Tennessee during the year. Net income for 2004 for each company separately was Dakota $300,000, Tennessee $100,000, Knoxville $100,000.

    Required:

    Determine the amount of *consolidated net income* to be reported by the business combination.

2. Pennsylvania Inc. purchased a 40% interest in Ohio Co. on January 1, 2005 at the same time that it purchased a 90% interest in Indiana Co. On January 1, 2006, Indiana purchased a 40% interest in Ohio. All companies account for investments using the equity method. At the time of purchase assets and liabilities were equal to their fair values. Pennsylvania determined that it had goodwill of $20,000 on the purchase of Ohio and $30,000 on the purchase of Indiana. Indiana had $10,000 goodwill when it purchased its interest in Ohio. During 2006, no intercompany dividends were paid and no intercompany transactions took place. For the year ending December 31, 2006, income was reported by the companies as follows:

Pennsylvania Inc.	$ 200,000
Ohio Co.	100,000
Indiana Co.	100,000

The income reported is for each company's own separate operations and does not include any income from the equity method due to its having investments.

Required:

A. Determine the amount of income to be reported by the business combination for 2006.

B. What is Indiana Co.'s income including its equity interest in Ohio Co.?

C. Can Pennsylvania Inc. include Ohio Co. in its consolidated financial statements? Explain.

3. Oregon Inc. owns 90% of the outstanding stock of Florida Co. During 2004, Oregon reports income exclusive of any income accrued from Florida of $100,000. Florida reported income of $60,000 and paid dividends of $10,000. There were no intercompany transactions during the period and Oregon found that Florida's assets and liabilities were fairly valued at the time of purchase and that there was no goodwill to be recognized.

Required:

A. Assuming that the companies qualify as an affiliated group and that they elect to file a consolidated income tax return, how much would consolidated income taxes be if the group pays a 40% marginal rate?

B. What would the total income tax be if each company filed separately?

Solutions to Multiple Choice Questions

1. **B**

Bronston's Operational Income	$ 400,000
Unrealized Gain Deferred	(120,000)
Bronston's Realized Income	$ 280,000

Software's Operational Income	$ 720,000
Unrealized Gain Deferred	(120,000)
Investment Income ($280,000 x 80%)	224,000
Software's Realized Income	$ 824,000

Perview's Operational Income	$ 1,250,000
Investment Income ($824,000 x 70%)	576,800
Perview's Realized Income	$ 1,826,800

2. **D**

Frank's Operational Income	$ 420,000
Unrealized Gain Deferred	(75,000)
Frank's Realized Income	$ 345,000
Outside Ownership Percentage	40%
Noncontrolling Interest in Frank Co.	$ 138,000

Sport's Operational Income	$ 600,000
Unrealized Gain Deferred	(100,000)
Investment Income ($345,000 x 60%)	207,000
Sport's Realized Income	$ 707,000
Outside Ownership Percentage	30%
Noncontrolling Interest in Sport Co.	$ 212,100
Noncontrolling Interest in Frank Co.	$ 138,000
Total Noncontrolling Interest	$ 350,100

3. **D** The accountant uses the following set of equations to calculate the appropriate income figures to be assigned to each company:

Patchner's Realized Income (PRI) = Patchner's operating income plus 80% of Spring's realized income.

Spring's Realized Income (SRI) = Spring's operating income plus 20% of Patchner's realized income.

By inserting the operational income figures, the simultaneous equations can be restated as follows:

PRI = $250,000 plus 80% of SRI.
SRI = $100,000 plus 20% of PRI.

To arrive at a single equation containing only one unknown, the equivalency of PRT in the first equation can be used as a replacement within the second equation, *with replacement*:

SRI = $100,000 + .20 ($250,000 + .8 SRI)
SRI = $100,000 + $50,000 + .16 SRI
.84 SRI = $150,000
SRI = $178,571

Since the noncontrolling interest owns 20% of Spring's common stock, **$35,714** ($178,571 x 20%) of consolidated net income is assigned to these outside owners.

4.   **E**

5.   **B**

6.   **B**   The noncontrolling interest is based on total income. Therefore:

Total Edinburg Co. income	$ 90,000
Noncontrolling interest percentage	20%
Noncontrolling interest in Edinburg Co. income	**$ 18,000**

7.   **D**

8.   **E**   According to *SFAS 109, Accounting for Income Taxes*, a *deferred tax liability* is created by the temporary timing difference of $50,000 ($350,000 fair market value less $300,000 tax basis). Given a 30% income tax rate, a *deferred income tax liability* of $15,000 ($50,000 x 30%) must be recognized by the newly formed business combination. Consequently, in a consolidated balance sheet prepared immediately after Packer obtains control over Silver River, the *net assets* would be recorded at a fair market value of $350,000. In addition, the new *deferred income tax liability* of $ 15,000 is recognized. Since the net value of these two accounts is $335,000, goodwill of $25,000 is also recorded as the figure remaining from the $360,000 purchase price. The goodwill is calculated as follows:

Purchase price		$ 360,000
Fair market value	$ 350,000	
Deferred income tax liability	(15,000)	(335,000)
Goodwill		$ 25,000

9. **E** On consolidated income tax returns, the unrealized gains are deferred until realized. Since eighty percent of the subsidiary's stock is owned, the dividends are nontaxable and no *deferred income tax liability* is required on the income not distributed by the subsidiary.

Calculation of Shelley Co.'s Realized Income:

Reported Income	$ 50,000
2003 Deferred Gains	20,000
2004 Deferred Gains	(10,000)
Realized Income	$ 60,000
Outside Ownership Percentage	20%
Noncontrolling Interest	$ 12,000

Due to Government (Consolidated Return):

Consolidated Net Income (Revenues - COGS - Expenses - Noncontrolling Interest)	$ 143,000
Elimination of Noncontrolling Interest	12,000
Income to be Taxed	$ 155,000
Income Tax Rate	30%
Income Tax Expense	$ 46,500

10. **B**

Current Expense (as per Consolidated Return)

Consolidated Net Income	$ 143,000
Elimination of Noncontrolling Interest	12,000
Income to be Taxed	$ 155,000
Income Tax Rate	30%
Income Tax Payable	$ 46,500

Answers to Brief Essay Questions

1. According to present income tax laws, an affiliated group can be comprised of all domestic corporations in which a parent holds 80% ownership. More specifically, the parent must also own (directly or indirectly) 80% of the voting stock of the subsidiary corporation as well as at least 80% of each class of nonvoting stock.

2. There are several advantages to business combinations that file a consolidated income tax return. **First**, intercompany profits are not taxed until realized. For companies with large amounts of intercompany transactions, the deferral of unrealized gains causes a delay in the making of significant tax payments. **Second**, losses incurred by one company can be used to reduce or offset taxable income earned by other members of the affiliated group. **Third**, intercompany dividends are not taxable but that exclusion applies to the members of an affiliated group regardless of whether a consolidated tax return or separate return is filed.

3. If a subsidiary owns shares of its parent, a mutual ownership is said to exist. The unique concerns raised by mutual ownership center on the handling of any parent company stock owned by a subsidiary. *ARB 51 (par. 12)* states that "the shares of the parent held by a subsidiary should not be treated as outstanding stock in the consolidated balance sheet." That is, the subsidiary's investment in a parent's stock is intercompany in nature and therefore must be eliminated for consolidation purposes. The amount to be removed and the income allocated to the subsidiary can be calculated in two different ways: (1) The *treasury stock approach* simply reclassifies the cost of these shares as treasury stock with no equity accrual being recorded. (2) In contrast, the *conventional approach* accounts for the shares as a regular investment in a related party. Under the *conventional approach*, equity income accruals are attributed to the subsidiary in connection with ownership of the parent. Since the companies are both in parent and subsidiary positions, the amount of realized income cannot be directly derived by either party. These figures can be found only by solving two simultaneous equations.

Solutions to Problems

1.

Tennessee Co.'s Income	$ 100,000
70% of Knoxville Co.'s Reported Income	70,000
Tennessee Co.'s Adjusted Income	$ 170,000
Dakota Inc.'s Ownership Percentage	80%
Dakota Inc.'s Accrual	$ 136,000
Dakota Inc.'s Reported Income	300,000
Consolidated Income	$ 436,000

2.   A.

Indiana Co.'s Reported Income	$ 100,000
40% of Ohio Co.'s Income	40,000
Amortization	-
Indiana Co.'s Income	$ 140,000
Pennsylvania Inc.'s Ownership Percentage	90%
Pennsylvania Inc.'s Share of Indiana Co's Income	$ 126,000
Amortization	-
Consolidated Income	$ 126,000

Ohio Co.'s Reported Income	$ 100,000
Pennsylvania Inc.'s Ownership Percentage	40%
Pennsylvania Inc.'s of Ohio Co.'s Income	40,000
Amortization	$ -
Accrual for Ohio Co.	40,000
Accrual for Indiana Co.	$ 126,000
Pennsylvania Inc.'s Reported Income	200,000
Consolidated Income	$ 366,000

B.   Indiana Co.'s Income = $ 140,000

C.   Yes, because Pennsylvania Inc.'s ownership is 76%

Direct Interest	40%
Indirect Interest (90% x 40%)	36%
Total Interest	76%

3.   A.

Oregon Inc.'s Income	$ 100,000
Florida Co.'s Income	60,000
Total Taxable Income	$ 160,000
Income Tax Rate	40%
Total Income Tax Expense	$ 64,000
Noncontrolling Interest Share ($64,000 x ($60,000 ÷ $160,000 x 10%))	(2,400)
Consolidated Income Tax Expense	$ 61,600

B.

Oregon Inc.'s Income	$ 100,000
Dividends	9,000
Dividends Exclusion	(7,200)
Taxable Income	$ 101,800
Income Tax Rate	40%
Oregon Inc.'s Income Tax Expense	$ 40,720

Florida Co.'s Income	$ 60,000
Income Tax Rate	40%
Florida Co.'s Total Income Tax Expense	$ 24,000
Noncontrolling Interest's Share ($24,000 x 10%)	(2,400)
Florida Co.'s Income Tax Expense	$ 21,600
Oregon Inc.'s Income Tax Expense	$ 40,720
Total Income Tax Expense for Consolidation	$ 62,320

Chapter 8

Reporting Segment and Interim Information
Chapter Outline

I. Disaggregated Information — Historical Perspective

    A. In the past, consolidation of financial information made the analysis of diversified companies quite difficult.

        1. The consolidation process tends to obscure the individual characteristics of the various component operations.

        2. Many groups (especially during the 1960s) called for the presentation of disaggregated financial data as a means of enhancing the informational content of corporate reporting.

    B. The move toward dissemination of disaggregated information culminated in December 1976 with the release by *SFAS 14, Financial Reporting for Segments of a Business Enterprise*.

        1. This pronouncement requires extensive disclosures pertaining to industry segments, domestic and foreign operations, export sales, and major customers.

        2. The information is not designed to allow comparisons to be made between companies but rather serves as a means of permitting a better evaluation of an enterprise's past performance and future prospects.

        3. Disclosure is not required of nonpublic enterprises.

II. FASB Statement 14 - *SFAS 14* required financial information to be presented portraying as many as four distinct aspects of a company's operations.

    A. *Industry segments* — A company was required to disclose for each reportable industry segment:

        1. Revenues

        2. Operating profit or loss

        3. Identifiable assets

        4. Aggregate amount of depreciation, depletion, and amortization expense

        5. Capital expenditures

6.   Equity in the net income from an investment in the net assets of equity investees

B.   *Domestic and foreign operations* — A company had to disclose for domestic operations as well as for operations in each significant foreign geographic area:

    1.   Revenues

    2.   Operating profit or loss

    3.   Identifiable assets

C.   *Export sales* — A company reported for domestic operations the amount of revenue derived from exporting products to unaffiliated customers in foreign countries.

D.   *Major customers* — A company was required to disclose the amount of revenue derived from sales to each major customer.

III.   Usefulness of Disaggregated Financial Information

A.   Academic research has empirically investigated the usefulness of *SFAS 14* disclosures, and discovered the following:

    1.   Industry segment data improve analysts' accuracy in predicting consolidated sales and earnings; this is true for both large and small firms.

    2.   The availability of industry segment data leads to greater consensus among analysts regarding their forecasts of sales and earnings.

    3.   Segment *revenue* data (both industry and geographic) appear to be more useful than segment *earnings* data in making forecasts.

    4.   The initial disclosure of geographic area data was used by stock market participants in assessing the riskiness of companies with foreign operations.

B.   The *Association for Investment Management and Research* (*AIMR*), *AICPA*, and *IASC* have all been instrumental in trying to improve segment reporting.

IV.   FASB Statement 131

A.   According to *SFAS 131*, the objective of segment reporting is to provide information about the different business activities in which an enterprise engages and the different economic environments in which it operates to help users of financial statements:

    1.   Better understand the enterprise's performance.

    2.   Better assess its prospects for future net cash flows.

    3.   Make more informed judgments about the enterprise as a whole.

B.	The *management approach* for determining segments is based on the way that management disaggregates the enterprise for making operating decisions.

    1.	The disaggregated components are *operating segments*, which will be evident from the enterprise's organization structure.

    2.	An *operating segment* is a component of an enterprise:

        a.	That engages in business activities from which it earns revenues and incurs expenses.

        b.	Whose operating results are regularly reviewed by the chief operating decision maker to assess performance and make resource allocation decisions.

        c.	For which discrete financial information is available.

V.	Determining Reportable Operating Segments

    A.	In determining whether business activities and environments are similar, management must consider these aggregation criteria:

        1.	The nature of the products and services provided by each operating segment.

        2.	The nature of the production process.

        3.	The type or class of customer.

        4.	The distribution methods.

        5.	If applicable — the nature of the regulatory environment.

    B.	*SFAS 131* retained the three tests from *SFAS 14* for identifying operating segments for which separate disclosure is required:

        1.	*Revenue test* — Determine if segment revenues, both external and intersegment, are ten percent or more of the combined revenue, internal and external, of all reported operating segments.

        2.	*Profit or loss test* — Determine if segment profit or loss is ten percent or more of the greater (in absolute terms) of the combined reported profits of all profitable segments or the combined reported loss of all segments incurring a loss.

        3.	*Asset test* — Determine if segment assets are ten percent or more of the combined assets of all operating segments.

VI.   Other Guidelines

    A.   FASB rules applying to the disclosure of operating segment information are designed to ensure that the disaggregated data is consistent from year to year and relevant to the needs of financial statement users.

    B.   If an operating segment newly qualifies for disclosure in the current year, prior period segment data presented for comparative purposes must be restated to reflect the newly reportable segment as a separate segment.

    C.   *SFAS 131* requires a substantial portion of a company's operations to be presented individually to enhance the value of the disaggregated information.

VII.   Information to be Disclosed by Operating Segment - *SFAS 131* has significantly expanded the amount of information to be disclosed for each operating segment:

    A.   *General information* about the operating segment:

        1.   Factors used to identify operating segments.

        2.   Types of products and services from which each operating segment derives its revenues.

    B.   *Segment profit or loss* and the following revenues and expenses included in segment profit or loss:

        1.   Revenues from external customers.

        2.   Revenues from transactions with other operating segments.

        3.   Interest revenue and interest expense (reported separately); net interest revenue may be reported for finance segments if this measure is used internally for evaluation.

        4.   Depreciation, depletion, and amortization expense.

        5.   Other significant noncash items included in segment profit or loss.

        6.   Unusual items (discontinued operations and extraordinary items).

        7.   Income tax expense or benefit.

    C.   *Total segment assets* and the following related items:

        1.   Investment in equity method affiliates.

        2.   Expenditures for additions to long-lived assets.

D. Even though requested by the AIMR, the FASB does not require cash flow information to be reported for each operating segment since this information often is not generated by segments for internal reporting purposes.

VIII. Enterprisewide Disclosures

A. Information about products and services – Revenues derived from transactions with external customers from each product or service must be disclosed, if operating segments have not been determined based on differences in products or services.

B. Information about Geographic areas

1. For the domestic country - Disclose revenues from external customers and long-lived assets.

2. For all foreign countries in which the enterprise derives revenues or holds assets - Disclose revenues from external customers and long-lived assets.

3. For each foreign country in which a material amount of revenues is derived or assets are held - Disclose revenues from external customers and long-lived assets.

4. These disclosures are required even if the company reports only one operating segment.

C. Information about Major Customers

1. When more than 10% of a company's revenues are derived from a single customer, reliance on that customer must be disclosed.

2. The amount of revenues from each major customer and the operating segment earning those revenues must be disclosed.

IX. Interim Reporting

A. The *management approach* should provide less costly disclosure since the information used has already been collected by management.

B. *SFAS 131* therefore requires segment disclosures to be made in interim reports.

C. The following items of information are required to be included in interim reports for each operating segment:

1. Revenues from external customers.

2. Intersegment revenues.

3. Segment profit or loss.

4. Total assets, if there has been a material change from the last annual report.

Multiple Choice Questions

1. Pennwick Inc. had the following expense items and appropriately determined *segment revenue* of $2,700,000 associated with its *sporting segment*.

Operating expenses (on sales to outsiders)	$ 1,750,000
Operating expenses (on sales to other segments)	380,000
Interest expense	180,000
Income tax expense	65,000
Cumulative effect of a change in accounting principal	10,000

    What is the appropriate *segment profit*?

    A. $950,000
    B. $570,000
    C. $390,000
    D. $325,000
    E. $315,000

2. Assuming that each of the items below is significant (constitutes more than ten percent of the appropriate total), which one would **not** have to be disclosed under *SFAS 131*?

    A.   types of products and services from which each operating segment derives its revenues
    B.   factors used to identify operating segments
    C.   the identity of a major customer who accounts for 12% of all sales
    D.   revenues from external customers
    E.   income tax expense or benefit

3. *SFAS 131* requires a company to disclose the following information for each *reportable operating segment*, **except for**

    A.   revenues
    B.   gross profit
    C.   total segment assets
    D.   expenditures for additions to long-lived assets
    E.   income tax expense or benefit

4. Which one of the following items of information are required to be included in *interim reports* for each operating segment?

    A.   revenues from external customers
    B.   intersegment revenues
    C.   revenues from internal customers
    D.   segment profit or loss
    E.   total assets, if there has been a material change from the last annual report

5. Which one of the following is a test for identifying operating segments for which separate disclosure is required?

    A. asset test
    B. liability test
    C. expense test
    D. gross profit test
    E. equity test

6. Reed Inc. has three operating segments with the following information:

	Boats	Aircraft	Publishing	Total
Sales to Outsiders	$4,000,000	$1,200,000	$5,200,000	$10,400,000
Intersegment Transfers	500,000	60,000	1,200,000	$1,760,000
Interest Income (outsiders)	200,000	0	400,000	$600,000
Interest Income (insiders)	160,000	16,000	100,000	$276,000
Expenses	3,600,000	735,000	4,800,000	$9,135,000
Assets	10,000,000	7,200,000	12,000,000	$29,200,000

Using the revenue test, what is the minimum amount of revenue that a segment can have and still be considered reportable?

    A. $1,040,000
    B. $1,216,000
    C. $1,303,600
    D. $1,276,000
    E. $ 362,500

7. Using the information in #6 above, which segments are reportable using the revenue test?

    A. Boats and Publishing
    B. Boats and Aircraft
    C. Aircraft and Publishing
    D. Aircraft only
    E. Boats, Aircraft, and Publishing

8. Ashley Inc. has a publishing industry operating segment. Which one of the following is included in calculating the segment's operating profit or loss?

    A. intersegment revenues
    B. interest expense
    C. extraordinary losses
    D. income taxes
    E. Intersegment interest income

9.   Masten Inc. has four identifiable industry segments:

	Paper	Wood	Furniture	Toys
Revenues	$30,000	$25,000	$23,000	$10,000
Intersegment Revenues	6,000	4,000	2,000	7,000
Intersegment COGS	4,000	2,000	1,000	5,000
Operating Expenses	10,000	8,000	12,000	18,000
Allocation of Common Costs	3,000	2,000	3,000	1,000
Interest Expense (outsiders)	1,000	3,000	4,000	2,000
Income Taxes (Savings)	4,500	4,000	1,200	(2,000)

What is the minimum operating profit or loss that a segment must have in order to be considered significant?

A. $3,200
B. $1,100
C. $2,700
D. $4,500
E. $4,600

10.   *SFAS 14* required a company to disclose the following information for each *reportable industry segment*, **except for**

A.   identifiable liabilities
B.   revenues
C.   operating profit or loss
D.   capital expenditures
E.   equity in net income from an investment in the net assets of equity investees

11.   Which one of the following organizations requested that the FASB require cash flow information to be reported for each operating segment?

A.   AICPA
B.   SEC
C.   CASB
D.   IASC
E.   AIMR

Brief Essay Questions

1.   What are the major findings of academic research relating to *SFAS 14* disclosures?

2.   Both the AIMR and the AICPA's special committee recommended that segment reporting be aligned with internal reporting with segments defined on the basis of how an enterprise is organized and managed. Segments based on an enterprise's internal organization structure would have what four advantages?

3.   An *operating segment* is a component of an enterprise that has what three attributes?

Problems

1. Examine the following information for Faru Co., and determine which segments are reportable.

Faru Co.
Business Segments

	Plastics	Metals	Lumber	Paper	Finance
Total Assets	$ 1,772,000	$ 4,351,000	$ 408,000	$ 791,000	$ 700,000
Sales to Outside Parties	8,215,000	2,787,000	827,000	451,000	-
Intersegment Revenues	138,000	170,000	125,000	140,000	-
Interest Income	-	25,000	8,000	-	242,000
Cost of Goods Sold	5,088,000	2,096,000	1,191,000	753,000	21,000
Other Expenses	79,000	21,000	66,000	40,000	113,000

2. Examine the following information for Hoyle Inc., and determine which segments are reportable.

Hoyle Inc.
Business Segments

	Textbooks	Study Guides	Tapes	Videos	Lecture
Total Assets	$ 50,000	$ 50,000	$ 25,000	$ 370,000	$ -
Sales to Outside Parties	250,000	180,000	72,000	450,000	1,960,000
Intersegment Revenues	400,000	20,000	8,000	-	-
Interest Income (external)	30,000	-	2,000	-	-
Cost of Goods Sold	425,000	140,000	15,000	185,000	-
Other Expenses	170,000	80,000	30,000	27,000	490,000

Solutions to Multiple Choice Questions

1. **B**

Segment revenue	$2,700,000
Operating expenses (on sales to outsiders)	(1,750,000)
Operating expenses (on sales to other segments)	(380,000)
Segment profit	**$ 570,000**

2. **C**

3. **B**

4. **C**

5. **A**

6. **D**

	Boats	Aircraft	Publishing	Total
Sales to Outsiders	$4,000,000	$1,200,000	$5,200,000	$10,400,000
Intersegment Transfers	500,000	60,000	1,200,000	1,760,000
Interest Income (outsiders)	200,000	0	400,000	600,000
Total Revenues for Purposes of the Revenue Test	$4,700,000	$1,260,000	$6,800,000	$12,760,000
Materiality Threshhold %				10%
Minimum Segment Profit				$1,276,000

7. **A**   Boats and Publishing are reportable. The total revenues for Boats ($4,700,000) and for Publishing ($6,800,000) exceed the $1,276,00 threshhold and would therefore be *reportable segments*. The Aircraft segment ($1,260,000) falls below the threshold and does not pass the revenue test.

8. **A.**

9. **D.**   The operating profit or loss test does not include interest expense or income taxes. Therefore, the operating profit or loss of a segment is its revenues and intersegment revenues less the cost of intersegment transfers, operating expenses, and the allocation of common costs.

Operating Profits:		Operating Losses:	
Paper	$19,000	Toys	$7,000
Wood	17,000		
Furniture	9,000		
Total	$45,000		$7,000

Total operating profits for segments with profits is $45,000. Total operating losses for segments with losses are $7,000. $45,000 > $7,000. We use 10% of the larger number. Therefore, any segment where the absolute value of the segment's operating gain or loss exceeds $4,500 will be a *reportable segment*.

10. **A**

11. **E**

Answers to Brief Essay Questions

1. The major findings of academic research relating to SFAS 14 disclosures are as follows:

   A. Industry segment data improve analysts' accuracy in predicting consolidated sales and earnings; this is true for both large and small firms.

   B. The availability of industry segment data leads to greater consensus among analysts regarding their forecasts of sales and earnings.

   C. Segment revenue data (both industry and geographic) appears to be more useful than segment earnings data in making forecasts.

   D. The initial disclosure of geographic area data was used by stock market participants in assessing the riskiness of companies with foreign operations.

2. Segments based on an enterprise's internal organization structure would have the following four advantages:

   A. Knowledge of an enterprise's organization structure is valuable because it reflects the risks and opportunities believed to be important by management.

   B. The ability to see the company the way it is viewed by management improves an analyst's ability to predict management actions that can significantly affect future cash flows.

   C. Because segment information already is generated for management's use on the basis of the company's internal structure, the incremental cost of providing that information externally should be minimal.

   D. Segments based on an existing internal structure should be less subjective than segments based on the term *industry*.

3. An *operating segment* is a component of an enterprise:

   A. that engages in business activities from which it earns revenues and incurs expenses,

   B. whose operating results are regularly reviewed by the chief operating decision maker to assess performance and make resource allocation decisions, and

   C. for which discrete financial information is available.

Solutions to Problems

1. Plastics and Metals each pass at least one test. The 75% rule is met, so no additional segments need to be added.

Revenue Test

	Revenues per Segment	Total Revenues	10% of Revenues	Does this segment pass this test?
Plastics	8,353,000	13,128,000	1,312,800	YES
Metals	2,982,000	13,128,000	1,312,800	YES
Lumber	960,000	13,128,000	1,312,800	NO
Paper	591,000	13,128,000	1,312,800	NO
Finance	242,000	13,128,000	1,312,800	NO

Identifiable Assets Test

	Assets per Segment	Total Assets	10% of Assets	Does this segment pass this test?
Plastics	1,772,000	8,022,000	802,200	YES
Metals	4,351,000	8,022,000	802,200	YES
Lumber	408,000	8,022,000	802,200	NO
Paper	791,000	8,022,000	802,200	NO
Finance	700,000	8,022,000	802,200	NO

Profit or Loss Test

	Gain or Loss per Segment	Greater of Total Profits or Total Losses	10% of Total Gains or Total Losses	Does this segment pass this test?
Plastics	3,186,000	4,159,000	415,900	YES
Metals	865,000	4,159,000	415,900	YES
Lumber	(297,000)	4,159,000	415,900	NO
Paper	(202,000)	4,159,000	415,900	NO
Finance	108,000	4,159,000	415,900	NO

75% Test

Total Revenues (external)	75% of Total Revenues (external)	Total External Revenues + Interest	Is 75% test met?
$ 12,555,000	$ 9,416,250	$ 11,027,000	YES

2. Textbooks, Study Guides, Videos, and Lectures each pass at least one test. The 75% rule is met, so no additional segments need to be added.

Revenue Test

	Revenues per Segment	Total Revenues	10% of Revenues	Does this segment pass this test?
Textbooks	680,000	3,372,000	337,200	YES
Study Guides	200,000	3,372,000	337,200	NO
Tapes	82,000	3,372,000	337,200	NO
Videos	450,000	3,372,000	337,200	YES
Lectures	1,960,000	3,372,000	337,200	YES

Identifiable Assets Test

	Assets per Segment	Total Assets	10% of Assets	Does this segment pass this test?
Textbooks	50,000	495,000	49,500	YES
Study Guides	50,000	495,000	49,500	YES
Tapes	25,000	495,000	49,500	NO
Videos	370,000	495,000	49,500	YES
Lectures	-	495,000	49,500	NO

Profit or Loss Test

	Gain or Loss per Segment	Greater of Total Profits or Total Losses	10% of Total Gains or Total Losses	Does this segment pass this test?
Textbooks	85,000	1,830,000	183,000	NO
Study Guides	(20,000)	1,830,000	183,000	NO
Tapes	37,000	1,830,000	183,000	NO
Videos	238,000	1,830,000	183,000	YES
Lectures	1,470,000	1,830,000	183,000	YES

75% Test

Total Revenues (external)	75% of Total Revenues (external)	Total External Revenues + Interest	Is 75% test met?
$ 2,944,000	$ 2,208,000	$ 2,870,000	YES

Chapter 9

Foreign Currency Transactions and Hedging Foreign Exchange Risk
Chapter Outline

I.   Global Economy - In today's world economy, a great many companies deal in currencies other than their reporting currencies.

    A.   Merchandise may be imported or exported with prices denominated in a foreign currency.

    B.   For the reporting purposes of a U.S. company, each transaction denominated in a foreign currency must be re-stated in U.S. dollars using an exchange rate that represents the value of the U.S. dollar relative to the foreign currency.

    C.   Exchange rates tend to fluctuate as the strength of the U.S. economy changes relative to the economies of other countries.

II.   Exchange Rate Mechanisms – Exchange rates have not always fluctuated.

    A.   From 1945-1973, foreign currency exchange rates were fixed to the U.S. dollar, which was in turn tied to the value of gold.

        1.   Called the "Gold Standard"

        2.   In 1973, the U.S. ended reliance on the Gold Standard

    B.   There are several different approaches to setting currency exchange rates

        1.   Independent Float – The value of currency is allowed to fluctuate freely.

        2.   Pegged to Another Currency – The value of currency is fixed to the value of another currency.

        3.   European Monetary System – 12 European countries agreed to use a single common currency. The value of the euro (€)

III. Foreign Exchange Rates

    A.   Foreign currency trades can be executed on a spot or forward basis.

        1.   The *spot rate* is the price at which a foreign currency can be purchased or sold today.

        2.   The *forward rate* is the price today at which foreign currency can be purchased or sold sometime in the future.

B. A *foreign currency option* gives its holder *the right but not the obligation* to trade foreign currency in the future.

1. The sale of foreign currency by the holder of the option is accomplished with a *put* option.

2. The exchange rate at which the option will be executed if the holder decides to exercise the option is the *strike price*.

3. Options must be purchased by paying an *option premium* which is a function of two components.

    a. The *intrinsic value* of an option is equal to the gain that could be realized by immediately exercising the option.

    b. The *time value* of an option relates to the possibility that the spot rate can change over time.

IV. Foreign Currency Transactions

A. Export sales and import purchases are international transactions that are components of a trade.

1. Export sale — a transaction exposure exists when the exporter allows the buyer to pay in a foreign currency and also allows the buyer to pay sometime after the sale has been transacted.

2. Import purchase — a transaction exposure exists when the importer is required to pay in a foreign currency and is allowed to pay sometime after the purchase has been transacted.

B. There are two alternative methods of accounting for changes in the value of a foreign currency transaction.

1. The *one-transaction perspective* assumes that an export sale is not complete until the foreign currency receivable has been collected and converted into U.S. dollars; any change in the dollar value of the foreign currency is accounted for as an adjustment to *Accounts Receivable* and *Sales*. This method is not acceptable under U.S. GAAP.

2. *SFAS 52* requires companies to use a *two-transaction perspective* that treats an export sale and the subsequent cash collection as two separate transactions.

    a. The U.S. dollar value of an export sale is recorded as of the date the sale.

    b. Any difference between the number of U.S. dollars that could have been received at the date of sale and the number of U.S. dollars actually received at the date of payment due to fluctuations in the exchange rate is treated as a *Foreign Exchange Gain or Loss* and reported separately from *Sales* in the *income statement*.

C. There are two alternative approaches to accounting for unrealized foreign exchange gains and losses.

    1. Under the *deferral approach*, unrealized foreign exchange gains and losses are deferred on the <u>balance sheet</u> until cash is actually paid or received. This approach is not acceptable under U.S. GAAP.

    2. *SFAS 52* requires companies to use the *accrual approach* to account for unrealized foreign exchange gains and losses.

        a. A firm reports unrealized foreign exchange gains and losses in *net income* for the period in which the exchange rate changes.

        b. Any change in the exchange rate from the date of sale to the balance sheet date would result in a *foreign exchange gain or loss* to be reported in income for that period.

        c. Any change in the exchange rate from the balance sheet date to the date of payment would result in a second *foreign exchange gain or loss* that would be reported in the second accounting period.

        d. SFAS 52 is criticized for violating the principle of conservatism when an *unrealized foreign exchange gain* arises at the balance sheet date.

V. Hedging Foreign Exchange Risk

    A. Foreign Forward Contracts

        1. agreements to exchange foreign currency for U.S. dollars at a predetermined exchange rate on a specified date in the future.

        2. forward contracts are non-cancelable.

    B. Foreign Currency Options

        1. essentially, these are forward contracts that the company can use or not use, at their own option.

        2. the "opt-out" option carries a cost.

VI. Fair Value of Derivatives – determined by measuring changes in the forward rate over the life of the contract.

    A. Three pieces of information are needed

        1. The forward rate when the forward contract was entered into.

2. The current forward rate for a contract that matures on the same date as the forward contract entered into.

3. A discount rate.

B. The value of a foreign currency option is determined using a pricing model such as the Black-Scholes Option Pricing model.

VII. Hedge of a Foreign Currency Transaction

A. SFAS 133 and SFAS 138 govern accounting for hedges of foreign currency.

B. Hedge relationships are created when a company uses a foreign currency derivative to minimize the adverse effect that changes in exchange rates have on cash flows and net income.

C. The gain/loss from the hedge is recognized in net income in the same period as the loss/gain on the transaction being hedged.

D. Hedge accounting can only be used if three conditions are met

1. The derivative is used to hedge either a fair value exposure or a cash flow exposure to foreign exchange risk.

2. The derivative is highly effective in offsetting changes in the fair value or cash flows related to the hedged item.

3. The derivative is properly documented as a hedge.

E. Nature of Hedged Risk

1. A fair value exposure exists when changes in exchange rates can affect the fair value of assets or liabilities.

2. A cash value exposure exists if changes in exchange rates affect the amount of cash flow to be realized from a transaction.

a. Recognized foreign currency assets and liabilities

b. Foreign currency firm commitments

c. Forecasted foreign currency transactions

F. Cash Flow Hedges – can only be used when the hedging instrument completely offsets the variability in the cash flows of a hedged transaction.

1. Adjust the hedged asset/liability to fair value based in changes in the spot rate. A foreign exchange gain/loss is recognized in net income.

2.   Adjust the derivative to fair value. The resulting gain/loss is recorded as part of Accumulated Other Comprehensive Income

3.   Transfer an amount equal to the foreign exchange gain/loss on the hedged asset/liability from AOCI to net income.

4.   An additional amount is removed from AOCI and recognized in net income to reflect

      a.   the current period's amortization of the original discount/premium on the forward contract, or

      b.   the change in the time value of the option, depending on which is being used.

    G.   Fair Value Hedge

1.   The hedged asset/liability is adjusted to fair value based on changes in the spot exchange rate. A foreign exchange gain/loss is recognized in net income.

2.   The derivative hedging instrument is adjusted to fair value. The resulting gain/loss is reporting in net income.

VIII.   Using a forward contract to hedge a foreign currency denominated asset

    A.   Steps for a Cash Flow Hedge

1.   On the date the forward contract is taken, the value is always $0, because the agreement is an executory contract.

2.   On the balance sheet date, determine the fair value of the forward contract.

      a.   Record a forward contract asset or liability.

          (1)   Determine the U.S. dollar equivalent of the amount hedged by the forward contract using the contract exchange rate.

          (2)   Determine the U.S. dollar equivalent of the amount hedged by the forward contract using the currently available contract with a maturity date that is the same as the original forward contract rate.

          (3)   The difference is the undiscounted value of the forward contract.

             i.   If (1) > (2), then record a forward contract asset

             ii.   If (1) < (2), then record a forward contract liability

(4)   Discount (3) using the pre-established discount rate and the forward contract due date as the future maturity date.

b.   Record the other side of the entry to Accumulated Other Comprehensive Income (AOCI)

c.   Remove enough from the AOCI account to offset any gain/loss recognized in the income statement related to the re-measurement of the underlying foreign currency asset.

e.   Record the amortization of the forward contract discount/premium. The corresponding entry is made to AOCI.

(1)   Compare the U.S. dollar amount of the original foreign currency asset to the U.S. dollar amount that will be realized when the forward contract matures.

(2)   The difference is identified as the "forward contract discount/premium"

3.   On the date that the forward contract matures

a.   Adjust the forward contract to the fair value on the maturity date.

(1)   determine the fair value by comparing the forward contract rate to the current spot rate.

(2)   record an adjustment to the Forward Contract account.

(3)   Record the other side of the entry in AOCI

b.   Remove enough from AOCI to offset any foreign exchange gain/loss realized from the re-measurement of the underlying foreign currency asset.

c.   Amortize the remaining Forward Contract Discount

d.   Note: That is done properly, these entries will cause the AOCI account to zero out.

B.   Steps for a Fair Value Hedge

1.   On the date the forward contract is taken, the value is always $0, because the agreement is an executory contract.

2.   On the balance sheet date, determine the fair value of the forward contract.

a.   Record a forward contract asset or liability.

(1)   Determine the U.S. dollar equivalent of the amount hedged by the forward contract using the contract exchange rate.

(2)   Determine the U.S. dollar equivalent of the amount hedged by the forward contract using the currently available contract with a maturity date that is the same as the original forward contract rate.

(3)   The difference is the undiscounted value of the forward contract.

(4)   Discount (3) using the pre-established discount rate and the forward contract due date as the future maturity date.

    b.   Record the other side of the entry to Gain/Loss on Forward Contract.

3.   On the date that the forward contract matures

    a.   Adjust the Forward Contract to fair value on the maturity date.

    b.   Record the settlement of the forward contract.

IX.   Foreign Currency Option as Hedge of Transaction

A.   Steps for a Cash Flow Hedge

1.   On the date the forward option contract is taken, the option is recorded at its cost.

2.   On the balance sheet date

    a.   Adjust the value of the option contract based on a pricing model. The adjustment amount is recorded in AOCI.

    b.   Remove enough from AOCI account to offset any gain/loss recognized in the income statement related to the re-measurement of the underlying foreign currency asset.

    c.   Record the change in time value of the option as an adjustment to AOCI.

3.   On the date that the option contract matures

    a.   Adjust the option contract to the fair value on the maturity date.

    b.   Remove enough from AOCI to offset any foreign exchange gain/loss realized from the re-measurement of the underlying foreign currency asset.

    c.   Record the change in time value of the option as an adjustment to AOCI.

B. Steps for a Fair Value Hedge

    1.   On the date the forward option contract is taken, the option is recorded at its cost.

    2.   On the balance sheet date, adjust the fair value of the option contract. Record a gain/loss on the income statement.

    3.   On the date that the forward contract matures, adjust the Forward Contract to fair value on the maturity date.

X.   Hedge of a Future Foreign Currency Commitment

    A.   Companies engaged in foreign currency transactions often enter into hedging arrangements as soon as an order has been accepted.

    B.   SFAS 133 requires the following procedures for a *fair value hedge of a foreign currency firm commitment*

        1.   The hedging instrument must be reported as either an asset or a liability on the balance sheet.

            a.   Changes in the fair value of the hedging instrument are recognized currently as gains and losses in income.

        2.   Although there is no transaction to account for, gains and losses on the foreign currency commitment must be recognized in income to offset gains and losses on the forward contract (*hedge accounting*).

    C.   According to *SFAS 133*, *hedge accounting* is allowed only when:

        1.   At inception of the hedge, there is formal documentation of the hedging relationship; and

        2.   The hedging relationship is expected to be highly effective.

    D.   If the SFAS 133 conditions are not met, then changes in the fair value of the hedging instrument are recognized currently as gains and losses in income, while gains and losses on the foreign currency commitment are NOT recognized.

        1.   This effectively means that hedge accounting for hedges of foreign currency commitments is not allowed.

    E.   Options can also be used as hedge instruments for firm foreign currency commitments.

XI.   Forecasted Transactions

    A.   *SFAS 133* allows the use of *hedge accounting* for forward contracts hedging forecasted transactions (also known as a *cash flow hedge*) and for options used for the same purpose.

B.   The accounting for a *cash flow hedge* differs from the accounting for a *fair value hedge* in two ways:

    1.   There is no recognition of gains and losses on a forecasted transaction, unlike the accounting for a firm commitment.

    2.   The foreign currency option is reported at *fair value*, but because there is no gain or loss on the forecasted transaction to offset against, changes in the fair value of the foreign currency option are not reported as gains or losses in net income.

        a.   They are reported instead as part of Accumulate Other Comprehensive Income.

        b.   On the projected date of the forecasted transaction, the *cumulative change in fair value* is transferred from AOCI to *net income*.

XII.   Uses of Hedging Instruments

    A.   Hedges of all foreign currency transactions.

    B.   The use of a foreign contract hedge when the *forward rate* results in a greater cash inflow or smaller cash outflow than with the *spot rate*.

    C.   *Proportional hedging policies* requiring hedging on some predetermined percentage of transaction exposure.

    D.   *Foreign currency swap.*

XIII.   Off Balance Sheet Nature of Forward Contracts

    A.   Most U.S. companies do not report forward contract assets and liabilities on their balance sheets since forward contracts are executory contracts.

    B.   Such companies prefer to keep forward contracts off their balance sheets because it allows them to report a smaller total amount of current liabilities, improving such financial ratios as the current ratio and debt-to-equity ratio.

XIV.   Foreign Currency Borrowing

    A.   Companies borrow foreign currency from foreign lenders to (a) finance foreign operations or (b) take advantage of more favorable interest rates.

    B.   Accounting is complicated by (a) the denomination of both the principal and interest in foreign currency and (b) the resulting exposure to foreign exchange risk.

    C.   Foreign exchange gains and losses on *intercompany foreign currency transactions that are of a long-term investment nature* are deferred in the stockholders' equity section of the balance sheet until the loan is repaid.

Multiple Choice Questions

1.   The foreign exchange rate for the immediate delivery of currencies exchanged is called the

   A.   forward rate.
   B.   historical rate.
   C.   spot rate.
   D.   market rate.
   E.   swap rate.

2.   For which of the following hedges does SFAS 133 allow hedge accounting to be used to record gains and losses related to the hedge instrument in net income?

	Forward Contract Hedge	Option Used as a Hedge of a Foreign Currency Firm Commitment	Foreign Currency Option Used as a Cash Hedge
A.	Yes	Yes	Yes
B.	Yes	No	Yes
C.	Yes	Yes	No
D.	No	Yes	No
E.	Yes	No	No

3.   A U.S. exporter has a 90-day account receivable denominated in Euro's (€) as a result of an export sale made on May 1, 2004, to a German customer. The exporter signed a 90-day forward contract on May 1, 2004, to sell Euro's. The spot rate was $.975 on that date and the 90-day forward rate was $.950. On June 30, 2004, the exporter's fiscal year-end, the spot rate was $.980 and the 30-day forward rate was $.956. Which one of the following would the U.S. exporter have reported in income for the year ending June 30, 2004?

   A.   Net Exchange Loss
   B.   Net Exchange Gain
   C.   No Exchange Gain or Loss
   D.   Net Credit Adjustment to Beginning Retained Earnings
   E.   Net Debit Adjustment to Beginning Retained Earnings

4.   Barger Co. ordered parts costing £250,000 from a British supplier on March 12 when the spot rate was $1.55 per pound. A one-month forward contract was signed on that date to purchase £250,000 at a forward rate of $1.52. On April 12, when the parts were received, the spot rate was $1.56. At what amount should the parts be carried on Barger's books?

   A. $387,500
   B. $390,000
   C. $380,000
   D. $388,750
   E. $250,000

Items 5 and 6 are based on the following information.

NOD Corp. (a U.S.-based company) sold parts to a Indian customer on December 15, 2004, with payment of 720,000 rupee's to be received on January 15, 2005. The following exchange rates apply:

Date	Spot Rate	Forward Rate to January 15
December 15, 2004	$0.0205	$0.0260
December 31, 2004	$0.0220	$0.0258
January 15, 2005	$0.0250	$0.0250

5. Assuming no forward contract was entered into, how much foreign exchange gain or loss should NOD report on its 2004 income statement with regard to this transaction?

     A.   no gain or loss
     B. $ 144 gain
     C. $ 144 loss
     D. $ 1,080 gain
     E. $ 1,080 loss

6. NOD uses a discount rate of 6%. The present value factor for 30 days is .9950. The present value factor for 15 days is .9975. Assuming a forward contract was entered into to hedge this foreign currency transaction, and that NOD wants to account for the forward contract as a fair value hedge, what would be the total net exchange gain or loss in 2004?

     A. $ 1,224.00 net loss
     B. $ 1,223.64 net gain
     C. $ 1,223.64 net loss
     D. $ 1080.00 net gain
     E. $ 144.00 net gain

Items 7 through 9 are based on the following information.

On November 15, 2004, Duster places an order for inventory items from their Japanese supplier. On December 15, 2004, Duster Inc. entered into a forward contract to purchase ¥1,200,000 in sixty days. The relevant exchange rates are as follows:

Date	Spot Rate	Forward Rate to February 15
November 15, 2004	$0.0075	$0.0086
December 15, 2004	$0.0081	$0.0083
December 31, 2004	$0.0089	$0.0085
February 15, 2005	$0.0084	$0.0084

7.   Duster entered into the forward contract to hedge a purchase of inventory made on December 15, 2004, payable on February 15, 2005. Duster uses a discount rate of 5%. The present value factor for 90 days is .9876. The present value factor for 60 days is .9917. The present value factor for 45 days is .9938. The present value factor for 30 days is .9958. At December 15, 2004, what is the fair value of this forward contract?

   A.   No difference. No value.
   B. $ 1,320 debit
   C. $ 1,320 credit
   D. $ 360 debit
   E. $ 360 credit

8.   Referring to #7 above, what is the fair value of the forward contract on December 31?

   A. $ 238.51 asset
   B. $ 238.51 liability
   C. $ 240.00 asset
   D. $ 240.00 liability
   E. $ 9,960 asset

9.   Referring again to the information in #7 above, what is the amount of gain or loss that Duster should record on February 15, 2005?

   A. $ 120.00 loss
   B. $ 120.00 gain
   C. $ 118.51 loss
   D. $ 118.51 gain
   E. $ - 0 –

10. The exchange rate at which an option will be executed if the holder decides to exercise the option is called the

   A.   strike price.
   B.   intrinsic value.
   C.   spot rate.
   D.   forward rate.
   E.   option price.

Brief Essay Questions

1.   Briefly list and describe the three *currency arrangements* covered early in the text chapter.

2.   Contrast the definitions of a *spot rate* and a *forward rate*.

3.   According to the text, why is the *one-transaction perspective* criticized?

Problems

1. Johnson Inc., a U.S.-based firm, sold some of its inventory to a British firm on November 27, 2004 when the exchange rate was $1.75 to the British pound. The agreement called for the British firm to remit £87,000 on January 26, 2005. Additional information regarding exchange rates is shown below:

December 1, 2004	$1.500
December 31, 2004	1.525
January 26, 2005	1.540

Required:

A. Show the entry to be made (if any) on Johnson's books on December 31, 2004 and provide supporting calculations.

B. Show the entry to be made on Johnson's books on January 26, 2005 when it receives payment from the British firm.

2. On December 1, 2004, Norton Inc. (a U.S. company) purchases inventory from a Japanese supplier for ¥5,000,000. Payment will be made in sixty days. To hedge the transaction, Norton signs a forward contract to buy ¥5,000,000 in sixty days. Norton uses a discount of 6%. Norton uses the straight-line method for amortizing discounts.

The appropriate yen exchange rates are as follows:

Date	Spot Rate	Forward Rate to 1/28/05
December 1, 2004	$0.0080 = ¥1	$0.0085 = ¥1
December 31, 2004	$0.0089 = ¥1	$0.0092 = ¥1
January 28, 2005	$0.0084 = ¥1	$0.0084 = ¥1

Required:

Prepare all journal entries for Norton Inc. in connection with the purchase and payment. Assume that Norton wants to account for this as a cash flow hedge.

3. Refer to the information in #2 above. Assume that Norton accounts for this as a fair value hedge.

Required:

Record the journal entries in connection with the purchase and payment.

4. New York Chili, Inc. (a U.S. company in Montana) has the following import/export transactions in 2004:

August 1   Sold inventory for 2,200,000 pesos, on account, to a Mexican customer. Payment is due on November 1. New York Chili took a forward contract to hedge this transaction.

November 1   Received payment for the August 1 sale.

New York Chili has a September 30 year-end and uses a 8% discount rate. Currency exchange rates are as follows:

Date	Spot Rate			Forward Rate to 11/1/04		
August 1, 2004	$0.1025	=	1 peso	$0.1028	=	1 peso
September 30, 2004	$0.1030	=	1 peso	$0.1032	=	1 peso
November 1, 2004	$0.1035	=	1 peso	$0.1035	=	1 peso

Required:

Assume New York Chili accounts for this transaction as a fair value hedge. Record the journal entries in connection with the purchase of inventory and sale of goods for New York Chili.

Solutions to Multiple Choice Questions
1.   C

2.   C

3.   B

4.   C   Actual cash outflow as established by the forward contract (£250,000 x $1.52) = **$380,000**

5.   D   Dollar value of receivable @ 12/31/04 (720,000 rupees x $.0220)$ 15,840
Dollar value of receivable @ 12/1/04 (720,000 rupees x $.0205)   (14,760)
Increase $ 1,080 gain

6.   B   @ the Contracted Forward Rate (720,000 rupees x $.0260) $ 18,720.00
@ the Currently Available Rate (720,000 rupees x $.0258)   (18,576.00)
Net change in value (Loss) $ 144.00 gain
Present Value Factor for 15 days @ 6%   x   .9975
Fair Value of Forward Contract on 12/31/04 $ 143.64
Plus Gain or Original Receivable   1,080.00 gain
Net gain $ 1,223.64 gain

7.   A   On December 15, 2004, the contracted rate for a February 15, 2005 delivery and the currently available forward rate to February 15, 2005 are both the same. Since there is no difference, there is no fair value recorded for the forward contract on December 15, 2004. This is considered an executory contract.

8.   A

@ the Contracted Forward Rate (1,200,000 ¥ x $.0083)	$ 9,960.00
@ the Currently Available Rate (1,200,000 ¥ x $.0085)	(10,200.00)
Net change in value (Loss)	$ (240.00)
Present Value Factor for 45 days @ 5%	x .9938
Fair Value of Forward Contract on 12/31/04	$ (238.51) debit

The ¥1,200,000 will be purchased on February 15, 2005 at the contracted rate of $.0083, or $9,960.00. If we had waited until December 31, 2004 to hedge the inventory purchase, we could have obtained a forward rate of $.0085, resulting in the ¥1,200,000 costing $10,200 on February 15, 2005. The difference is $240. The present value of that $240 over 45 days (to Feb. 15), using a discount rate of 5% is $238.51 an asset.

9.   C   The value of the forward contract on December 31, 2004, was a $238.51 debit balance. The fair value of the forward contract on February 15, 2005, is determined by comparing the dollars that Duster is required to pay on the forward contract ($9,960.00) to the dollars Duster would have had to pay if they had not hedged the transaction (¥1,200,000 x .0084 = $10,080). The current fair value is a $120 debit balance, a loss of $118.51.

10.   A

Answers to Brief Essay Questions

1.   Three currency arrangements:

      A.   *Independent float* — the value of the currency is allowed to fluctuate freely according to market forces with little or no intervention from the central bank.

      B.   *Pegged to another currency* — the value of the currency is fixed (pegged) in terms of a particular currency and the central bank intervenes as necessary to maintain the fixed value.

      C.   *European monetary System (EMS)* — the currencies of most of the members of the European Union float jointly against non-EMS currencies.

2.   The *spot rate* is the price at which a foreign currency can be purchased or sold today. In contrast, the *forward rate* is the price today at which foreign currency can be purchased or sold sometime in the future.

3.   The *one-transaction perspective* is criticized because it sometimes hides the fact that a company could have received a larger dollar amount if the foreign customer had been required to pay at the time of the sale.

Solutions to Problems

1.   Entries to be made on Johnson Inc.'s books:

Date	Accounts	Debit	Credit
ENTRY A			
12/31/2004	Foreign Exchange Loss	2,175	
	Accounts Receivable (£)		2,175
ENTRY B			
1/26/2005	Cash	133,980	
	Accounts Receivable (£)		132,675
	Foreign Exchange Gain		1,305

2.   Entries to record Norton's purchase of inventory and accompanying hedge entries when the hedge is accounted for as a cash value hedge.

Date	Accounts	Debit	Credit
12/1/2004	Inventory	40,000.00	
	Accounts Payable		40,000.00
	To record payable at the 12/1 spot rate		
	Note: There is no entry on 12/1 to record the forward contract.		
12/31/2004	Foreign Exchange Loss	4,500.00	
	Accounts Payable		4,500.00
	To adjust the payable to the 12/31 spot rate		
12/31/2004	Accumulated Other Comprehensive Income	4,500.00	
	Gain on Forward Contract		4,500.00
	To record an offsetting gain against the foreign exchange loss associated with the A/P		
12/31/2004	Forward Contract	3,483.71	
	AOCI		3,483.71
	to record the fair value of the forward contract.		
12/31/2004	Discount Expense	1,250.00	
	AOCI		1,250.00
	to allocate the forward contract discount equally over the term of the forward contract.		

Date	Accounts	Debit	Credit
1/28/2005	Accounts Payable	2,500.00	
	Foreign Exchange Gain		2,500.00
	to adjust accounts payable to the current exchange rate value		
1/28/2004	Loss on Forward Contract	2,500.00	
	AOCI		2,500.00
	to record an offsetting loss to the foreign exchange gain		
1/28/2004	AOCI	3,983.71	
	Forward Contract		3,983.71
	to adjust forward contract to fair value		
1/28/2004	Discount Expense	1,250.00	
	AOCI		1,250.00
	to allocate the forward contract discount equally over the term of the forward contract		
1/28/2004	Foreign Currency (¥)	42,500.00	
	Cash		42,500.00
	to acquire yen at the contracted exchange rate of $.0085		
1/28/2004	Accounts Payable	42,000.00	
	Forward Contract	500.00	
	Foreign Currency (¥)		42,500.00
	to record payment to the Japanese supplier		

3. Entries to record Norton's purchase when the hedge is accounted for as a fair value hedge.

Date	Accounts	Debit	Credit
12/1/2004	Inventory	40,000.00	
	Accounts Payable		40,000.00
	To record payable at the 12/1 spot rate		
	Note: There is no entry on 12/1 to record the forward contract.		
12/31/2004	Foreign Exchange Loss	4,500.00	
	Accounts Payable		4,500.00
	To adjust the payable to the 12/31 spot rate		
12/31/2004	Forward Contract	3,483.71	
	Loss on Forward Contract		3,483.71
	to record the fair value of the forward contract.		
1/28/2004	Accounts Payable	2,500.00	
	Foreign Exchange Gain		2,500.00
	to adjust A/P to current spot rate value		
1/28/2004	Loss on Forward Contract	3,983.71	
	Forward Contract		3,983.71
	to adjust forward contract to fair value		
1/28/2004	Foreign Currency (¥)	42,500.00	
	Cash		42,500.00
	to acquire yen at the contracted exchange rate of $.0085		
1/28/2004	Accounts Payable	42,000.00	
	Forward Contract	500.00	
	Foreign Currency (¥)		42,500.00

4. Entries to record New York Chili's sale the hedge is accounted for as a fair value hedge.

Date	Accounts	Debit	Credit
8/1/2004	Accounts Receivable	225,500.00	
	Sales		225,500.00
	to record sale to Mexican customer		
	Note: There is no entry on 12/1 to record the forward contract.		
9/30/2004	Accounts Receivable	1,100.00	
	Foreign Exchange Gain		1,100.00
	To adjust the A/R to the 9/30 spot rate		
9/30/2004	Loss on Forward Contract	800.00	
	Forward Contract		800.00
	to record the fair value of the forward contract.		
11/1/2004	Accounts Receivable	1,100.00	
	Foreign Exchange Gain		1,100.00
	to adjust A/R to the 11/1 spot rate value		
11/1/2004	Loss on Forward Contract	740.00	
	Forward Contract		740.00
	to adjust forward contract to fair value		
11/1/2004	Foreign Currency (pesos)	227,700.00	
	Accounts Receivable		227,700.00
	to record receipt of pesos from Mexican customer		
11/1/2004	Cash	226,160.00	
	Forward Contract	1,540.00	
	Foreign Currency (pesos)		227,700.00

Chapter 10

Translation of Foreign Currency Financial Statements
Chapter Outline

I. Exchange Rates Used in Translation

    A. There are two major theoretical issues in regard to the translation process:

        1. which **translation method** should be used and

        2. where the resulting **translation adjustment** should be reported in the consolidated financial statements.

    B. Two types of *exchange rates* are used in translating financial statements:

        1. *Historical exchange rate* — the exchange rate that exists when a transaction occurs.

        2. *Current exchange rate* — the exchange rate that exists a the balance sheet date.

II. Translation Methods

    A. The Current Rate Method

        1. Required by SFAS 52 for foreign subsidiaries that:

            a. Use something other than the US $ as their *functional currency* (discussed later)

            b. Operate fairly independently of the US parent company.

        2. The basic assumption underlying the *current rate method* is that a company's *net investment* in a foreign operation is *exposed* to foreign exchange risk.

        3. All assets of the foreign subsidiary are converted to US $ using the rate in effect on the date of the translation. (current rate)

        4. All revenues and expenses are converted to US $ using the rate in effect on the date of the transaction (historical rate).

            a. For revenues and expenses that are earned throughout the period, where using the historical rate would be impractical, the weighted average rate for the period is acceptable.

b. For revenues and expenses that occur at a readily identifiable point in time, the actual historical rate is still mandated.

5. Capital Accounts (such as Common Stock and Paid-In Capital) are converted using the historical rates in effect at the date the stock was originally issued.

6. Beginning Retained Earnings is defined by the US $ Retained Earnings from the previous period.

7. Ending Retained Earnings is determined by:

a. starting with Beginning Retained Earnings (which is already in US $)

b. adding Net Income (from the translated Income Statement), and

c. subtracting Dividends (translated at the historical rate in effect on the date the dividends are declared)

8. Any imbalance between the translated net assets and the translated equity section of the balance sheet is recorded in an account called *Cumulative Translation Adjustment*

a. This account is usually located in the equity section of the translated balance sheet and is reported as a component of *Comprehensive Income*.

B. The Temporal Method

1. Established originally by SFAS 8 and required by SFAS 52 for foreign subsidiaries that:

a. Use the US $ as their *functional currency* (discussed later)

b. Use the US $ for most of their transactions

c. Also required for foreign subsidiaries operating in a high inflation economy.

2. The basic objective of the *temporal method* is to produce a set of U.S. dollar translated financial statements as if the foreign subsidiary had used U.S. dollars in conducting its operations.

3. *Assets and liabilities* on the foreign operation's balance sheet at *historical cost* are translated at *historical* exchange rates to yield an equivalent historical cost in U.S. dollars.

4. *Assets and liabilities* carried at a *current or future value* are translated at the *current* exchange rate to yield an equivalent current value in U.S. dollars.

5. All revenues and expenses are converted to US $ using the rate in effect on the date of the transaction (historical rate).

a. For revenues and expenses that are earned throughout the period, where using the historical rate would be impractical, the weighted average rate for the period is acceptable.

b. For revenues and expenses that occur at a readily identifiable point in time, the actual historical rate is still mandated.

6. Capital Accounts (such as Common Stock and Paid-In Capital) are converted using the historical rates in effect at the date the stock was originally issued.

7. Beginning Retained Earnings is defined by the US $ Retained Earnings from the previous period.

a. Ending Retained Earnings is determined by:

i. taking Beginning Retained Earning (which is already in US $)

ii. adding Net Income (from the translated Income Statement), and

iii. subtracting Dividends (translated at the historical rate in effect on the date the date declared)

8. Any imbalance between the translated net assets and the translated equity section of the balance sheet is recorded in an account called "Translation Gain or Loss"

a. The amount is recorded as a gain or loss on the income statement.

III. Complicating Aspects of the Temporal Method

A. With the *temporal method*, a record must be kept of the exchange rates when inventory, prepaid expenses, fixed assets, and intangible assets are acquired since these assets, carried at *historical cost*, are translated at *historical* exchange rates.

B. Keeping track of *historical* rates for these assets is unnecessary under the *current rate method*.

IV. Disposition of Translation Adjustment

A. There are two major issues relating to foreign currency financial statement translation.

1. The *first issue* is selecting the appropriate method.

2. The *second issue* relates to deciding *where the resulting translation adjustment should be reported in the consolidated financial statements*.

B. There are two prevailing schools of thought regarding the second issue.

1. *Translation gain or loss* — the translation adjustment is considered to be a gain or loss similar to a gain or loss arising from foreign currency transactions and

should be reported as income in the period in which the fluctuation in the exchange rate occurs (required by SFAS 8 when using the Temporal Method).

2.   *Cumulative translation adjustment in stockholders' equity* — the translation adjustment is taken directly to stockholders' equity (required by SFAS 52 when using the Current Rate Method).

V.   U.S. Rules

A.   *SFAS 8* required the use of the *temporal method* with *translation gains and losses* being reported in the income statement by all companies for all foreign operations.

   1.   *SFAS 8* was criticized in 1978.

   2.   As a result of the negative feedback, the FASB agreed to reconsider the translation issue.

B.   *SFAS 52,* issued in December of 1981, required the use of the *current rate method* to replace the *temporal method* in most cases where the accounts of the foreign subsidiary are being reported.

   1.   Under *SFAS 52,* the foreign subsidiary has to first record all account balances in its own *functional currency*, the currency of its primary environment.

      a.   The *functional currency* is the currency a foreign subsidiary uses to conduct most of its operating and financing functions such as (1) settlement of sales transactions, (2) payment of employees, and (3) loans with banks.

      b.   The *functional currency* may be (1) the foreign entity's local currency, (2) another foreign currency, or (3) the U.S. dollar.

      c.   *SFAS 52* recommends that management consider several economic factors when determining a foreign entity's *functional currency*, such as (1) the location of the primary sales markets, (2) sources of materials and labor, (3) intercompany transactions, and (4) sources of financing.

      d.   Next, the financial statements of the subsidiary are adjusted to be in compliance with U.S. GAAP.

      e.   *All* of the subsidiary's asset and liability balances are *translated* into the parent company's *reporting currency* based on the exchange rate at the balance sheet date.

      f.   Other accounts are translated at the historical exchange rate that was in effect at the time of original accounting recognition.

      g.   Any increases or decreases created by translating assets and liabilities at new currency rates will be accumulated over the years and reported as a separate component in the *stockholders' equity section* of the *balance sheet*; no income effect is created by a translation.

    h.   The *translation adjustment* to be reported is determined by monitoring the change in value of the *exposed net asset or liability position* held by the subsidiary.

    i.   To make this calculation, all changes made in the *net asset or liability position* during the period are identified along with the corresponding value at that time; this total is compared to the translated balance of the assets and liabilities at year-end.

2.   *Remeasurement* (rather than *translation*) is mandated by *SFAS 52* in several specific situations.

    a.   Recording individual transactions that are carried out by a company (parent or subsidiary) in a currency other than its own *functional currency*.

    b.   Restating a foreign subsidiary's account balances into the parent's *reporting currency* (in anticipation of consolidation) when the subsidiary operates in a highly inflationary environment.

    c.   Restating a foreign subsidiary's account balances into the parent's *reporting currency* when both companies have the same *functional currency*.

3.   Remeasurement applies the rules of the *temporal method* to foreign currency account balances.

    a.   Cash, monetary receivables, monetary liabilities, and market-valued assets are remeasured at *current* exchange rates whereas all other accounts are remeasured at *historical* rates as of the date of the original transaction.

    b.   The net increase or decrease in value created by restating monetary accounts at current rates is reported as a component of income.

VI.   Comparison of the Results from Applying the Two Different Methods

    A.   The *current rate method* does not always result in greater *net income* and a larger amount of *equity* than the *temporal method*.

    B.   The determination of the *functional currency* and resulting translation method can have a material impact on the amounts reported by a parent company in its *consolidated financial statements*.

    C.   The *temporal method* distorts financial ratios as measured in the foreign currency.

D. Conceptually, when the *current rate method* is used, *income statement items* can be translated at either the *average* or the *current* exchange rate.

VII. Hedging Balance Sheet Exposure

    A. Translation adjustments and remeasurement gains or losses are a function of two factors:

        1. changes in the exchange rate and

        2. balance sheet exposure.

    B. *Forward contracts* are a popular means of hedging *balance sheet exposure*.

VIII. Disclosures Related to Translation

    A. *SFAS 52 (par. 31)* requires firms to present an analysis of the change in the *Cumulative Translation Adjustment* account in (a) either the *balance sheet* of the *income statement* or (b) *notes to the financial statements*.

    B. Many companies comply with this requirement by including a *translation adjustment* column in the *Statement of Stockholders' Equity*.

    C. Other firms provide separate disclosure in the notes.

IX. Consolidation of a Foreign Subsidiary

    A. Special attention needs to be paid to the treatment of the *excess of cost over book value*.

    B. A *cumulative translation adjustment* will be required to actually balance the *trial balance*.

    C. The following typical *consolidation entries* need to be made on the *consolidation worksheet*:

        1. **Entry S** - Eliminates the subsidiary's *stockholders' equity* accounts as of the beginning of the current year along with the equivalent book value component within the parent's purchase price in the *Investment* account.

        2. **Entry A** - Allocates the *excess of cost over book value* at the date of acquisition to *plant and equipment* and eliminates that amount within the parent's purchase price from the *Investment* account.

        3. **Entry I** - Eliminates the amount of equity income recognized by the parent in the current year and included in the *Investment* account under the *equity method*.

        4. **Entry D** - Eliminates the subsidiary's dividend payment that was a reduction in the *Investment* account under the *equity method*.

5.   **Entry T** - Eliminates the *cumulative translation adjustment* included in the *Investment* account under the *equity method* and eliminates the *cumulative translation adjustment* carried on the parent's books.

6.   **Entry E** - Revalues the *excess cost over book value* for the change in exchange rate since the date of acquisition with the counterpart recognized as an increase in the *consolidated cumulative translation adjustment*.

Multiple Choice Questions

1. Foreign subsidiaries of U.S. parent companies that operate in highly inflationary economies are required by SFAS 52 to use which method for translating the financial statements:

   A.   Temporal Method, with the *Translation Gain or Loss* to be reported as part *of Comprehensive Income*.
   B.   Current Rate Method, with the *Cumulative Translation Adjustment* to be reported as part of *Comprehensive Income*.
   C.   Temporal Method, with the *Translation Gain or Loss* to be reported as part of Net Income.
   D.   Current Rate Method, with the *Cumulative Translation Adjustment* to be reported as part of Net Income.
   E.   Equity Method, with the *Translation Gain or Loss* to be reported as part of *Noncontrolling Interest in Subsidiary*.

2. A subsidiary of Harris Inc. is located in Germany. The *functional currency* of this subsidiary is the Euro (€). The subsidiary acquires inventory on October 31, 2004 for 300,000 € which is sold on January 15, 2005 for 420,000 €. Collection of the money takes place on February 4, 2005. Applicable exchange rates are as follows:

Date	Spot Rate	
October 31, 2004	0.9800 =	1 €
December 31, 2004	0.9850 =	1 €
January 15, 2005	0.9750 =	1 €

What amount is reported for this inventory on the December 31, 2004 US $ balance sheet?

   A. $295,500
   B. $294,000
   C. $292,500
   D. $411,600
   E. $413,700

3.   A subsidiary of Shaw Inc. has one asset (*Inventory*) and one liability (*Accounts Payable*). The *functional currency* of this subsidiary is the Kuwaiti Dinar. The inventory was acquired for 90,000 dinars when the *exchange rate* was $3.2500 = 1 dinar. *Accounts Payable*, which has a balance of 50,000 dinars, was established when the *exchange rate* was $3.2875 = 1 dinar. At year-end, the *exchange rate* was $3.3000 = 1 dinar. What kind of exposure is Shaw exposed to?

   A.   Net asset balance sheet exposure.
   B.   Net liability balance sheet exposure.
   C.   Translation adjustment exposure.
   D.   Transaction exposure.
   E.   Currency rate fluctuation exposure.

4.   A U.S.-based company has a subsidiary located in Germany. The Euro (€) is the *functional currency* of the subsidiary. What exchange rate should be used to translate the following items reported in the subsidiary's year-end financial statements?

	Inventory	Machinery	Depreciation Expense
A.	Current rate	Current rate	Average rate
B.	Historical rate	Current rate	Current rate
C.	Current rate	Historical rate	Average rate
D.	Average rate	Historical rate	Current rate
E.	Average rate	Current rate	Current rate

5.   If a company has no foreign subsidiaries, then the issues related to hedging of receivables and payables denominated in foreign currencies are irrelevant.

   A.   True
   B.   False

6.   At what point in the process should the parent company adjust the foreign subsidiary's accounts to bring them in accordance with GAAP?

   A.   Prior to the beginning of the Translation process.
   B.   After Translation, but prior to consolidation.
   C.   After consolidation, but prior to reporting.
   D.   No adjustments are necessary, since most foreign countries already use GAAP.
   E.   No adjustment should be necessary. Foreign subsidiaries are required by the SEC to have an accounting system that is consistent with GAAP.

7. Packstone Inc. owns a subsidiary in England. The subsidiary's *functional currency* is the pound. Therefore, translation is necessary in order to prepare *consolidated financial statements*. The subsidiary began 2004 with £500,000 in cash and no other assets or liabilities. On March 1, 2004, the subsidiary used £100,000 to purchase equipment. On April 20, 2004, the subsidiary used cash to purchase merchandise inventory costing £80,000. This merchandise was sold on May 16, 2004, for £120,000 in cash. On November 1, 2004, the subsidiary paid a cash dividend to Packstone in the amount of £60,000 and recorded depreciation on the equipment for the year of £50,000. The appropriate exchange rates were as follows:

Date	Spot Rate	
January 1, 2004	1.4800	= £1
March 1 2004	1.5000	= £1
April 20, 2004	1.5200	= £1
May 16, 2004	1.5500	= £1
November 1, 2004	1.5300	= £1
December 31, 2004	1.5600	= £1
Average for 2004	1.6000	= £1

What is the *translation adjustment* to be reported in the *stockholders' equity* section of the *consolidated balance sheet*?

A. $ –0–
B. $31,000 debit
C. $31,000 credit
D. $37,600 debit
E. $37,600 credit

8. Which one of the following translation methods has as its basic assumption the premise that a company's *net investment* in a foreign operation is *exposed* to foreign exchange risk?

A. current rate method
B. average rate method
C. current/noncurrent method
D. monetary/nonmonetary method
E. temporal method

9. The primary currency of the foreign entity's operating environment is known as the

A. translation currency.
B. functional currency.
C. reporting currency.
D. temporal currency.
E. prime-time currency.

10. Bean Inc. started 2004 with two assets: *Cash* of ¥30,000 and *Land* which originally cost ¥50,000 when acquired on June 30, 2002. On August 18, 2004, the company rendered services to a customer for ¥80,000, an amount that was immediately paid in cash. On November 15, 2004, the company incurred an operating expense of ¥26,000, which was immediately paid. No other transactions occurred during the year. Currency exchange rates were as follows:

Date	Spot Rate
June 30, 2002	0.0080 = ¥1
January 1, 2004	0.0084 = ¥1
August 18, 2004	0.0090 = ¥1
November 15, 2004	0.0096 = ¥1
December 31, 2004	0.0102 = ¥1
January 4, 1900	0.0098 = ¥1

Assume that this company is a Japanese subsidiary of an American company. Also assume that the U.S. dollar is the *functional currency* of the parent and the subsidiary so that remeasurement is required. What is the *remeasurement gain or loss* for 2004?

A. $210.40
B. $243.10
C. $188.10
D. $134.40
E. $132.50

Items 11 and 12 are based on the following information:

A subsidiary of Parket Inc. purchased marketable equity securities and inventory on March 1, 2004, for 80,000 pesos each. Both of these items were paid for on May 1, 2004, and were still on hand at year-end. Inventory is carried at cost under average lower-of-cost-or-market valuation. Currency exchange rates are as follows:

Date	Spot Rate
January 1, 2004	$0.1900 = ¥1
March 1, 2004	$0.2000 = ¥1
May 1, 2004	$0.2200 = ¥1
December 31, 2004	$0.2400 = ¥1

11. Assuming that the peso is the subsidiary's *functional currency*, what balances are reported on the December 31, 2004 *consolidated balance sheet*?

	Marketable Securities	Inventory
A.	$ 16,000	$ 16,000
B.	$ 17,600	$ 17,600
C.	$ 19,200	$ 16,000
D.	$ 19,200	$ 19,200
E.	$ 17,600	$ 16,000

12. Assuming that the U.S. dollar is the subsidiary's *functional currency*, what balances are reported on the December 31, 2004 *consolidated balance sheet*?

	Marketable Securities	Inventory
A.	$ 16,000	$ 16,000
B.	$ 17,600	$ 17,600
C.	$ 19,200	$ 16,000
D.	$ 19,200	$ 19,200
E.	$ 17,600	$ 16,000

Problems

1. Nelson Inc. has a $2,500 translation loss due to foreign currency exchanges before any year-end adjustments on December 31, 2004. The following information exists at year-end and has not yet been taken into account:

- Nelson's wholly-owned foreign subsidiary, Jennings Inc., when translated, shows a $5,000 foreign currency translation loss for the year ended December 31, 2004.

- In transactions with an unrelated supplier, Nelson recognized a payable denominated in the currency of the supplier in U.S. dollars, the payable was $19,000 on November 1, 2004, when the transaction originated; on December 31, 2004, the U.S. dollar equivalent of the payable was $19,750.

Required:

In Nelson's 2004 *income statement*, what amount should be shown as a *foreign exchange loss*?

2. Kent Inc. has a wholly-owned foreign subsidiary in Canada called Barbel Co. Barbel maintains certain accounts in Canadian dollars as follows:

	Canadian $
Depreciation on building acquired on August 1, 2004	$ 7,500
Equipment rental expense for 2004	6,000

Assume that the Canadian dollar is Barbel Co.'s *functional currency*. Selected exchange rates are shown below:

	US $ Equivalent of Canadian $
August 1, 2004	$ 1.25
December 31, 2004	$ 1.20
Average for 2004	$ 1.15

Required:

What dollar amount should be included in Ken's Income Statement on December 31, 2004 to reflect the expenses shown above?

3. On 1/1/2004, Awlamer, Inc., a U.S. company, acquires 90% of Justa Minuto Incorporato, located in Quadaleemoro, South America. Justa Minuto was incorporated in 1988 when the exchange rate was $.520 = 1 bobb. Justa Minuto's only asset is 2,000 acres of land that was acquired in 1988 on the date of incorporation at a cost of 55,000 bobbs. The exchange rate in effect on the date of incorporation was $.520 per bobb. At 1/1/2004, Justa Minuto's R/E balance in $US was $19,975. At 12/31/2004, Awlamer must convert Justa Minuto's financial statements into $US for consolidation purposes. Justa Minuto's dividends were paid on 10/1/2004. On June 30, Justa Minuto sold land originally costing 20,000 bobbs for 23,000 bobbs. Assuming no intercompany transactions and that Justa Minuto uses GAAP for accounting purposes, prepare the translated financial statements at 12/31/2004. Uses the bobb for most of its transactions. Use the foreign currency exchange rates listed below.

Exchange Rates:

1/1/2004	1 bobb = $ .850 US	6/30/2004	1 bobb = $ .640
10/1/2004	1 bobb = $ .800 US	Weighted Avg	1 bobb = $ .785
12/31/2004	1 bobb = $ .660 US		

Financial Balances

Revenues	84,000 bobbs
COGS	62,000 bobbs
Salary Expense	11,000 bobbs
Gain on Sale of Land	3,000 bobbs
Other Operating Exp	8,500 bobbs
Cash	14,000 bobbs
A/R	28,000 bobbs
Inventory	57,000 bobbs
Land	35,000 bobbs
A/P	10,000 bobbs
Common Stock (par)	100,000 bobbs
R/E(Beginning)	23,500 bobbs
Dividends Paid	5,000 bobbs

Required:

Prepare a TRANSLATED Income Statement, a Statement of Changes in Retained Earnings, and a Balance Sheet for Justa Minuto Incorporato (in proper format).

Solutions to Multiple Choice Questions

1. **C**

2. **A**   A translation is appropriate since the € is the *functional currency* of the subsidiary. All assets are translated and reported using the *current* exchange rate, as of the balance sheet date.

      Translated value at 12/31/04 (300,000 € x $.9850) =   **$295,500**

3. **A**   Shaw is exposed to net asset exposure, because assets translated at the current exchange rate exceed liabilities translated at the current exchange rate.

4. **A**

5. **B**

6. **A**

7. **E**   Only changes in the *net assets* have an impact on the calculation of the *translation adjustment*. The equipment purchase does not change net assets since the increase in the *Equipment* account is offset by the reduction in the *Cash* account. The sale of inventory increases *net assets* by the amount of the *gross profit*.

Beginning cash balance	£ 500,000 x $1.48 =	$ 740,000
Sale of merchandise for a gain	40,000 x $1.55 =	62,000
Payment of cash dividend	(60,000) x $1.53 =	(91,800)
Recording of depreciation	(50,000) x $1.54 =	(77,000)
	£ 430,000	633,200

Actual value of net assets at 12/31/04   £430,000 x $1.56/ £= $670,800
Translation adjustment (**credit**) $ 37,600

8. **A**

9. **B**

10. **C**

Net monetary assets - cash	¥	30,000 x $ 0.0084 =	$ 252.00
Increase in monetary assets - revenues	¥	80,000 x $ 0.0090 =	$ 720.00
Decrease in monetary assets - expenses	¥	(26,000) x $ 0.0096 =	$ (249.60)
Net monetary assets @ 12/31/04 - value			$ 722.40
Prior to rate change	¥	84,000 x $ 0.0102 =	$ 856.80
Remeasurement gain			$ 134.40

11. **D**   Translation of marketable equity securities (80,000 pesos x $.24) **$ 19,200**
            Translation of inventory (80,000 pesos x $.24)   **$ 19,200**

12. **C**   Translation of marketable equity securities (80,000 pesos x $.24) **$ 19,200**
            Translation of inventory (80,000 pesos x $.20)   **$ 16,000**

Solutions to Problems

1. Translation loss before adjustment $ 2,500
    Loss on transaction with supplier ($19,750 – $19,000)   750
    Foreign exchange loss $ 3,250

    The loss associated with the wholly-owned foreign subsidiary would not be shown on the *income statement*; instead, that adjustment is shown in the *equity section* of the *balance sheet*.

2. Depreciation in Canadian dollars   C$ 7,500
    Equipment rental expense in Canadian dollars   6,000
    Total expenses   C$ 13,500

    Average exchange rate for 2004   1.15
    Depreciation and equipment rental
    expenses included in Kent Inc.'s 2004
    income statement in U.S. dollars $ 15,525

3. This translation requires the application of the current rate method.

Justa Minuto
Statement of Income
For the Period Ending 12/31/2004

	bobbs	Exchange Rate	U.S. $
Revenues	(84,000.00)	0.7850	(65,940.00)
Cost of Goods Sold	62,000.00	0.7850	48,670.00
Gross Margin	(22,000.00)		(17,270.00)
Salaries Expense	11,000.00	0.7850	8,635.00
Other Operating Expense	8,500.00	0.7850	6,672.50
Gain on Sale of Land	(3,000.00)	0.6400	(1,920.00)
Net Income	(5,500.00)		(3,882.50)

Advanced Accounting – 7/e

Justa Minuto
Statement of Changes in Retained Earnings
For the Period Ending 12/31/2004

	bobbs	Exchange Rate	U.S. $
Retained Earnings, 1/1/04	(23,500.00)	N/A	$ (19,975.00)
Add: Net Income	(5,500.00)		(3,882.50)
Less: Dividends	5,000.00	0.8000	4,000.00
Retained Earnings, 12/31/04	(24,000.00)		$ (19,857.50)

Justa Minuto
Balance Sheet
12/31/2004

	bobbs	Exchange Rate	U.S. $
Assets			
Cash	14,000.00	0.6600	$ 9,240.00
Accounts Receivable	28,000.00	0.6600	18,480.00
Inventory	57,000.00	0.6600	37,620.00
Land	35,000.00	0.6600	23,100.00
Total Assets	134,000.00		$ 88,440.00
Liabilities and Owners' Equity			
Accounts Payable	(10,000.00)	0.6600	$ (6,600.00)
Common Stock	(100,000.00)	0.5200	(52,000.00)
Retained Earnings, 12/31/04	(24,000.00)	N/A	(19,857.50)
Cumulative Translation Adjustment			(9,982.50)
Total Liabilities and Owners' Equity	(134,000.00)		$ (88,440.00)

Chapter 11

Worldwide Accounting Diversity and International Standards

Chapter Outline

I. Evidence of Accounting Diversity

    A.   To function in today's changing world, business leaders must be able to utilize and assess information that is generated in many different countries.

    B.   Accounting principles are not uniform, as they have developed country by country.

II. Reasons for Accounting Diversity.

    A.   The following 5 items have been identified as commonly accepted factors influencing a country's financial reporting practices:

        1.   Legal system – Countries with codified Roman law usually have a corporation law that establishes the basic legal parameters governing business enterprises; while, in countries with a tradition of common law, the accounting profession or an independent nongovernmental body representing a variety of constituencies establishes specific accounting rules.

        2.   Taxation – In some countries, financial statements constitute the basis for taxation; in other countries, financial statements are adjusted for income tax purposes and submitted to the government separately from the reports sent to stockholders.

        3.   Providers of financing – There is less pressure for public accountability and information disclosure in countries where company financing is dominated by families, banks, or the state.

        4.   Inflation – Countries with high inflation must adopt accounting rules requiring the inflation adjustment of historical cost amounts.

        5.   Political and economic ties – Accounting rules have been transmitted from country to country through political and economic linkages.

    B.   There is a high degree of correlation among the legal system, income tax conformity, and source of financing.

        1.   Common law countries separate taxation from accounting and rely more heavily on the stock market as a source of capital.

2. Code law countries link taxation to accounting statements and rely less on financing provided by stockholders.

III. Problems Caused by Diverse Accounting Practices – The diversity in accounting practice in various countries causes problems that can be serious for some parties.

   A. One problem relates to the preparation of *consolidated financial statements* by companies with foreign operations – all of the foreign operations of a U.S. company must be converted from local GAAP to U.S. GAAP by the *balance sheet* date.

   B. A second problem relates to companies obtaining access to foreign capital markets – a U.S. company that wants to obtain capital in a foreign country will usually be required to present financial statements prepared in accordance with the GAAP of the foreign country.

   C. A third problem relates to the lack of comparability of financial statements among companies from different countries.

IV. Accounting Clusters

   A. Clusters of countries share common accounting practices and one classification scheme identifies four major accounting models.

      1. British-American describes the approach utilized in the U.K. and the U.S. where information is developed for creditors and investors with adequate disclosure serving as a major objective.

      2. The Continental model emphasizes compliance with government laws and the reduction of income taxes.

      3. The South American model must deal with the impact of significant inflation rates.

      4. The Mixed Economy model describes the approach recently developed in Eastern Europe and the former Soviet Union that combines elements of the former planned economic system and the recent market economy reforms.

   B. The terms micro-based and macro-uniform describe the British-American and Continental models, respectively.

      1. The micro-based class is divided into two subclasses:

         a. The first micro-based subclass is heavily influenced by business economics and accounting theory.

         b. The second micro-based subclass is of British origin and is more pragmatic and oriented toward business practice, relying less on economic theory in the development of accounting rules.

2. The macro-uniform class is divided into two subclasses:

    a. The only country in the government and economics subclass is Sweden.

    b. The Continental government, tax, legal subclass contains Continental European countries divided into two families.

V. Major Deviations from GAAP – The items most frequently requiring adjustment in foreign reconciliations to U.S. GAAP are:

    A. Depreciation and amortization

    B. Deferred or capitalized costs

    C. Deferred taxes

    D. Pension costs (including other post-retirement benefits)

    E. Foreign currency translation

    F. Gain/loss on disposal of assets

    G. Business combinations (including goodwill)

    H. Extraordinary items, discontinued operations, and accounting changes

    I. Employee compensation

    J. Investments in associated entities (equity method)

VI. International Harmonization of Financial Reporting

    A. Harmonization is the process of reducing differences in financial reporting practices across countries, thereby increasing the comparability of financial statements.

    B. Supporters of accounting harmonization argue that comparability of financial statements worldwide is necessary for the globalization of capital markets.

    C. The biggest obstacle of harmonization is the magnitude of the current differences among countries and the fact that the political cost of eliminating those differences would be tremendous.

VII. Major Harmonization Efforts

  A. The European Union (EU) has endeavored to harmonize financial reporting practices within the community.

  B. The UD Forum of standard setters has been created and has not yet issued any pronouncements, proving to be little more than a discussion group so far.

  C. The EU Directives have served as a basic framework of accounting that has been adopted by other countries in search of an accounting model.

VIII. International Accounting Standards Committee

  A. The International Accounting Standards Committee (IASC) was formed in 1973 in hopes of improving and promoting the worldwide harmonization of accounting principles.

  B. The goals of the IASC were:

    1. To formulate and publish in the public interest accounting standards to be observed in the presentation of financial statements and to promote their worldwide acceptance and observance.

    2. To work generally for the improvement and harmonization of regulations, accounting standards and procedures relating to the presentation of financial statements.

  C. Succeeded by the International Accounting Standards Board (IASB) in April 2001.

IX. International Accounting Standards Board (IASB)

  A. Formed in April, 2001.

  B. 14 members; 12 full time, 2 part time

    1. Five members must have a background as practicing auditors.

    2. Three members must have a background as preparers of financial statements.

    3. Three members must have a background as users of financial statements.

    4. One member must come from academia.

  C. Full time members must sever all ties with former employers. They may not engage in any activities that might be a conflict of interest.

172

D. As of 2001, 41 International Accounting Standards have been issued.

    1. 39 of those standards were issued by the IASC.

    2. The Standing Interpretations Committee (SIC) has issued 31 interpretations of International Accounting Standards

E. The FASB has identified 218 items covered both by U.S. GAAP and IASB standards.

    1. 135 of those items are accounting for using either the same approach or a similar approach.

    2. 56 items have a different accounting approach.

    3. 27 items have an alternative approach.

X. The IOSCO Agreement

A. The International Organization of Securities Commissions (IOSCO) is a member of the IASC's Consultative Group.

B. Supported the IASC's Comparability Project "to eliminate most of the choices of accounting treatment currently permitted under International Accounting Standards"

    1. Resulted in revision of 26 IAS's between 1993 – 1998.

    2. Agreed with the IASC on a group of "core" standards for use in financial statements of companies involved in cross-border securities offerings and listings.

C. In 1996, the SEC announced criteria that would allow IAS's to be accepted for cross-border purposes. The standards must:

    1. Constitute a comprehensive, generally accepted basis of accounting,

    2. Be of high quality, resulting in comparability and transparency, and providing for full disclosure,

    3. Be regorously interpreted and applied.

D. Since 1994, the SEC no longer requires reconciliation to U.S. GAAP if a foreign registrant uses the relevant IAS related to:

    1. Statement of Cash Flows

    2. Amortization of Goodwill

3.   Translation of Financial Statements of Subsidiaries in Highly Inflationary Economics

4.   Distinction between Purchase and Pooling of Interests.

XI.   Use of International Accounting Standards

     A.   Over 200 companies and organizations worldwide refer to the use of IAS's in their annual reports.

     B.   China requires companies with B-shares that trade in both China and overseas to use IAS's.

     C.   Over 50 companies in Germany voluntarily use IAS's.

     D.   U.S. companies have largely ignored IAS's.

XII.   The Accounting Profession and Financial Statement Presentation

     A.   The accounting profession in the United Kingdom is the oldest and has the world's best reputation.

        1.   Legal regulation is provided by the Companies Act of 1989.

        2.   Professional organizations have historically been quite important in the development of accounting in the United Kingdom.

        3.   In 1990, the Accounting Standards Board was formed as the accounting standard-setting organization.

        4.   Directives of the European Economic Community also influence accounting principles.

        5.   Several different formats are available for the financial statements.

           a.   The balance sheet differs from that found in the U.S. in that fixed assets are presented first.

           b.   Reserves and adjustments are commonly reported within the equity section.

           c.   The income statement begins with a turnover figure (net sales).

     B.   Accounting principles in Germany are set by the national legislature (Bundestag)

        1.   These mandatory principles are outlined in detail in the Third Book of the Commercial Code (Handelsgesetzbuch).

2. German accounting rules are quite conservative.

3. Accounting principles vary somewhat based on the size of the reporting entity.

4. Financial statement requirements are somewhat different than in the U.S.

    a. The balance sheet begins with fixed assets and stockholders' equity is shown prior to liabilities.

    b. Reserve balances are common within stockholders' equity.

    c. The income statement can be shown according to a cost of sales approach (similar to that found in the U.S.) or in what is called the type of cost format.

C. In Japan, and most other code law countries, primarily the government sets basic accounting principles.

1. The Business Accounting Deliberation Council, a body whose members are appointed by the government, develops most principles.

2. The Japanese Institute of Certified Public Accountants (JICPA) is not a powerful organization.

3. Financial statements required by the Japanese Commercial Code consist of (1) balance sheet, (2) income statement, (3) proposal of appropriation of profit or disposition of loss, and (4) business report.

    a. Reserves frequently appear in the stockholders' equity section of the balance sheet.

    b. On the income statement, a number of gains and losses are shown separately as extraordinary (or special) items.

    c. Rules are influenced by the laws.

XIII. The Handling of Specific Accounting Problems Around the World

A. Valuation of assets – Although historical cost is prevalent, some countries allow increases to market value to be recorded.

B. Business combinations – Consolidation is common although not iniversal, and the allowed use of either the purchase method or the pooling of interests method varies from country to country.

C. Goodwill – Amortizing the cost as an expense is the most common approach although in the United Kingdom a direct reduction in an equity reserve is allowed. The permitted life of goodwill varies significantly by country.

D.   Accounting changes – The reporting of accounting changes is handled in many different ways throughtout the world, and no one approach seems to be predominant.

E.   Inventory methods – FIFO and averaging are prevalent although LIFO is also allowed in many places.

Multiple Choice Questions

1.   The International Accounting Standards Committee was replaced in April 2001 by the

    A.   International Accounting Oversight Board.
    B.   International Accounting Standards Board.
    C.   European Union
    D.   The Third Directive
    E.   The United Nations Accounting Standards Committee

2.   Which one of the following countries does **not** follow the British-American model of accounting?

    A.   Australia
    B.   Netherlands
    C.   Canada
    D.   Ireland
    E.   Spain

3.   Which one of the following countries does **not** follow the Continental Model of accounting?

    A.   Spain
    B.   Japan
    C.   Germany
    D.   Ireland
    E.   France

4.   How many members are on the new board for setting international accounting standards?

    A.   10
    B.   12
    C.   14
    D.   15
    E.   20

5.   The single most important source of accounting standards in Japan is the

    A.   Business Accounting Deliberation Council (BADC).
    B.   Japanese Accounting Standards Board (JASB).
    C.   French Accounting Pronouncements Board (FAPB).
    D.   Chinese Accounting Standards Board (CASB).
    E.   German Accounting Standards Board (GASB).

6. Which one of the following financial statements is **not** required by the Japanese Commercial Code?

    A. business report
    B. balance sheet
    C. income statement
    D. statement of cash flows
    E. proposal of appropriation of profit or disposition of loss

7. Regarding financial statements in the United Kingdom, which one of the following statements is **incorrect**?

    A. The balance sheet begins with current assets.
    B. The balance sheet is similar in appearance to that used in the United States.
    C. The capital and reserves section of the balance sheet can include adjustments that have no impact on the calculation of net income.
    D. The profit and loss statement begins with turnover (the British term for net sales)
    E. Discontinued operations are reported in the profit and loss account before taxation.

8. Which of the following is **not** one of the 5 common factors that influence a country's financial reporting practices?

    A. Legal system.
    B. Population.
    C. Inflation.
    D. Providers of financing.
    E. Taxation.

9. How many International Accounting Standards have been issued by the IASC as of January 2000?

    A. 32
    B. 35
    C. 39
    D. 41
    E. 26

10. The process of reducing differences in financial reporting practices across countries is referred to as:

    A. Cooperation
    B. Reconciliation
    C. Joint Compromise
    D. Joint Adoption
    E. Harmonization

Advanced Accounting 7/e

Brief Essay Questions

1. What are the most common items that require reconciliation to GAAP?

2. Explain the function of the Business Accounting Deliberation Council (BADC) in Japan.

3. What are the three key criteria that International Accounting Standards must meet before a company's international financial statements can be cross-listed in the United States?

Solutions to Multiple Choice Questions

1. B

2. E

3. D

4. C

5. A

6. D

7. B

8. B

9. D

10. E

Answers to Brief Essay Questions

1. Most common items requiring reconciliation:
   - Depreciation and amortization
   - Deferred or capitalized costs
   - Deferred taxes
   - Pension costs (including other post-retirement benefits)
   - Foreign currency translation
   - Gain/loss on disposal of assets
   - Business combinations (including goodwill)
   - Extraordinary items, discontinued operations, and accounting changes
   - Employee compensation
   - Investments in associated entities (equity method)

2.   The Business Accounting Deliberation Council (BADC) is the most important source of accounting principles in Japan. It is comprised of individuals drawn from (1) the government, (2) business, (3) education, and (4) the accounting profession. Membership in the council is by the appointment of the Ministry of Finance, allowing governmental control.

3.   The three key criteria are:

A.   The standards must constitute a comprehensive, generally accepted basis of accounting.

B.   The standards must be of high quality, resulting in comparability and transparency, and providing for full disclosure.

C.   The standards must be rigorously interpreted and applied.

Chapter 12

Financial Reporting and the Securities and Exchange Commission

Chapter Outline

I. The work of the Securities and Exchange Commission (SEC)

    A. The primary mission of the U.S. SEC is to protect investors and maintain the integrity of the securities markets.

    B. The SEC is an independent agency of the federal government created by the Securities Exchange Act of 1934.

    C. The SEC is headed by 5 commissioners

        1. Appointed by the President.

        2. Serve 5-year staggered terms.

        3. The Chairman of the SEC is usually from the same political party as the President.

    D. The SEC is composed of 18 offices and 4 divisions, including:

        1. The **Division of Corporation Finance** has responsibility for ensuring that disclosure requirements are met by publicly held companies.

        2. The **Division of Market Regulation** oversees the securities markets in the US and is responsible for registering and regulating brokerage firms.

        3. The **Division of Enforcement** helps to ensure compliance with federal security laws by investigating possible violations of securities laws and recommends appropriate remedies.

        4. The **Division of Investment Management** overses the $15 trillion investment management industry and administers the securities laws affecting investment companies including mutual funds and investment advisers.

        5. The **Office of Investment Technology** supports the SEC and its staff in all aspects of information technology. This office operates the Electronic Data Gathering Analysis and Retrieval System (EDGAR).

        6. The **Office of Compliance Inspections and Examinations** determines whether brokers, dealers, and investment companies and advisors are in compliance with federal securities laws.

7. The **Office of the Chief Accountant** is the principal advisor to the commission on accounting and auditing matters that arise in connection with the securities laws. Works closely with the AICPA and the FASB.

E. Important pieces of securities legislation enacted by Congress:

1. The *Securities Act of 1933* – Regulates the initial offering of securities by a company or underwriter.

2. The *Securities Exchange Act of 1934* – Regulates the subsequent, secondary-market, trading of securities through brokers and exchanges.

3. Public Utilities Holding Company ACT of 1935

4. Trust Indenture Act of 1939

5. Investment Company Act of 1940

6. Investment Advisers Act of 1940

7. Foreign Corrupt Practices Act of 1977

8. Insider Trading Sanctions Act of 1984

9. Insider Trading and Securities Fraud Enforcement Act of 1988

10. Sarbanes-Oxley Act of 2002

F. Four basic goals of the SEC:

1. Ensuring that full and fair information is disclosed to all investors before the securities of a company are allowed to be bought and sold.

2. Prohibiting the dissemination of materially misstated information.

3. Preventing the misuse of information especially by inside parties.

4. Regulating the operation of securities markets such as the New York Stock Exchange and the American Stock Exchange.

G. The SEC specifies most of its disclosure requirements in two basic documents:

1. *Regulation S-K* establishes requirements for all nonfinancial information contained in filings with the SEC.

2. *Regulation S-X* prescribes the form and content of the financial statements (as well as the accompanying notes and related schedules) included in the various reports filed with the SEC.

II.   The SEC's Authority over GAAP

    A.   The SEC holds the legal authority for establishing accounting principles for most publicly held companies in the U.S.

        1.   The SEC has delegated much of its standards setting authority to the AICPA and the FASB, allowing the accounting profession to set its own standards.

        2.   On occasion, when the SEC disagrees with the profession, the SEC will effectively mandate a particular standard.

    B.   *Financial Reporting Releases* (FRR's) are currently issued by the SEC as needed to supplement Regulations S-K and S-X.

    C.   The SEC staff published a series of *Staff Accounting Bulletins* (SAB's) as a means of informing the financial community of its views on current matters relating to accounting and disclosure practices.

    D.   The SEC may require the disclosure of additional data if current rules are viewed as insufficient.

    E.   The SEC can also exert its power by declaring a moratorium on the use ofr specified accounting practices.

    F.   Forcing a specific registrant to change its filed statements is another method used by the SEC to control the financial reporting process.

    G.   The SEC retains the authority to override or negate any pronouncements produced in the private sector.

III.   The SEC's impact on Financial Reporting and Disclosures

    A.   Rule 14c-3 requires the following proxy information to be included in annual reports.

        1.   5-year summary of operations including sales, total assets, income from continuing operations, and cash dividends per share.

        2.   Description of the business activities including principal products and sources and availability of raw materials.

        3.   Three-year summary of industry segments, export sales, and foreign and domestic operations.

        4.   Listing of company directors and executive officers.

        5.   Market price of the company's common stock for each quarterly period within the two most recent fiscal years.

6.   Any restrictions on the company's ability to continue paying dividends.

7.   Management's discussion and analysis of financial condition, changes in financial condition, and results of operations.

B.   The SEC requires certain other disclosures in proxy statements

     1.   All nonaudit services provided by the independent auditing firm.

     2.   A statement as to whether the board of directors (or its audit committee) approved all nonaudit services after considering the possibility that such services might impair the external auditor's independence.

     3.   The percentage of nonaudit fees to the total annual audit fee.

     4.   Individual nonaudit fees that are larger than 3% of the annual audit fee.

IV.   Sarbanes-Oxley Act of 2002

A.   Eliminated self-regulation of the accounting profession by the AICPA by setting up the Public Companies Accounting Oversight Board

     1.   Five-member board appointed to staggered 5-year terms.

     2.   Only 2 members can be accountants.

     3.   Enforces auditing, quality control, and independence standards and rules.

B.   All public accounting firms performing audits of publicly traded companies must be registered with the SEC

     1.   Fees will be collected and used to fund the PCAOB.

     2.   Registered firms will be inspected.

C.   Audit committees are now responsible for appointing and compensating the external auditor.

     1.   The members of the Audit Committee must be independent from management.

D.   The lead partner for the audit firm performing the audit must be rotated off the job after 5 years.

E.   The SEC still maintains ultimate control over accounting standards through Regulation S-X

V.   Filings with the SEC

A.   The SEC reporting process can be divided into two broad categories.

1.   *Registration statements* are required prior to the issuance of any new security.

2.   Periodic filings with the SEC are required of registrants by a number of federal laws; the most important of which is the Securities Exchange Act of 1934.

B.   In regard to registration statements, the SEC is charged with ensuring full and fair disclosure of relevant financial information.

1.   The registrant is responsible for supplying the data.

2.   The decision to invest must remain with the public.

C.   Depending on specific circumstances, specific forms are required for this purpose:

1.   **Form S-1** – Used when no other form is prescribed; usually used by new registrants or by companies that have been filing reports with the SEC for less than 36 months.

2.   **Form S-2** – Used by companies that have filed with the SEC for 36 months or longer, but are not large enough to file a Form S-3.

3.   **Form S-3** – Used by companies that are large in size and already have a significant following in the stock market.

   a.   at least 75% of its voting stock is held by nonaffiliates

   b.   Disclosure is reduced for these organizations because the public is assumed to have access to a considerable amount of information.

4.   **Form S-4** – Used by securities issued in connection with business combination transactions.

5.   **Form S-8** – Used as a registration statement for employee stock plans.

6.   **Form S-11** – Used for the registration of securities by certain real estate companies.

7.   **Form SB-1** – Used by small business issuers to register up to $10 million of securities but only if the company has not registered more than $10 million of securities in the previous twelve months.

8.   **Form SB-2** – Used by small business issuers to register securities to be sold for cash.

D.   Registration Statements

    A.   Part I – Prospectus

        1.   Financial statements for the issuing company audited by an independent CPA along with appropriate supplementary data.

        2.   An explanation of the intended use of the proceeds to be generated by the sale of the new securities.

        3.   A description of the risks associated with the securities.

        4.   A description of the business and the properties owned by the company.

    B.   Part II – Optional additional data such as marketing arrangements, expenses of issuance, sales to special parties, etc.

E.   Registration Process

    1.   When the SEC receives a registration statement, the Division of Corporation Finance reviews it.

        a.   The registrant will receive a letter of comments from the SEC indicating the changes or explanations that are requested for the registration statement to proceed in the approval process.

    2.   When the Division of Corporation Finance is satisfied that all SEC regulations have been fulfilled, the registration statement is made effective and the securities can be sold.

    3.   Large companies are allowed to use a process known as shelf registration.

        a.   The company files once with the SEC.

        b.   The filing is then good for the subsequent 2 years without having to go back to the SEC.

F.   Companies that have their securities publicly traded on an exchange must also make regular periodic filings with the SEC.

    1.   10-K – An annual report filed with the SEC within 60 days of the end of a registrant's fiscal year to provide information and disclosures required by Regulation S-K and Regulation S-X.

    2.   10-Q – Contains condensed Interim financial statement for the registrant and must be filed with the SEC within 30 days of the end of each quarter.

3.   8-K – Used to disclose a unique or significant happening. Must be filed within 2 days of the event.

G.   A proxy statement solicits voting power to be used at stockholders' meetings and must be filed with the SEC at least 10 days before being distributed.

H.   Exempt Offerings - Examples

1.   Securities sold strictly to the residents of the state in which the issuing company is chartered and principally doing business.

2.   Securities issued by governments, banks, and savings and loan associations.

3.   Securities issued that are restricted to a company's own existing shareholders where no commission is paid to solicit the exchange.

4.   Securities issued by nonprofit organizations such as religious, educational, or charitable groups.

5.   Small offerings of no more than $5 million.

6.   Offerings of no more than $1 million made to any number of investors within a 12-month period, with no specific disclosure requirements. General solicitations are allowed.

7.   Offerings of no more that $5 million made to 35 or fewer purchasers in a 12-month period, with no general soliciation.

8.   The private placement of securities to no more than 35 sophisticated investors whom already have sufficient information available to them about the issuing company. General solicitation is not allowed.

VI.   Electronic Data Gathering, Analysis, and Retrieval System (EDGAR)

A.   Development began in 1984.

B.   System not fully operational until 1994.

C.   Disseminates over 500,000 financial statements to financial information users.

D.   Most statements are posted to EDGAR within 24 hours.

E.   Allows financial information to be accessed via the Internet.

Multiple Choice Questions

1. Which one of the following is **not** a major goal of the SEC?

    A. Protecting investors against financial losses.
    B. Ensuring that full and fiar information is disclosed to all investors before the securities of a company are allowed to be bought and sold.
    C. Prohibiting the dissemination of materially misstated information.
    D. Preventing the misuse of information especially by inside parties.
    E. Regulating the operation of securities markets.

2. Which one of the following statements is correct?

    A. The U.S. Senate appoints the five commissioners of the SEC.
    B. Regulation S-K provides the regulations for all financial information including the form and content of financial statements.
    C. Regulation S-X establishes requirements for all nonfinancial information contained in filings with the SEC.
    D. The SEC's authority for financial accounting principles is only in the gray area of accounting where the FASB's rules are not clear.
    E. Companies issuing securities in connection with business combination transactions must file Registration Statement S-4 with the SEC.

3. A letter sent to a company by the SEC indicating needed changes or clarifications in a registration statement is known as a(n)

    A. Post-audit letter.
    B. Letter of comments.
    C. Staff accounting bulletin.
    D. Advisory letter.
    E. Memorandum of modifications.

4. Filing information with the SEC by indicating that the information is already available in another document is called

    A. Single reporting.
    B. Summary financial reporting.
    C. Incorporation by reference.
    D. Proxy information reporting.
    E. Reporting by referral.

5. What is the nickname of the system that was designed for the SEC to allow electronic filings?

    A. EDGAR
    B. MADONNA
    C. OCSAR
    D. FIONA
    E. CHARLIE

Advanced Accounting – 7/e

6. A registration statement is a(n)

    A. Annual filing made with the SEC.
    B. Required filing with the SEC before an outside party can obtain a large quantity of stock.
    C. Filing made with the SEC to indicate that a significant change has occurred.
    D. Document that must be filed with the SEC before a company can begin its initial offering of securities to the public.
    E. Form used for securities issued in connection with business combination transactions.

7. Which one of the following regulations prescribes the form and content of financial statements included in the various reports filed with the SEC?

    A. Regulation S-K
    B. Regulation S-1
    C. Regulation S-2
    D. Regulation 8-K
    E. Regulation S-X

8. A Form 10-K is filed with the SEC within

    A. 90 days of the end of each quarter.
    B. 90 days of the end of the registrant's fiscal year.
    C. 45 days of the end of each quarter.
    D. 45 days of the end of the registrant's fiscal year.
    E. 60 days of the end of the registrant's fiscal year.

9. Which one of the following divisions or offices of the SEC helps to draft rules for the form and content of financial statements and other reporting requirements?

    A. The Division of Corporation Finance.
    B. The Division of Enforcement.
    C. The Division of Investment Management.
    D. The Office of the Chief Accountant.
    E. The Office of Compliance Inspections and Examinations.

10. What is the purpose of Staff Accounting Bulletins (SAB's)?

    A. To supplement Regulation S-K.
    B. To supplement Regulation S-X.
    C. To inform the financial community of the SEC's views on current matters relating to accounting and disclosure practices.
    D. To prescribe the form and content of financial statements filed with the SEC.
    E. To request clarifications or additional information from a company that is filing an incomplete registration statement.

11. The Public Companies Accounting Oversight Board (PCAOB) effectively the accounting professions' self-regulating process previously overseen by

   A. The old Public Oversight Board
   B. The Securities and Exchange Commission
   C. The FASB
   D. The AICPA
   E. The Congress

12. How many years does a member of the PCAOB serve?

   A. 3
   B. 5
   C. 10
   D. 15
   E. 25

13. How often must the lead partner on an audit be rotated off the job?

   A. Every 2 years
   B. Every 3 years
   C. Every 4 years
   D. Every 5 years
   E. Every 6 years

14. Which form is used to disclose unique or significant happenings for a publicly traded company?

   A. Form 10-K
   B. Form 10-Q
   C. Form 8-K
   D. Form S-8
   E. Form S-1

Brief Essay Questions

1. What are the four interconnected goals that the SEC has attempted to achieve?

2. What are the eight common forms used in the filing of SEC registration statements?

3. What kinds of stock issuances are exempt from filing with the SEC?

Solutions to Multiple Choice Questions

1. A

2. E

3. B

4. C

5. A

6. D

7. E

8. E

9. D

10. C

11. D

12. B

13. D

14. C

Answers to Brief Essay Questions

1. The four interconnected goals are:

   A. Ensuring full and fair information is disclosed to all investors before the securities of a company are allowed to be bought and sold.

   B. Prohibiting the dissemination of materially misstated information.

   C. Preventing the misuse of information especially by inside parties.

   D. Regulating the operation of securities markets such as the New York Stock Exchange and American Stock Exchange.

2.   The eight common forms are:

   A. **Form S-1** – Used when no other form is prescribed; usually used by new registrants or by companies that have been filing reports with the SEC for less than 36 months.

   B. **Form S-2** – Used by companies that have filed with the SEC for 36 months or longer, but are not large enough to file a Form S-3.

   C. **Form S-3** – Used by companies that are large in size and already have a significant following in the stock market. At least 75% of its voting stock is held by nonaffiliates and disclosure is reduced for these organizations because the public is assumed to have access to a considerable amount of information.

   D. **Form S-4** – Used by securities issued in connection with business combination transactions.

   E. **Form S-8** – Used as a registration statement for employee stock plans.

   F. **Form S-11** – Used for the registration of securities by certain real estate companies.

   G. **Form SB-1** – Used by small business issuers to register up to $10 million of securities but only if the company has not registered more than $10 million of securities in the previous twelve months.

   H. **Form SB-2** – Used by small business issuers to register securities to be sold for cash.

3.   Exempt Companies – Examples

   A. Securities sold strictly to the residents of the state in which the issuing company is chartered and principally doing business.

   B. Securities issued by governments, banks, and savings and loan associations.

   C. Securities issued that are restricted to a company's own existing shareholders where no commission is paid to solicit the exchange.

   D. Securities issued by nonprofit organizations such as religious, educational, or charitable groups.

   E. Small offerings of no more than $5 million.

   F. Offerings of no more than $1 million made to any number of investors within a 12-month period, with no specific disclosure requirements. General solicitations are allowed.

G. Offerings of no more that $5 million made to 35 or fewer purchasers in a 12-month period, with no general solicitation.

H. The private placement of securities to no more than 35 sophisticated investors whom already have sufficient information available to them about the issuing company. General solicitation is not allowed.

Chapter 13

Accounting for Legal Reorganizations and Liquidations

Chapter Outline

I.   Accounting for Legal Reorganizations and Liquidations

    A.   For many different reasons, a company sometimes becomes insolvent, a state referred to as *bankruptcy*.

    B.   Legal guidance is provided primarily by *the Bankruptcy Reform Act of 1978*.

        1.   Attempts to arrive at a fair distribution of a debtor's assets.

        2.   Seeks to discharge the obligations of an honest debtor.

    C.   Bankruptcy proceedings can be formally instigated either the debtor or a group of creditors.

        1.   When the insolvent company petitions the court, this is referred to as a *voluntary* petition.

        2.   When a minimum number of creditors (in some cases, only one creditor is necessary) petitions the court, this is referred to as an *involuntary* petition.

        3.   After the petition is filed with the court, the court will normally grant an *order of relief* to halt all actions against the debtor, until such time as the debtor is either liquidated or emerges from the protection of the bankruptcy court.

    D.   Within the bankruptcy process, determining the appropriate classification of all creditors is an important step in achieving a fair settlement.

        1.   *Fully secured creditors* hold a collateral interest in assets of the insolvent company. The collateral must be sufficient to cover the amount of the liability owed to the creditor.

            a.   Any excess over the amount owed to the creditor will be available to help cover unsecured liabilities in a liquidation.

            b.   The determination of whether the collateral is sufficient is based on the *net realizable value* of the collateral, not the book value.

        2.   *Partially secured creditors* also have a collateral interest in the assets of the insolvent company. By definition, the net realizable value of the collateral is insufficient to cover the amount of the liability.

a. The uncovered part of the liability is included as part of the total unsecured liabilities of the company.

b. This situation may occur with assets that decrease in value over time, such as equipment, while the loan balance decreases at a slower rate. This situation may also occur with inventory.

3. *Unsecured liabilities with priority* are a special group of liabilities for which there is no collateral interest, but that are given special treatment because of their nature.

   a. Included in this category are

      i. Claims for administrative expenses related to the bankruptcy process. Included in this group are expenses of the trustee, lawyers, and accountants.

      ii. Obligations arising between the date that a petition is filed with the bankruptcy court and the appointment of a trustee or the issuance of an order for relief.

      iii. Employee claims for wages earned, but not paid, during the 90 days preceding the filing of a petition. The claim is limited to $4,300 per employee. This group does not include salaries of company officers.

      iv. Employee claims for contributions to benefit plans earned, but not paid, during the 180 days preceding the filing of a petition. The claim is limited to $4,300 per employee.

      v. Claims for return of deposits made by customers to acquire property or services that have not been delivered by the insolvent company. The claims are limited to $1,950 per deposit.

      vi. Government claims for unpaid taxes.

   b. Some of these liabilities are given priority to encourage individuals, firms, or companies to continue their business relationship with insolvent company while it attempts to sort out its finances. Without such encouragement, employees might leave, or accounting or law firms might refuse to lend their services when those services would be most needed.

4. *Unsecured liabilities* include all other liabilities of the insolvent.

   a. Creditors holding unsecured liabilities often only receive a portion of the total amount due to them in liquidation.

b.   The low likelihood of receiving full payment is often an incentive for unsecured creditors to look for ways to help the insolvent company stay in business.

5.   *Equity shareholders* only get paid in a liquidation after all creditors have been paid.

E.   A statement of financial affairs may be produced by an insolvent company to assist in disclosing its current financial position. Given that the business may close its doors at any time, the going concern assumption is no longer valid. Thus, the rules for disclosure change.

    1.   Assets are reported at net realizable value.

    2.   Assets are generally grouped and labeled as follows:

       a.   Pledged with fully secured creditors.

       b.   Pledged with partially secured creditors

       c.   Available for priority liabilities and unsecured creditors

    3.   Liabilities are generally grouped and labeled as follows:

       a.   Liabilities with priority

       b.   Fully secured creditors

       c.   Partially secured creditors

       d.   Unsecured creditors

    4.   The statement of financial affairs can be useful at the beginning of the bankruptcy process to assist all parties in evaluating the prospective outcomes of the various alternatives.

    5.   Most of the asset balances reported in the statement are estimated projections of net realizable value, and do not usually represent firm commitments to sell on the part of the insolvent company.

II.   Liquidation – A Chapter 7 Bankruptcy

A.   In a Chapter 7 Bankruptcy, proceedings conclude with the assets of the insolvent company being liquidated to satisfy creditor claims.

B.   A trustee, appointed by the court, oversees the termination of business activities, liquidation of the noncash properties, and distribution of cash to the creditors and stockholders. The trustee's duties include:

1. Changing locks and moving assets and records to locations controlled by the trustee.

2. Posting notices that all assets of the insolvent company are in the possession of the U.S. Trustee.

3. Notifying the U.S. Post Office that all mail for the company is to be forwarded to the trustee.

4. Opening a new bank account in the name of the trustee, and notifying banks that no withdrawals are allowed from the insolvent company's accounts except by the trustee.

5. Compiling all financial records and placing them in the custody of the trustee's own accountant.

6. Obtaining possession of all other corporate records.

C. The trustee prepares periodic reports, showing the result of liquidating the insolvent company's assets. This report is often referred to as *a statement of realization and liquidation*.

1. The statement indicates the book value and classification of all remaining assets and liabilities.

2. The report also discloses the effects of all transactions that have occurred to date.

III. Reorganization – A Chapter 11 Bankruptcy

A. In a Chapter 11 Bankruptcy, the insolvent company seeks to stay in business. While under the temporary protection of the court from the actions of creditors, the company will develop a plan to reorganize the business with hopes that the reorganized company will be profitable.

B. A reorganization plan must be devised that can win the approval of each class of creditors and each class of stockholders as well as the court.

C. Reorganization plans often include the following actions:

1. Proposed changes in operations.

2. Plans for generating additional monetary capital.

3. Plans for changes in the management of the company.

4. Plans to settle the debts of the company that existed when the order for relief was entered.

IV. Acceptance of the Reorganization Plan

    A.   Each class of creditors must approve the plan with a vote that represents 2/3 of the dollar amount and more than ½ of the votes cast.

    B.   Each class of shareholders must approve the plan with a vote of 2/3 of the owners casting votes.

    C.   If the plan is not approved, but the court believes it to be a good plan, the judge can impose the plan over the objections of the owners and creditors in a "cram down" reorganization.

V. AICPA Statement of Position 90-7 (SOP 90-7) provides guidance for the preparation of financial statements by companies during Chapter 11 reorganization.

    A.   An income statement prepared during the period of reorganization should disclose operating activities separately from reorganization items.

        1.   Any gains, losses, revenues, or expenses resulting from the reorganization must be reported separately.

        2.   Reorganization items would include gains and losses from the sale of assets necessitated by the reorganization.

        3.   Professional fees incurred in connection with the reorganization must be expenses immediately.

        4.   Any interest income earned during reorganization because of an increase in the company's cash reserves (remember, they have this cash because the court is allowing them to postpone payment of liabilities) should be reported as a reorganization item.

    B.   Since a new entity is not created when a company moves into reorganization, traditional GAAP continues to apply.

        1.   Assets are reported at their book value.

        2.   Liabilities are reported at the amount owed, though some of those amounts may be renegotiated to a lower amount during the reorganization process.

        3.   The current/noncurrent classification is not applicable during reorganization.

    C.   During reorganization, liabilities are reported as either *subject to compromise* or *not subject to compromise*.

        1.   *Liabilities subject to compromise* include all unsecured and partially secured debts that existed on the day the order for relief was granted.

2. According to SOP 90-7, *liabilities subject to compromise* are reported on the basis of the expected amount of the allowed claims as opposed to the amounts for which those allowed claims may be settled.

VI. Fresh Start Accounting

A. SOP 90-7 also provides accounting guidance for companies emerging from reorganization.

    1. If certain conditions are met, fresh start accounting may be required when a company emerges from reorganization. The emerging company is viewed as a new entity for accounting purposes which means that the company adopts a new basis of accounting.

    2. The emerging company adjusts its assets and liabilities to current value.

B. A company emerging from Chapter 11 Bankruptcy must use fresh start accounting if two criteria are met.

    1. The reorganization value (which approximates the fair market value of the emerging company's assets) is less than the total liabilities.

    2. The original owners are left with less than 50% of the voting stock of the reorganized company.

C. To make the necessary asset adjustments to reorganization value and fresh start accounting, *additional paid-in capital* is normally increased or decreased. Any write-down of a liability creates a recognized gain.

D. Because the company is viewed as a new entity, it must leave the reorganziation with a zero balance in retained earnings.

E. According to SOP 90-7, the reorganization value is determined by discounting future cash flows for the emerging company.

    1. The reorganization value is then assigned to the company's specific tangible and intangible assets in the same way as in a purchase combination.

    2. Any excess of reorganization value over the amounts assigned to specific assets is assigned to an intangible asset similar to goodwill.

    3. Following a reorganization, SOP 90-7 requires that all liabilities (except for *deferred income taxes*) must be reported at the present value of the future cash payments.

Multiple Choice Questions

1. Information useful to the creditors of a business filing for bankruptcy is found in the

    A. Statement of Financial Affairs
    B. Charge and Discharge Statement
    C. Realization and Liquidation Statement
    D. Plan of Reorganization
    E. Statement of Bankruptcy

2. Under a voluntary Chapter 7 bankruptcy, the assets would

    A. Remain in the custody of the company.
    B. Be placed in the custody of the trustee.
    C. Be placed in the custody of the court.
    D. Be given to the creditors to satisfy their claims.
    E. Be sold at auction for cash.

3. Charles Turner Construction Inc. is a creditor of ABC Co. Turner constructed the office building in which ABC has its headquarters. At the time the building was constructed, Turner attached a lien on the building as security for the $80,000 note which Turner accepted. Now, ABC Co. has filed for bankruptcy and it is estimated that the building has a net realizable value of $70,000. Turner's status is

	Fully Secured	Partially Secured	Unsecured
A.	Yes	No	Yes
B.	No	No	Yes
C.	No	Yes	No
D.	No	Yes	Yes
E.	Yes	No	No

Items 4 through 6 are based on the following information.

Veltri Inc. has the following assets and liabilities (assets are stated at net realizable value).

Assets pledged with secured creditors	$ 80,000
Assets pledged with partially secured creditors	60,000
Other assets	150,000
Secured liabilities	40,000
Partially secured liabilities	95,000
Liabilities with priority	75,000
Unsecured liabilities	225,000

4. In a liquidation, what is the amount of free assets after payment of liabilities with priority?

    A. $190,000
    B. $120,000
    C. $ 75,000
    D. $ 95,000
    E. $115,000

5. In a liquidation, what percentage of unsecured liabilities will be paid?

    A. 84%
    B. 34%
    C. 54%
    D. 44%
    E. 64%

6. In a liquidation, how much money would be paid on the partially secured liabilities?

    A. $35,400
    B. $65,200
    C. $75,400
    D. $95,200
    E. $67,800

Items 7 through 9 are based on the following information.

ABC Co. is beginning the process of liquidation. ABC has prepared a statement of financial affairs that discloses the following data:

Assets pledged with secured creditors	$210,000
Secured liabilities	125,000
Assets pledged with partially secured creditors	290,000
Free assets (not including excess to be received from assets pledged on secured liabilities)	225,000
Unsecured liabilities with priority	121,000
Unsecured liabilities	450,000

7. What percentage of unsecured liabilities will be paid?

    A. 69%
    B. 37%
    C. 50%
    D. 48%
    E. 42%

8. ABC owes $45,000 to Wallace Co., an unsecured creditor (without priority). How much money can Wallace Co. expect to collect from ABC?

    A. $42,600
    B. $ -0-
    C. $21,800
    D. $18,900
    E. $17,200

9.   ABC owes $90,000 to a bank on a note payable that is secured by a security interest attached to the property with an estimated net realizable value of $75,000. How much can the bank expect to collect?

    A. $81,300
    B. $37,800
    C. $75,600
    D. $45,500
    E. $60,100

10. Before a company can use fresh start accounting, which one of the following conditions must exist?

    A.   The reorganization value of the company must exceed the value of the liabilities.
    B.   The fair market value of the assets of the emerging company must be less than the allowed claims as of the date of the order of relief (plus liabilities incurred during reorganization).
    C.   The original owners must hold at least 50% of the stock of the company when it emerges from bankruptcy.
    D.   The reorganization value of the emerging entity's assets must exceed the sum of all postpetition liabilities and allowed claims.
    E.   The reorganization value of the company must be less than the value of all liabilities.

Brief Essay Questions

1.   The statement of financial affairs is prepared for the debtor and is especially important in assisting the unsecured creditors as they decide whether to push for reorganization or liquidation. The debtor's assets are reported according to the classifications relevant to a liquidation. Consequently, how are assets labeled?

2.   The statement of financial affairs is prepared for the debtor and is especially important in assisting the unsecured creditors as they decide whether to push for reorganization or liquidation. The debtor's liabilities are reported according to the classifications relevant to a liquidation. Consequently, how are debts labeled?

3.   A limited amount of unpaid wages to employees is given priority in a distribution of cash resulting from a liquidation of an insolvent company. What is that limit? What happens to the amount of unpaid wages to employees that exceed the limit and therefore do not get the priority treatment?

Solutions to Multiple Choice Questions

1.   **A**   The statement of financial affairs is the statement most useful for this purpose. The charge and discharge statement is associated with estates and the realization and liquidation statement is associated with Chapter 7 bankruptcies that have been approved by the court.

2. **B**   All Chapter 7 bankruptcies, whether voluntary or unvoluntary, result in the assets being placed in the custody of either a permanent or interim trustee.

3. **C**   The net realizable value of the asset is insufficient to cover the debt. This means that the creditor is partially secured rather than fully secured. A partially secured creditor joins the unsecured creditors without priority for an amount equal to the difference between the value of the loan and the amount realized from the sale of the asset.

4. **E**   Free assets:

Other assets	$150,000
Excess from assets pledged with secured	
creditors ($80,000 - $40,000)	40,000
Total	$190,000
Liabilities with priority	(75,000)
Free assets after payment of liabilities with priority	$115,000

5. **D**   The percentage of unsecured liabilities to be paid is 44%. This is determined by dividing free assets by the amount of total unsecured liabilities.

Excess of partially secured liabilities over partially	
pledged assets ($95,000 - $60,000)	$ 35,000
Unsecured creditors	225,000
Total unsecured liabilities	$260,000
Free assets	$115,000
Total unsecured liabilities	÷260,000
Percentage of unsecured liabilities to be paid	44%

6. **C**

Assets pledged with partially secured creditors	$60,000
44% of partially secured liabilities not covered by	
pledged assets ($35,000 × 44%)	15,400
Total paid on partially secured liabilities	$75,400

7. **E**

Unsecured creditors	$ 225,000
Excess to be received from assets pledged on secured	
liabilities ($210,000 - $125,000)	85,000
Amount available for unsecured creditors	$ 310,000
Unsecured liabilities with priority	(121,000)
Net amount available for unsecured creditors	189,000
Unsecured liabilities	÷ 450,000
Percentage of unsecured liabilities that will be paid	42%

8. **D**   Amount Wallace Co. can expect to collect ($45,000 × 42%) = $18,900

9. **A**

Security interest net realizable value	$75,000
Expected payment on unsecured remainder	
($15,000 × 42%)	6,300
Amount bank can expect to receive	$81,300

10. **E**

Answers to Brief Essay Questions

1. The assets are labeled as:

   A. Pledged with fully secured creditors.
   B. Pledged with partially secured creditors.
   C. Available for priority liabilities and unsecured creditors (often referred to as free assets)

2. The debts are labeled as:

   A. Liabilities with priority.
   B. Fully secured creditors.
   C. Partially secured creditors.
   D. Unsecured creditors.

3. The wage limit for determining unsecured liabilities with priority is $4,300 per employee, covering the 90 days preceding the filing of the petition. Any excess over the $4,300 limit is included with unsecured liabilities without priority.

Chapter 14

Partnerships: Formation and Operation

Chapter Outline

I. Partnerships – Advantages and Disadvantages

    A.   Advantages of the partnership format include:

        1.   ease of formation, and

        2.   single taxation.

    B.   Partnerships rarely grow to a significant size (when compared with large corporate organizations) primarily because of the unlimited liability being assumed by each general partner.

    C.   Alternate Legal Forms

        1.   Subchapter S Corporation – limited to 75 stockholders, created as a corporation, under certain circumstances it will be taxed as a partnership.

        2.   Limited Partnership (LP) – Ownership consists of General Partners and Limited Partners. Limited Partners contribute investment capital, but do not participate in management of the partnership.

        3.   Limited Liability Partnership (LLP) – Same characteristics as a partnership, but the liability of the partners is limited to their own acts and omissions and the acts and omissions of those who are supervised by them.

        4.   Limited Liability Corporation (LLP) – Similar to a Subchapter S, but the number of owners is usually not restricted.

II. Partnership Accounting – Initial Capital Accounts

    A.   The basis of accounting for these capital balances are the *Articles of Partnership* which establish provisions for initial investments, withdrawals, admission of new partners, etc.

    B.   The tangible contribution made by the partners should be recorded at fair market value.

C. Two different approaches are available when one or more partners bring intangible assets to the partnership (such as expertise or name recognition).

    1. The *bonus method*

        a. Identifiable, tangible assets are recorded at their fair market value.

        b. The capital account balances for each of the partners are adjusted to indicate tangible and intangible contributions made by each partner.

    2. The *goodwill method*

        a. The implied value of the business is computed.

        b. The difference between the implied value and the fair market value of the tangible asset contributions is called "goodwill".

III. Partnership Accounting – Allocation of partnership income or loss.

A. At the end of each fiscal period, the revenue and expense accounts must be closed out with the resulting income figure being assigned to the individual capital accounts.

B. The method of allocating income to the capital accounts should be established in the *Articles of Partnership*.

    1. The partners can simply assume an equal division of profits and losses, or can negotiate different profit and loss sharing percentages for each partner.

    2. The income or loss of the partnership is often allocated to the partners after being adjusted for various factors. Essentially, these factors represent pre-allocations of "chunks" of the partnership's income/loss to the partners prior to applying the negotiated profit/loss sharing percentages.

        a. Partners may receive credit for interest based on their capital account balances. This will reduce the amount of income available for allocation to the partners using the profit/loss sharing percentages.

        b. Partners may receive credit for "unpaid" compensation or bonuses. These "salaries" or "bonuses" reduce the amount of income available for allocation to the partners using the profit/loss sharing percentages.

IV.   Partnership Accounting – Admitting New Partners

    A.   Book Value Method

        1.   Cash Paid Directly to the Partners

           a.   Reduce the capital account balances of each of the "old" partners by a percentage equal to the ownership percentage purchased by the new partner.

           b.   Set up the new partner's capital account balance.

        2.   Cash Paid to the Partnership

           a.   Debit the *Cash* account for the amount of cash contributed to the partnership by the new partner.

           b.   Credit the capital account balance of the new partner for the new partner's percentage of the tangible assets of the partnership (the tangible net assets of the partnership prior to the new partner's admittance plus the cash contribution).

           c.   Any difference between "a" and "b" above should be allocated to the original partners based on the profit and loss sharing percentages established in the *Articles of Incorporation*.

    B.   Revaluation Method

        1.   Cash Paid Directly to the Partners

           a.   Determine the implied value of the partnership based on the new partner's payment to the partners and the percentage of the partnership acquired (Cash Payment ÷ Percentage Ownership Acquired).

           b.   Determine amount of Goodwill generated by the transaction. (Implied Value – Net Tangible Assets of the Partnership).

           c.   Allocate the goodwill to the original partners based on the original partners' profit/loss sharing percentages.

           d.   Reduce the capital account balances of each of the "old" partners by a percentage equal to the ownership percentage purchased by the new partner.

        2.   Cash Paid to the Partnership

           a.   Determine the implied value of the partnership based on the new partner's payment to the partners and the percentage of the partnership acquired (Cash Payment ÷ Percentage Ownership Acquired).

b. Determine amount of Goodwill generated by the transaction. (Implied Value – Net Tangible Assets of the Partnership, Including the Contributed Cash).

c. Allocate the goodwill to the original partners based on the original partners' profit/loss sharing percentages.

d. Increase the assets by the amount of the contributed cash and establish the capital account balance of the new partner.

V. Partnership Accounting – Dissolution of the Partnership

A. Each change in composition serves to dissolve the original partnership. The old partnership ceases to exist, and a new partnership is formed.

B. When a partner withdraws from the partnership, and the remaining partners continue with the business, assets are usually distributed to the withdrawing partner.

C. The amount of the distribution to the withdrawing partner is often determined by the Articles of Partnership.

1. The difference between the amount distributed to the withdrawing partner and the withdrawing partner's capital balance can be recorded as an adjustment to the remaining partners' capital accounts.

2. Alternatively, goodwill and all capital accounts can be adjusted to fair market value, based on the distribution amount.

Multiple Choice Questions

1. Which one of the following is a reason for the popularity of partnerships as a legal form for businesses?

    A. Partnerships avoid the double taxation of income that is found in corporations.
    B. Partnerships need only be formed by an oral agreement.
    C. In some cases, losses may be used to offset gains for income tax purposes.
    D. Partners in partnerships are not subject to unlimited liability.
    E. Partnerships avoid mutual agency.

Items 2 and 3 are based on the following information:

Marea and Ashley began a partnership on January 4, 2004. Marea invested cash of $90,000 as well as inventory costing $8,000, but with a current appraised value of $10,000. Ashley contributed land with a $30,000 book value and a $65,000 fair market value. The partnership also accepted responsibility for a $5,000 note payable owed in connection with the land. The partners agreed to begin operations with equal capital balances.

2. Assuming that the bonus method was used by this partnership, what was Marea's initial capital balance?

    A. $ 61,500
    B. $ 80,000
    C. $ 82,500
    D. $100,000
    E. $ 81,000

3. Assuming that the goodwill method was used by this partnership, what is the amount of goodwill and the amount of Ashley's initial capital balance?

	Goodwill	Ashely's Initial Capital Balance
A.	$ 15,000	$ 80,000
B.	$ 45,000	$ 90,000
C.	$ 20,000	$ 65,000
D.	$ 40,000	$100,000
E.	$ 30,000	$ 85,000

Items 4 through 6 are based on the following information:

The partnership of Albert and Beach decided to admit Collins as a partner with a 25% interest. Collins invested $50,000 in cash into the partnership. Albert's and Beach's capital accounts and their profit and loss sharing ratios are shown below:

	Capital	Profit and Loss Sharing Ratio
Albert	$90,000	60%
Beach	$30,000	40%

4. If the partnership used the goodwill (revaluation) method, how much goodwill should be recognized by this transaction?

    A. $80,000
    B. $50,000
    C. $45,000
    D. $25,000
    E. $30,000

5. If the partnership used the goodwill (revaluation) method, what would be the capital balances for Albert, Beach, and Collins after Collins' investment was recorded?

	Albert	Beach	Collins
A.	$ 90,000	$30,000	$50,000
B.	$120,000	$50,000	$30,000
C.	$108,000	$42,000	$50,000
D.	$108,000	$42,000	$57,000
E.	$ 90,000	$30,000	$90,000

6. If the partnership used the bonus method, what would be the capital balances for Albert, Beach, and Collins after Collins' investment was recorded?

	Albert	Beach	Collins
A.	$ 90,000	$30,000	$50,000
B.	$120,000	$50,000	$50,000
C.	$ 90,000	$37,500	$42,500
D.	$150,000	$62,500	$57,000
E.	$108,000	$37,500	$50,000

Items 7 and 8 are based on the following information:

A partnership was formed on January 5, 2004 with the following capital balances:

Curtis	$ 300,000
Donald	$ 250,000
Edward	$ 450,000

The Articles of Partnership stipulated that profits and losses are assigned as follows:

- Each partner is allocated interest equal to 10% of the beginning capital balance.
- Donald is allocated a $75,000 salary
- Any remaining profits/losses are allocated on a 3:2:5 basis, respectively.
- Each partner is allowed to withdraw up to $20,000 per year.

Net income of $190,000 was earned by the business in 2004.

7.   How much income is allocated to Donald in 2004?

        A. $ 38,000
        B. $103,000
        C. $ 75,000
        D. $ 30,000
        E. $ 25,000

8.   Assuming that each partner withdraws the maximum amount, what is each partner's capital account balance at the end of 2004?

	Curtis	Donald	Edward
A.	$314,500	$333,000	$482,500
B.	$357,000	$288,000	$545,000
C.	$337,000	$268,000	$525,000
D.	$300,000	$250,000	$450,000
E.	$280,000	$230,000	$430,000

Items 9 and 10 are based on the following information:

As of December 31, 2004, the Manhattan Co. partnership had the following capital balances:

Scott, Capital	$ 400,000
Adams, Capital	$ 300,000
Baxter, Capital	$ 200,000
Walters, Capital	$ 100,000

Profits/Losses are split on a 4:3:2:1 basis, respectively. Adams decided to leave the partnership and was paid $324,000 from the business based on the original contractual agreement.

9.   If the goodwill method is applied, what is the total amount of goodwill?

        A. $50,000
        B. $72,000
        C. $21,000
        D. $80,000
        E. $89,000

10.   If the goodwill method is applied, what is the capital for Scott after Adams' withdrawal?

        A. $425,000
        B. $432,000
        C. $416,000
        D. $475,000
        E. $437,000

Items 11 and 12 are based on the following information:

The following condensed balance sheet is presented for the partnership of Cooke, Dorry, and Evans who share profits and losses in the ratio of 4:3:3, respectively.

Cash	$ 90,000
Other Assets	820,000
Loan Rec. - Cooke	30,000
Total Assets	$ 940,000
Accounts Payable	$ 210,000
Loan Payable - Evans	40,000
Cooke, Capital	300,000
Dorry, Capital	200,000
Evans, Capital	190,000
Total Liabs. & Capital	$ 940,000

11. Assume that Fisher is going to pay $300,000 to the partnership for her 25% interest. Using the goodwill method, what will Dorry's capital balance be after admitting Fisher?

   A. $ 290,000
   B. $ 63,000
   C. $ 263,000
   D. $ 360,000
   E. $1,200,000

12. Assume that Fisher is going to pay $300,000 to the individual partners for a 25% interest. Using the bonus method, what will Fisher capital balance be?

   A. $ 75,000
   B. $ 300,000
   C. $ 235,000
   D. $ 172,500
   E. $ 247,500

Brief Essay Questions

1. How does *partnership accounting* differ from *corporate accounting*?

2. What are the meaning and purpose of the *Articles of Partnership*?

3. When a partner sells his or her interest in a partnership, what rights are conveyed to the new partner?

Advanced Accounting – 7/e

Problems

1. The Albright & Baker partnership had the account balances shown below on January 1, 2004 when the partners decided to admit Clark as a new partner. Clark was to contribute $20,000 cash to the partnership for a 25% interest in the firm.

Cash	$ 10,000
Other current assets	$ 40,000
Buildings and equipment – net	$ 50,000
Land	$ 20,000
Accounts payable	$ 40,000
Albright, Capital	$ 50,000
Baker, Capital	$ 30,000

Required:

A. What entry would have been made to admit Clark as a partner under the goodwill method?

B. What entry would have been made to admit Clark as a partner under the bonus method is Albright and Baker had shared profits and losses according to their relative capital balances?

C. If Clark was to receive a 40% interest in the partnership and if no goodwill or bonus was to be recognized, how much cash would Clark have contributed? Show supporting calculations.

2. The partners of the XYZ partnership had the following capital balances on January 1, 2004:

X, Capital	$ 52,000
Y, Capital	$ 82,000
Z, Capital	$ 92,000

The *Articles of Partnership* provided that each partner might draw $1,000 per month and the profit and losses for the year would be allocated as follows:

- Z would be allowed a $2,000 per month salary allocation.
- Each partner would be allocated interest as income at the rate of 10% per year based on his or her end-of-year balance (after drawing but before income allocation).
- Any remaining balance (positive or negative) is to be allocated based on the capital balances of the partners.

Before any allocation could take place, the XYZ partnership had to allow for sales of $312,000 and expenses of $231,000 for 2004.

Required:

For the year ending December 31, 2004, develop a *Schedule of Income Allocation* for the XYZ partnership. Also, show the entries necessary to close the *Profit and Loss Summary* account and the *Drawing* accounts into the capital balances.

3. A partnership has the following balances and profit/loss sharing percentages:

	Capital Balances	Profit/Loss Sharing %
Fesler	$ 80,000	50%
Swanson	$ 100,000	40%
Galbreath	$ 70,000	10%

Required:

A. Booker is going to buy into the partnership by paying $100,000 to the partners in exchange for a 20% ownership in the partnership. Using the **book value method**, what are the four capital balances after admitting Booker to the partnership?

B. Booker is going to buy into the partnership by paying $100,000 to the partners in exchange for a 20% ownership in the partnership. Using the **goodwill method**, what are the four capital balances after admitting Booker to the partnership?

C. Booker is going to buy into the partnership by paying $100,000 directly to the partnership in exchange for a 20% ownership in the partnership. Using the **bonus method**, what are the four capital balances after admitting Booker to the partnership?

D. Booker is going to buy into the partnership by paying $100,000 directly to the partnership in exchange for a 20% ownership in the partnership. Using the **goodwill method**, what are the four capital balances after admitting Booker to the partnership?

Solutions to Multiple Choice Questions

1. **A**

2. **B**   Under the bonus method, all contributed property is recorded at fair market value. As specified by the *Articles of Partnership*, total capital is then divided equally between the partners. Total capital (net assets) is calculated as follows:

Cash	$ 90,000
Inventory	10,000
Land	65,000
Total assets	$ 165,000
Less: Notes payable	(5,000)
Total capital	$ 160,000
Marea's percentage	50%
Marea, Capital	$ 80,000

3. **D**   The fair market value of Marea's contribution is $100,000, whereas Ashley is investing only a net amount of $60,000 (the value of the land less the accompanying debt). Because the capital accounts are initially to be equal, Ashley is presumed to be contributing goodwill of $40,000. The initial capital balances are calculated as follows:

Cash	$ 90,000
Inventory	10,000
Land	65,000
Goodwill	40,000
Total assets	$ 205,000
Less: Notes payable	(5,000)
Total capital	$ 200,000
Marea's percentage	50%
Marea, Capital	$ 100,000

4. **E**

Implied value of the business ($50,000 ÷ 25%)	$ 200,000
Total capital ($80,000 + $40,000 + $50,000)	(170,000)
Goodwill	$ 30,000

5. **C**

	Albert	Beach	Collins
Original capital	$ 90,000	$ 30,000	
Goodwill ($30,000 x 60% or 40%)	18,000	12,000	
Collins' payment ($200,000 x 25%)			$ 50,000
Capital balances	$108,000	$ 42,000	$ 50,000

6.   C

	Albert	Beach	Collins
Original capital	$ 90,000	$ 30,000	
Collin's Cash ($50,000 x 60% or 40%)	30,000	20,000	
Allocation to Collins (25%)	(30,000)	(12,500)	$42,500
Capital balances	$ 90,000	$ 37,500	$ 42,500

7.   B

	Curtis	Donald	Edward	Total
Interest - 10% of Beginning Capital	$ 30,000	$ 25,000	$ 45,000	$ 100,000
Salaries		75,000		75,000
Allocation of remaining income ($15,000 allocated 3:2:5)	4,500	3,000	7,500	15,000
Total Income Allocation	$ 34,500	$ 103,000	$ 52,500	$ 190,000

8.   C

	Curtis	Donald	Edward	Total
Beginning Capital	$ 300,000	$ 250,000	$ 450,000	$ 1,000,000
Net income	34,500	103,000	52,500	190,000
Withdrawals	(20,000)	(20,000)	(20,000)	(60,000)
Ending Capital	$ 314,500	$ 333,000	$ 482,500	$ 1,130,000

9.   D   Goodwill ($24,000 ÷ 30% = $80,000)

10.   B

	Scott	Baxter	Walters
Original Capital	$ 400,000	$ 200,000	$ 100,000
Goodwill Allocation	32,000	16,000	8,000
Capital Balances	$ 432,000	$ 216,000	$ 108,000

11.   C

Fisher's contribution	$ 300,000
÷ Fisher's % ownership	25%
Implied value of the partnership	$ 1,200,000
Implied value of the partnership	$ 1,200,000
Less: Tangible partnership assets	(990,000)
Goodwill	$ 210,000
Dorry, Capital - Beginning	$ 200,000
Add: Dorry's share of the goodwill	63,000
Dorry, Capital - Ending	$ 263,000

12.   **D**

Tangible Net Partnership Assets	$	690,000
× Fisher's % ownership		25%
Implied value of the partnership	$	172,500

Answers to Brief Essay Questions

1.   Partnership accounting issues focus on the equity (or capital) section of the balance sheet. In a corporation, stockholders' equity is divided between earned capital (retained earnings) and contributed capital. Conversely, for a partnership, each partner has an individual capital account which is not differentiated according to its sources. Virtually all accounting issues encountered in connection with the partnership format are related to recording and maintaining these capital balances.

2.   The Articles of Partnership is a legal document that defines the rights and responsibilities of the partners in relation to the business and in relation to each other. Because the Articles of Partnership serves as a governing document for the partnership, it should be created as a prerequisite for the formation of a partnership. It may contain any number of provisions but should normally specify each of the following:

   A.   Name and address of each partner.
   B.   Business location.
   C.   Description of the nature of the business.
   D.   Rights and responsibilities of each partner.
   E.   Initial investment to be made by each partner along with the method to be used for valuation.
   F.   Specific method by which profits and losses are to be allocated.
   G.   Periodic withdrawals to be allowed each partner.
   H.   Procedures for admitting new partners.
   I.   Method for arbitrating disputes.
   J.   Method for setting a partner's share of the business upon withdrawal, retirement, or death.

3.   In selling an interest in a partnership, three rights are conveyed to the new owner:

   A.   The right of co-ownership of the business property.

   B.   The right to a specified allocation of profits and losses generated by the partnership's business, and

   C.   The right to participate in the management of the business.

   No problem exists in selling or assigning the first two of these rights. However, *the right to participate in management decisions* can only be transferred with the consent of all partners.

Solutions to Problems

1. A.

Date	Accounts	Debit	Credit
	Cash	20,000	
	Goodwill	6,667	
	Clark, Capital		26,667

The key to the solution is to determine the net assets (total capital) of the partnership after Clark's contribution in order to determine his 25% share.

Assets before contribution	$ 120,000
Clark's contribution	20,000
Assets after contribution	$ 140,000

Assets after contribution	$ 140,000
Less: Liabilities	(40,000)
Net Assets	$ 100,000
Clark's percentage	25%
Clark's share of the partnership's net assets	$ 25,000

Goodwill is then attributable to Clark's capital account. Goodwill is solved algebraically, as follows:

$20,000 + G = 25\% \times (\$100,000 + G)$
$.75G = \$5,000$
$G = \$6,667$ (rounded)

B.

Date	Accounts	Debit	Credit
	Cash	20,000	
	Albright, Capital	3,125	
	Baker, Capital	1,875	
	Clark, Capital		25,000

Observe that in order to provide Clark with a 25% interest in the firm, Albright's and Baker's capital accounts must be reduced. For example, the amount of the reduction for Albright is based on Albright's profit sharing ratio:

$50,000 \div (\$50,000 + \$30,000) \times \$5,000 = \$3,125$

C.   Let X = Cash to be contributed by Clark
      X = .4 x ($80,000 + X)
      X = $32,000 + .4X
      .6X = $32,000
      X = $53,333 (rounded)

2.   Schedule of Income Allocation

XYZ Partnership
Schedule of Income Allocaiton
For Year Ending December 31, 2004

	Total	X	Y	Z
Income	$ 81,000			
Z's Salary	(24,000)			$ 24,000
Remainder	57,000			
Interest	(19,000)	$ 4,000	$ 7,000	8,000
Remainder	38,000			
Remaining balance	(38,000)	8,000	14,000	16,000
Totals	$ -	$ 12,000	$ 21,000	$ 48,000

Date	Accounts	Debit	Credit
	Income Summary	81,000	
	X, Capital		12,000
	Y, Capital		21,000
	Z, Capital		48,000
	to close Income Summary to the capital accounts		
	X, Capital	12,000	
	Y, Capital	12,000	
	Z, Capital	12,000	
	X, Drawing		12,000
	Y, Capital		12,000
	Z, Drawing		12,000
	to close Income Summary to the capital accounts.		

3.   A.   Book value method, Cash paid to the partners

Each partner gives up 20% of their current balance to Booker.

Fesler, Capital			Swanson, Capital	
	80,000			100,000
16,000			20,000	
	64,000			80,000

Galbreath, Capital			Booker, Capital	
	70,000			
14,000				50,000
	56,000			50,000

B.   Goodwill method, Cash contribution paid to partners

Booker's contribution	$ 100,000
÷ Booker's % ownership	20%
Implied value of the partnership	$ 500,000
Implied value of the partnership	$ 500,000
Less: Tangible partnership assets	(250,000)
Goodwill	$ 250,000

The goodwill is allocated to the three original partners. Then 20% of each balance is allocated to Booker.

Fesler, Capital			Swanson, Capital	
	80,000			100,000
41,000	125,000		40,000	100,000
	164,000			160,000

Galbreath, Capital			Booker, Capital	
	70,000			
19,000	25,000			100,000
	76,000			100,000

C.   Book value method, Cash contribution paid to partnership

Assets before contribution	$ 250,000
Booker's contribution	100,000
Assets after contribution	$ 350,000

After identifying the total assets of the new partnership, Cash is debited for $100,000. Booker's capital account is credited for 20% of the total assets ($350,000 x 20%). The difference is allocated to the other partners.

Fesler, Capital		Swanson, Capital	
	80,000		100,000
	15,000		12,000
	95,000		112,000

Galbreath, Capital		Booker, Capital	
	70,000		
	3,000		70,000
	73,000		70,000

D.   Goodwill method, Cash contribution paid to partnership

First, compute the implied value of the new partnership, and the amount of Goodwill to be recorded.

Booker's contribution	$ 100,000
÷ Booker's % ownership	20%
Implied value of the partnership	$ 500,000
Implied value of the partnership	$ 500,000
Less: Tangible partnership assets	(350,000)
Goodwill	$ 150,000

Second, allocate the Goodwill to the three original partners. Then, credit Booker's account for the amount of Booker's contribution.

Fesler, Capital		Swanson, Capital	
	80,000		100,000
	75,000		60,000
	155,000		160,000

Galbreath, Capital		Booker, Capital	
	70,000		
	15,000		100,000
	85,000		100,000

Chapter 15

Partnerships: Termination and Liquidation

Chapter Outline

I. Termination and Liquidation – Protecting the Interests of all Parties

    A.   The termination of a partnership and liquidation of its property may take place for a number of reasons.

        1.   The death, withdrawal, or retirement of a partner can lead to cessation of business activities.

        2.   The bankruptcy of an individual partner or the partnership as a whole can also necessitate this same conclusion.

    B.   The procedures involved in terminating and liquidating a partnership are basically mechanical.

        1.   Partnership assets are converted into cash that is used to pay business obligations as well as liquidation expenses.

        2.   Any remaining assets are then distributed to the individual partners based on their final capital balances.

        3.   The partnership's books are permanently closed since no general ledger accounts remain.

        4.   If each partner has a capital balance large enough to absorb all liquidation losses, the accountant should be able to easily record the series of transactions.

    C.   Because of the importance of liquidating and distributing assets, the accountant can play an important role in the process.

        1.   The accountant provides timely financial information to all parties involved.

        2.   The accountant works to ensure an equitable settlement of all claims.

II.   Schedule of Liquidation

    A.   The liquidation process usually involves the (1) disposal of noncash assets, (2) payment of liabilities and liquidation expenses, and (3) the distribution of any remaining cash to the partners based on their final capital balances.

B.   A *schedule of liquidation* should be produced periodically by the accountant to disclose.

    1.   Transactions to date.

    2.   Property still being held by the partnership.

    3.   Liabilities remaining to be paid.

    4.   Current cash and capital balances.

III.   Deficit Capital Balance

A.   By the end of the liquidation process, one or more partners may have a negative capital balance (*deficit*), usually as a result of losses incurred in disposing of assets.

B.   Legally, any deficit should be eliminated by having that partner contribute enough additional assets to offset the amount of the deficit.

C.   If this contribution is not received immediately, the remaining partners may request a *preliminary distribution* of any partnership cash that is available.

    1.   This payment is based on *safe capital balances* – the amounts that would remain in the individual capital accounts even if all deficits and other properties prove to be losses that must be absorbed by the remaining partners.

    2.   If a portion (or all) of a deficit is subsequently recovered, a further distribution to the partners is made based on newly *calculated safe capital balances*.

    3.   Any deficit that is not recovered must be charged to the remaining partners based on their relative profit and loss ratio.

IV.   Marshaling of Assets

A.   To provide an equitable system for distributing assets during liquidation, the *Uniform Partnership Act* states that claims against an insolvent partner shall be ranked as follows:

    1.   Those owing to separate creditors.

    2.   Those owing to partnership creditors.

    3.   Those owing to Partners by way of contribution.

B.   This priority listing is referred to as the *marshaling of assets doctrine*.

C. The *marshaling of assets doctrine* specifies that personal creditors can claim a partner's share of partnership assets; but, a recovery of all or a portion of the total amount is possible only if two specific criteria are met:

1. Payment of all partnership debts must be assured.

2. The insolvent partner has to have a positive capital balance.

V. Preliminary Distribution of Partnership Assets

A. The liquidation process can extend for a lengthy period of time as a business activities wind down and property is sold.

B. More cash may be generated than the amount needed to extinguish all potential liabilities and liquidation expenses.

C. If possible, the distribution of excess cash amounts should be made as quickly as possible to enable the partners to make use of their funds.

1. The accountant may choose to produce a proposed schedule of liquidation at such times to determine the equitable distribution of available cash amounts.

2. The proposed schedule of liquidation is developed based upon simulating the accounting recognition that would be required by a possible series of transactions: assets are sold, expenses are paid, etc.

   a. These events are designed with the anticipation of maximum losses in each case.

   b. Noncash assets are assumed to have no resale value, maximum possible liquidation expenses are included, and all partners are considered to be personally insolvent.

   c. Since numerous capital distributions may be required, this process if often called a liquidation made in installments.

3. Ending capital figures that remain on a proposed schedule of liquidation are safe capital balance – the amounts that could be immediately paid to each partner without jeopardizing future payments.

4. Safe capital balances indicate that the partner currently has a sufficient interest in the partnership to absorb all potential losses even after a preliminary distribution.

VI. Predistribution Plan

A. The proposed schedule of liquidation indicates safe capital balances but a newly revised statement must be produced frequently.

B. Accountants often prefer to produce a single predistribution plan at the start of a liquidation to provide guidance for all payments made to the partners throughout this process.

C. Information for the predistribution plan is generated by assuming the occurrence of a series of losses, each just large enough to eliminate one partner's claim to any partnership property.

D. Once a series of losses has been simulated that would eliminate the capital balances of all partners, the actual plan is developed by measuring the effects that occur if the losses do not materialize.

E. By working backwards through this series of possible losses, a predistribution plan can be produced that will cover all payments made within the liquidation.

Multiple Choice Questions

1. In a partnership liquidation, how is the final allocation of business assets made to the partners?

   A. equally
   B. according to the profit and loss ratio
   C. according to the balances of the partners' loan and capital accounts
   D. according to the initial investments made by the partners
   E. according to the method stipulated by the partnership agreement

2. A partnership is in the process of liquidating and is currently reporting the following capital balances.

Marla, Capital (50% share of all profits and losses)	$ 80,000
Barbara, Capital (30%)	60,000
Roberta, Capital (20%)	(24,000)

   Roberta has indicated that the $24,000 deficit will be covered by a forthcoming contribution. However, the two remaining partners have asked to receive the $116,000 in cash that is presently available. How much of this money should each partner be given?

	Marla	Barbara
A.	$65,000	$51,000
B.	$81,000	$35,000
C.	$58,000	$58,000
D.	$85,000	$31,000
E.	$72,000	$44,000

3. A partnership is considering the possibility of liquidation because one of the partners, Stewart, is insolvent. Capital balances at the current time are as follows, and profits and losses are divided on a 6:3:1 basis, respectively.

George, Capital	$ 65,000
Stewart, Capital	82,000
Thomas, Capital	53,000

   Stewart's creditors have filed a $40,000 claim against the partnership's assets. The partnership currently holds assets reported at $300,000 and liabilities of $100,000. If the assets can be sold for $125,000, what is the minimum amount that Stewart's creditors would receive?

   A. $25,000
   B. $26,000
   C. $21,000
   D. $30,000
   E. $27,000

Items 4 and 5 are based on the following information.

The following condensed balance sheet is for the partnership of Andrews, Carroll, and Murray, who share profits and losses in the ratio of 6:2:2, respectively.

Cash	$ 80,000
Other assets	120,000
Total assets	$ 200,000
Liabilities	$ 140,000
Andrews, Capital	30,000
Carroll, Capital	25,000
Murray, Capital	5,000
Total liabilities and partners' equity	$ 200,000

4.   Which partner is most vulnerable to a loss?

   A.   Andrews
   B.   Carroll
   C.   Andrews and Carroll are equally vulnerable
   D.   Murray
   E.   Andrews and Murray are equally vulnerable

5.   If the other assets are sold for $80,000, how should the available cash be distributed?

	Andrews	Carroll	Murray
A.	$ 6,000	$14,000	$ -0-
B.	$ 3,750	$16,250	$ -0-
C.	$16,250	$ 3,000	$ 750
D.	$ 3,750	$13,250	$ 3,000
E.	$ 7,350	$11,750	$ 900

6.   Which one of the following statements is **incorrect** regarding a predistribution plan?

   A.   A predistribution plan is developed by simulating a series of losses that are just large enough to eliminate, one at a time, all of the partners' claims to cash.
   B.   A predistribution plan recognizes that the individual capital accounts exhibit differing degrees of sensitivity to losses.
   C.   A predistribution plan serves as a guideline for all future cash payments in a liquidation.
   D.   A predistribution is prepared at the end of a liquidation to confirm actual cash distributions.
   E.   A series of absorbed losses forms the basis for the predistribution plan.

7. The following condensed balance sheet is for the Ashley, Bart, and Charles partnership. The partners share profits and losses in the ratio of 5:3:2, respectively.

Cash	$ 125,000
Inventory	100,000
Other assets	300,000
Total assets	$ 525,000
Liabilities	$ 270,000
Ashley, Capital	100,000
Bart, Capital	85,000
Charles, Capital	70,000
Total liabilities and partners' equity	$ 525,000

The partners have decided to liquidate the business. Liquidation expenses are estimated to be $8,000. The other assets are sold for $180,000. What distribution can be made to the partners?

	Ashley	Bart	Charles
A.	$14,000	$ 6,600	$ 6,400
B.	$ -0-	$ 8,200	$18,800
C.	$ 4,000	$ 6,400	$16,600
D.	$ -0-	$ 8,400	$18,600
E.	$ 4,500	$ 7,400	$15,100

8. A partnership has the following capital balances:

Monica, Capital (50% of profits and losses)	$100,000
Patricia, Capital (30%)	60,000
Susan, Capital (20%)	50,000

If the partnership is to be liquidated and $20,000 becomes immediately available, who gets the money?

	Monica	Patricia	Susan
A.	$ 5,000	$ 3,000	$12,000
B.	$ 7,000	$ 8,000	$ 5,000
C.	$ -0-	$14,000	$ 6,000
D.	$ 5,000	$ 6,000	$ 9,000
E.	$ 4,000	$ 8,000	$ 8,000

9. To enable an orderly and fair distribution during liquidation, the Uniform Partnership Act establishes a priority listing for all claims. This ranking of claims is called the

A. predistribution plan.
B. schedule of distribution.
C. schedule of liquidation.
D. schedule of termination.
E. marshaling of assets.

10.   Stanley, a partner of the Newtown partnership, made a loan to the partnership. The partnership is now in liquidation. Which one of the following statements is **incorrect** regarding the status of this loan during the liquidation process?

A.   The loan must be repaid before any cash distribution is made to the other partners, even if Stanley does not have a sufficient amount of capital to absorb all possible losses.
B.   The loan has a lower priority than obligations to outside creditors.
C.   If the partner has a negative safe capital balance, a portion or even all of the loan should be retained as an offset against the capital account.
D.   The loan is accounted for in liquidation as if it were a component of the partner's capital.
E.   If Stanley is insolvent and reports a negative capital balance, the handling of the loan becomes significant.

Brief Essay Questions

1.   What four types of transactions must be recorded in regard to the termination and liquidation of a partnership?

2.   When a partner has become bankrupt or his estate is insolvent, what are the claims against his separate property in the order in which they should be ranked?

Problems

1.   The partners of ABC Partnership have decided to liquidate and terminate the parntership. Prior to liquidating, the partnership balance sheet is as follows:

ABC Partnership
Balance Sheet
May 15, 2001

Cash	$	10,000
Inventory		50,000
Property, Plant & Equipment - Net		80,000
Total assets	$	140,000
Liabilities	$	60,000
A, Capital		30,000
B, Capital		40,000
C, Capital		10,000
Total liabilities and partners' equity	$	140,000

The profit and loss sharing ratio is 6:3:1 for A, B, and C respectively.

Required:

A. Prepare a schedule of liquidation for ABC Partnership, given that the partnership sold the inventory for $20,000 and the property, plant, and equipment for $60,000.

B. Prepare a schedule of liquidation for ABC Partnership, given that the inventory was sold for $5,000 and the property, plan, and equipment for $50,000.

2. Richards, Kidd, Brown, and Marley are partners who share profits and losses on a 4:3:2:1 basis, respectively. On March 31, 2004, the partners were presently beginning to liquidate the business. At the beginning of this process, capital balances were as follows:

Richards, Capital	$50,000
Kidd, Capital	40,000
Brown, Capital	36,000
Marley, Capital	24,000

Required:

Based on the information that has been provided, prepare a predistribution plan for the partnership.÷

Solutions to Multiple Choice Questions

1. **C**

2. **A**

	Marla	Barbara	Roberta
Reported Capital Balances	$ 80,000	$ 60,000	$ (24,000)
Potential Loss from Roberta's Deficit (split on a 5:3 basis)	(15,000)	(9,000)	24,000
	$ 65,000	$ 51,000	$ -

3. **A**

	George	Stewart	Thomas
Reported Capital Balances	$ 65,000	$ 82,000	$ 53,000
Allocate loss on sale of assets ($175,000 split on a 6:3:1 basis)	(105,000)	(52,500)	(17,500)
Adjusted Balances	$ (40,000)	$ 29,500	$ 35,500
Potential Loss from George' Deficit (split 3:1)	40,000	(30,000)	(10,000)
Assignment of Stewart's Loss to Thomas		500	(500)
Minimum Cash Distributions	$ -	$ -	$ 25,000

4.   **D**   A loss of only $25,000 will completely eliminate Murray's capital balance.

Andrews	$30,000 ÷ 60% = $ 50,000 loss to eliminate capital
Carroll	$25,000 ÷ 20% = $125,000 loss to eliminate capital
Murray	$ 5,000 ÷ 20% = $ 25,000 loss to eliminate capital

5.   **B**

	Andrews	Carroll	Murray
Reported Capital Balances	$ 30,000	$ 25,000	$ 5,000
Allocate loss on sale of assets ($40,000 split on a 6:2:2 basis)	(24,000)	(8,000)	(8,000)
Adjusted Balances	$ 6,000	$ 17,000	$ (3,000)
Potential Loss from Murray's Deficit (split 6:2)	(2,250)	(750)	3,000
Minimum Cash Distributions	$ 3,750	$ 16,250	$ -

Reported cash balance	$ 80,000
Proceeds from sale of other assets	80,000
Adjust balance	$ 160,000
Cash used to pay creditors	(140,000)
Available cash	$ 20,000

6.   **D**

7.   **B**

	Ashley	Bart	Charles
Reported Capital Balances	$ 100,000	$ 85,000	$ 70,000
Allocate loss on sale of assets ($120,000 split on a 5:3:2 basis)	(60,000)	(36,000)	(24,000)
Adjusted Balances	$ 40,000	$ 49,000	$ 46,000
Anticipated liquidation expenses ($8,000 split on a 5:3:2 basis)	(4,000)	(2,400)	(1,600)
Anticipated loss on inventory ($100,000 split on a 5:3:2 basis)	(50,000)	(30,000)	(20,000)
Potential balances	(14,000)	16,600	24,400
Potential loss from Ashley deficit (split 3:2)	14,000	(8,400)	(5,600)
Current Cash Distributions	$ -	$ 8,200	$ 18,800

8. **C**

Since the partnership currently has total capital of $230,000, the $20,000 that is available would indicate maximum potential losses of $210,000.

	Monica	Patricia	Susan
Reported Capital Balances	$ 100,000	$ 80,000	$ 50,000
Allocate loss ($210,000 split on a 5:3:2 basis)	(105,000)	(63,000)	(42,000)
Potential balances	$ (5,000)	$ 17,000	$ 8,000
Potential loss from Monica's deficit (split 3:2)	5,000	(3,000)	(2,000)
Minimum Cash Distributions	$ -	$ 14,000	$ 6,000

9. **E**

10. **A**

Answers to Brief Essay Questions

1. The four types of transaction that must be recorded in regard to the termination and liquidation of a partnership are:

    A. The conversion of partnership assets into cash.
    B. The allocation of the resulting gains and losses.
    C. The payment of liabilities and expenses.
    D. The distribution of any remaining assets to the partners based on their final capital balances.

2. The claims against the partner's separate property in the order in which they should be ranked are:

    A. Those owing to separate creditors.
    B. Those owing to partnership creditors.
    C. Those owing to Partners by way of contribution.

Solutions to Problems

1.   A.

ABC Partnership
Schedule of Liquidation
May 15, 2004

	Cash	Other Assets	Liabilities	A, Capital	B, Capital	C, Capital
	10,000	130,000	60,000	30,000	40,000	10,000
Inventory Sold	20,000	(50,000)		(18,000)	(9,000)	(3,000)
	30,000	80,000	60,000	12,000	31,000	7,000
PP&E Sold	60,000	(80,000)		(12,000)	(6,000)	(2,000)
	90,000	-	60,000	-	25,000	5,000
Creditors Paid	(60,000)		(60,000)			
	30,000	-	-	-	25,000	5,000
Cash Distributed	(30,000)				(25,000)	(5,000)
	-	-	-	-	-	-

B.

	Cash	Other Assets	Liabilities	A, Capital	B, Capital	C, Capital
	10,000	130,000	60,000	30,000	40,000	10,000
Inventory Sold	5,000	(50,000)		(27,000)	(13,500)	(4,500)
	15,000	80,000	60,000	3,000	26,500	5,500
PP&E Sold	50,000	(80,000)		(18,000)	(9,000)	(3,000)
	65,000	-	60,000	(15,000)	17,500	2,500
A's deficit (3:1)				15,000	(11,250)	(3,750)
	65,000	-	60,000	-	6,250	(1,250)
C's deficit					(1,250)	1,250
	65,000	-	60,000	-	5,000	-
Creditors Paid	(60,000)		(60,000)			
	5,000	-	-	-	5,000	-
Cash Distributed	(5,000)				(5,000)	
	-	-	-	-	-	-

2.

Richards, Kidd, Brown, and Marley Partnership
Predistribution Plan
March 31 2004

	Richards	Kidd	Brown	Marley
Beginning Balances	$ 50,000	$ 45,000	$ 36,000	$ 24,000
Assumed loss of $125,000 (see Sch. 1; allocated 4:3:2:1)	(50,000)	(37,500)	(25,000)	(12,500)
Step one balances	$ -	$ 7,500	$ 11,000	$ 11,500
Assumed loss of $15,000 (see Sch. 2; allocated 3:2:1)		(7,500)	(5,000)	(2,500)
Step two balances		$ -	$ 6,000	$ 9,000
Assumed loss of $9,000 (see Sch. 3; allocated 2:1)			(6,000)	(3,000)
Step three balances			$ -	$ 6,000

Schedule 1

Partner	Capital Balance/Loss Allocation			Maximum Loss That Can Be Absorbed
Richards	$ 50,000	÷	40%	$125,000
Kidd	$ 45,000	÷	30%	$150,000
Brown	$ 36,000	÷	20%	$180,000
Marley	$ 24,000	÷	10%	$240,000

Schedule 2

Partner	Capital Balance/Loss Allocation			Maximum Loss That Can Be Absorbed
Kidd	$ 7,500	÷	50%	$15,000
Brown	$ 11,000	÷	33%	$33,000
Marley	$ 11,500	÷	17%	$69,000

Schedule 3

Partner	Capital Balance/Loss Allocation			Maximum Loss That Can Be Absorbed
Brown	$ 6,000	÷	67%	$9,000
Marley	$ 9,000	÷	33%	$27,000

Chapter 16

Accounting for State and Local Governments (Part I)

Chapter Outline

I.   Introduction to Governmental Accounting

    A.   Generally Accepted Accounting Principles for State and Local Governments

        1.   Prior to 1984, the AICPA and the National Council on Governmental Accounting established governmental accounting standards.

        2.   Since 1984, the Governmental Accounting Standards Board (GASB) has set governmental accounting standards.

    B.   In GASB Concepts Statement No. 1, "Objectives of Financial Reporting," three groups of primary users of governmental accounting information were identified:

        1.   Citizenry

        2.   Legislative and oversite bodies

        3.   Investors and creditors

    C.   The primary objective of governmental accounting is to "measure and identify the public funds generated and expended by each of a government's diverse activities."

    D.   Governmental financial statements attempt to answer three questions:

        1.   Where did the financial resources come from?

        2.   Where did the financial resources go?

        3.   What amount of financial resources is presently held?

    E.   State and local governments use *fund accounting*

        1.   Each activity is monitored in a separate reporting unit called a fund

            a.   Each fund is a self-balancing set of accounts that is used to record data generated by an identifiable governmental function.

            b.   All of the funds taken together make up the government's financial reporting system.

            c.   Accounting for an entity as a group of funds is probably the most unique element of all not-for-profit accounting.

2. State and local government funds can be classified into three broad categories:

    a. Governmental Funds – These funds are used to account for the activities of a government that are carried out primarily to provide services to citizens and that are financed primarily through taxes and intergovernmental revenues.

        i. The General Fund

        ii. Special Revenue Funds

        iii. Capital Projects Funds

        iv. Debt Service Funds

        v. Permanent Funds

    b. Proprietary Funds – These funds are used to account for a government's ongoing organizations and activities that are similar to those often found in the private sector.

        i. Enterprise Funds

        ii. Internal Service Funds

    c. Fiduciary Funds – These funds are used to account for monies held by the government in a trustee capacity. These funds are only used to account for funds that are held for external parties.

        i. Investment Trust Funds

        ii. Private Purpose Trust Funds

        iii. Pension Trust Funds

        iv. Agency Funds

II. Governmental Financial Statements – GASB Statement No. 34 identified two distinctly different groups of financial statements that a governmental unit must produce.

    A. Fund-Based Financial Statements

        1. Different types of funds require different types of accounting

            i. The Governmental Funds require the use of the *current financial resources measurement focus* using the modified accrual basis of accounting.

ii. The Proprietary Funds require the use of the *economic resources measurement focus* using the accrual basis of accounting.

iii. The Fiduciary Funds require the use of the *economic resources measurement focus* using the accrual basis of accounting.

2. Balance Sheet

a. Includes columns for each major Fund.

b. Includes three basic sections:

i. Assets

ii. Liabilities

iii. Fund Balances

3. Statement of Revenues, Expenditures, and Changes in Fund Balance

a. Includes columns for each major Fund.

b. Includes three basic sections:

i. Revenues

ii. Expenditures

iii. Other Financing Sources

B. Government-Wide Financial Statements

1. Different types of funds require different types of accounting

i. The Governmental Funds require the use of the *economic resources measurement focus* using the accrual basis of accounting.

ii. The Proprietary Funds require the use of the *economic resources measurement focus* using the accrual basis of accounting.

iii. The Fiduciary Funds are not reported in the government-wide financial statements.

2. Statement of Net Assets

a. Includes separate columns for information related to Governmental Funds and for information related to Business-Type Funds (Proprietary).

        b.   Includes three sections:

               i.   Assets

               ii.   Liabilities

               iii.   Fund Balance

    3.   Statement of Activities

        a.   Includes columns (horizontally) for Expenses, Revenues, Net Revenue(Expense) from Governmental Activities, and Net Revenue(Expense) from Business-Type Activities.

        d.   Includes three basic sections (vertically):

               i.   Governmental Activities – List the revenues and expenses for each different fund.

               ii.   Business-Type Activities – List the revenues and expenses for each different fund.

               iii.   General Revenues – for recording revenues not related to a specific fund (for example, property taxes, interest, or grants).

III.   Accounting for Fund-Based Financial Statements

    A.   **Budgets**

        1.   Record the budget for each fund with a debit to *Estimated Revenues* and credits to various *Appropriations* accounts.

Estimated Revenues	xxxx	
Appropriations – Salaries		xxxx
Appropriations – Utilities		xxxx
Appropriations – Other		xxxx

        2.   These entries will serve as control accounts during the period and will be closed out at the end of the period.

    B.   **Encumbrances**

        1.   Financial commitments such as purchase commitments, contracts, or orders for goods.

Encumbrances Control	xxxx	
Fund Balance – Reserved for Encumbrances		xxxx

2.   When the goods are received, or the services are performed, the entry is reversed and replaced by a legal payable.

Fund Balance – Reserved for Encumbrances	XXXX	
Encumbrances Control		XXXX
Inventory, Supplies, etc	XXXX	
Voucher Payable		XXXX

C.   **Recognition of Expenditures for Operation**s - When the government makes expenditures, *Expenses* are **not** recorded. All expenditures are debited to an Expenditures account.

Expenditures – Salaries	XXXX	
Voucher Payable		XXXX

D.   **Recognition of Expenditures for Capital Additions** - When the government makes capital acquisitions, fixed assets are **not** recorded. All expenditures are debited to an Expenditures account.

Expenditures – Building	XXXX	
Voucher Payable		XXXX

E.   **Revenue Recognition for Derived Revenues such as Income Taxes and Sales Taxes**

    1.   Revenues are recognized when the **resources** become available for use.

    2.   Because the cash must be in-hand, record both a debit to *Cash* and a *Revenue*.

Cash	XXXX	
Revenues – Taxes		XXXX

F.   **Revenue Recognition for Imposed Nonexchange Revenues such as Property Taxes and Fines**

    1.   Record as soon as the government has an enforceable claim.

    2.   Record both a *Receivable,* an *Allowance for Uncollectible Amounts*, and a *Revenue*.

Property Tax Receivable	XXXX	
Allowance for Uncollectible Amounts		XXXX
Revenues		XXXX

G.   **Revenue Recognition for Government-Mandated Nonexchange Transactions and Voluntary Nonexchange Transactions**

    1.   The amounts must be available for revenue recognition. Includes such items as grants or donations.

2.   Record both a debit to *Cash* and a credit to *Revenues*.

Cash	xxxx	
Revenues - Grants		xxxx

H.   Issuance of Bonds

1.   Bonds serve as an important source of funds for government.

2.   Record the proceeds as *Other Financing Sources – Bond Proceeds*.

Cash	xxxx	
Other Financing Sources Bond Proceeds		xxxx

I.   Interfund Transactions

1.   It is important to keep track of transfers of cash between various funds.

2.   Requires two entries; one entry to record the transfer from one account and an entry to record the receipt of the transfer by the other account.

General Fund

Other Financing Uses - Transfer to Capital Projects Fund	xxxx	
Due to Capital Projects Fund		xxxx

Capital Projects Fund

Due from General Fund	xxxx	
Other Financing Sources - Transfer from General Fund		xxxx

IV.   Accounting for Government-Wide Financial Statements

A.   Budgets

1.   Record the budget for each fund with a debit to *Estimated Revenues* and credits to various *Appropriations* accounts.

2.   These entries will serve as control accounts during the period and will be closed out at the end of the period.

B.   Encumbrances

1.   Encumbrances are not recorded for Government-Wide Financial Statements, because no liability has yet to be incurred.

2.   When the goods are received, or the services are performed for the government, a legal liability is recorded.

Inventory, Supplies, etc	xxxx	
Voucher Payable		xxxx

C.   **Recognition of Expenditures for Operations** - When the government makes expenditures, *Expenses* are recorded, just as in a business-type organization.

Salaries Expense	xxxx	
Voucher Payable		xxxx

D.   **Recognition of Expenditures for Capital Additions** - When the government makes capital acquisitions, fixed assets are recorded, just as in a business-type organization.

Building	xxxx	
Voucher Payable		xxxx

E.   **Revenue Recognition for Derived Revenues such as Income Taxes and Sales Taxes**

1.   Revenues are recognized when the **information** about the amount of revenues due to the government becomes available.

2.   Both a receivable and a Revenue are recorded.

Accounts Receivable – Taxes	xxxx	
Revenues – Taxes		xxxx

F.   **Revenue Recognition for Imposed Nonexchange Revenues such as Property Taxes and Fines**

1.   Record as soon as the government has an enforceable claim.

2.   Record both a *Receivable*, an *Allowance for Uncollectible Amounts*, and a *Revenue*.

Property Tax Receivable	xxxx	
Allowance for Uncollectible Amounts		xxxx
Revenues		xxxx

G.   **Revenue Recognition for Government-Mandated Nonexchange Transactions and Voluntary Nonexchange Transactions**

1.   Revenue recognition occurs at the time of eligibility. Includes such items as grants or donations.

2.   Record both a debit to *Receivables* and a credit to *Revenues*.

Receivables	xxxx	
Revenues - Grants		xxxx

H. **Issuance of Bonds**

    1.   Bonds serve as an important source of funds for government.

    2.   Record just as with a business-type organization.

Cash	xxxx	
Bonds Payable		xxxx

I. **Interfund Transfers** – These transactions are seen as internal transfers and are not recorded.

Multiple Choice Questions

1. Which of the following is **not** considered part of the primary group of users of governmental accounting information?

    A.   Citizens
    B.   Management
    C.   Legislature
    D.   Governmental Oversite Groups
    E.   Creditors

2. A fund is

    A.   a term used for money collected and spent by a governmental unit.
    B.   an account used to accumulate donations by non-profit groups.
    C.   a self-balancing set of accounts used to record data generated by an identifiable governmental unit.
    D.   not used when preparing government-wide financial statements.
    E.   not used when preparing fund-based financial statements.

3. Which of the following group of funds uses the *current financial resources measurement focus* for the fund-based financial statements?

    A.   Donated Funds
    B.   Proprietary Funds
    C.   Fiduciary Funds
    D.   Charitable Funds
    E.   Governmental Funds

4. Which of the following statements would show an account called *Expenditures*?

    A.   Fund-Based Balance Sheet
    B.   Fund-Based Statement of Revenues, Expenditures, and Changes in Fund Balance.
    C.   Government-Wide Statement of Net Assets
    D.   Government-Wide Statement of Activities
    E.   Government-Wide Statement of Revenues, Expenditures and Changes in Fund Balance.

5.   Which of the following statements would show an account called *Expenses*?

    A.   Fund-Based Balance Sheet
    B.   Fund-Based Statement of Revenues, Expenditures, and Changes in Fund Balance.
    C.   Government-Wide Statement of Net Assets
    D.   Government-Wide Statement of Activities
    E.   Government-Wide Statement of Revenues, Expenditures and Changes in Fund Balance.

6.   When preparing fund-based financial statements, what account should be debited when office supplies are ordered?

    A.   Expenditures
    B.   Vouchers Payable
    C.   Fund Balance
    D.   Encumbrances
    E.   Appropriations

7.   When preparing fund-based financial statements, what account should be debited when office equipment is purchased?

    A.   Expenditures
    B.   Vouchers Payable
    C.   Fund Balance
    D.   Encumbrances
    E.   Appropriations

8.   Property taxes are classified as what kind of revenues?

    A.   Derived Revenues
    B.   Imposed Nonexchange Revenues
    C.   Voluntary Nonexchange Transactions
    D.   Government-Mandated Nonexchange Transactions
    E.   Earned Revenues

9.   Federal grants for road construction are classified as what kind of revenues?

    A.   Derived Revenues
    B.   Imposed Nonexchange Revenues
    C.   Voluntary Nonexchange Transactions
    D.   Government-Mandated Nonexchange Transactions
    E.   Earned Revenues

10. When preparing government-wide financial statements, what account is debited when funds are transferred from the Proprietary Utilities Fund to the General Fund?

A. No entry is required, because transfers from a Proprietary Fund to the General Fund are not allowed.
B. Revenue
C. Fund Balance
D. No entry is required, because transfers between funds are viewed as internal transfers not requiring recognition when preparing government-wide financial statements.
E. No entry is required, because Proprietary Funds are not included in government-wide financial statements.

11. Which type of funds are **not** included in government-wide financial statements?

A. Donated Funds
B. Proprietary Funds
C. Fiduciary Funds
D. Charitable Funds
E. Governmental Funds

Brief Essay Questions

1. The following balances were included in the subsidiary records of Dartwell Village's Parks and Recreation Department at March 31, 2004:

Appropriations – Supplies	$ 125,000
Expenditures – Supplies	86,000
Encumbrances – Supply Orders	24,250

How much does the department have available for additional purchases of supplies?

2. Identify the three basic fund groups and the individual funds that are usually found in each group.

3. Are encumbrances recorded in the accounting process used to prepare government-wide financial statements? Why?

Problems

1. Examine the following transactions for Dwelling Township's General Fund.

    a. On July 1, 2004, the city council approves the budget for the General Fund. Included in this budget is $4,900,000 in anticipated property taxes, $32,000,000 in anticipated sales tax revenues, $3,000,000 for utilities, $12,000,000 for salaries and wages, $1,400,000 for rent, 5,600,000 for administrative expenses, and $14,900,000 for capital improvements.

    b. On July 5, the purchasing office orders $42,000 of office supplies.

    c. On July 7, a cash transfer of $300,000 is made to the Public School Superintendent's office for a new roof on the town high school. The project will begin on August 1.

    d. On July 12, $600,000 of computer equipment is purchased with payment due in 30 days. The computers will have an estimated useful life of 3 years.

    e. On July 15, the office supplies ordered on July 7 arrive. The bill is for $43,700 and it is due in 30 days. The supplies are not considered assets, but are treated just the same as utilities.

    f. On July 20, property tax bills totaling $5,200,000 are mailed to city residents.

    g. On July 25, $78,000 in property tax payments are received by the city tax assessor's office.

    h. On July 30, the city receives a payment from the state revenue office for June's sales taxes collections. The check is for $3,400,000.

    Required:

    Assume you are going to prepare fund-based financial statements. Prepare all the journal entries for the above transactions and events.

2. Use the information for Problem 1 above.

    Required:

    Assume you are going to prepare government-wide financial statements. Prepare all the journal entries for the above transactions and events.

Answers to Multiple Choice Questions

1. B

2. C

3. E

4. B

5. D

6. D

7. A

8. B

9. D

10. D

11. C

Answers to Brief Essay Questions

1. The Recreation Department has $14,750 available for the purchase of supplies. Approved expenditures (appropriations) were $125,000. However $86,000 of this amount has already been spent and an additional $24,750 is committed. Therefore, the available spending authority for supplies is equal to *Appropriations – (Expenditures + Outstanding Encumbrances)*.

2. The three groups of funds are: *Governmental Funds, Proprietary Funds* (Business-Type), and *Fiduciary Funds*.

   General Funds include: the General Fund, Special Revenue Funds, Capital Projects Funds, Debt Service Funds, and Permanent Funds.

   Proprietary Funds include: Enterprise Funds and Internal Service Funds.

   Fiduciary Funds include: Pension Trust Funds, Investment Trust Funds, Private-Purpose Funds, and Agency Funds.

3. Government-Wide Financial Statements are prepared primarily using accrual accounting principles. Implied in that approach is the traditional prohibition against recording commitments or contracts. Since Encumbrances are exactly that; commitments and contracts; they are not recorded for Government-Wide Financial Statements.

Solutions to Problems

1. The journal entries for the fund-based financial statements are as follows:

Date	Accounts	Debit	Credit
07/01/01	Estimated revenues - Property Taxes	4,900,000	
	Estimated revenues - Sales Taxes	32,000,000	
	Appropriations Utilities		3,000,000
	Appropriations - Salaries		12,000,000
	Appropriations - Rent		1,400,000
	Appropriations - Administrative Expenses		5,600,000
	Appropriations - Capital Improvements		14,900,000
07/05/01	Encumbrances Control	42,000	
	Fund Balance - Reserve for Encumbrances		42,000
07/07/01	Other Financing Uses - Transfer to Capital Projects Fund	300,000	
	Cash		300,000
07/12/00	Expenditures - Computers	600,000	
	Cash		600,000
07/15/01	Fund Balance - Reserve for Encumbrances	42,000	
	Encumbrances Control		42,000
	Expenditures - Office Supplies	43,700	
	Voucher Payable		43,700
07/20/01	No entry until resources are available.		
07/25/01	Cash	78,000	
	Revenues - Property Taxes		78,000
07/30/01	Cash	3,400,000	
	Revenues - Sales Taxes		3,400,000

2.   The journal entries for the government-wide financial statements are as follows:

Date	Accounts	Debit	Credit
07/01/04	Estimated revenues - Property Taxes	4,900,000	
	Estimated revenues - Sales Taxes	32,000,000	
	Appropriations Utilities		3,000,000
	Appropriations - Salaries		12,000,000
	Appropriations - Rent		1,400,000
	Appropriations - Administrative Expenses		5,600,000
	Appropriations - Capital Improvements		14,900,000
07/05/04	No entry when preparing government-wide financial statements.		
07/07/04	No entry when preparing government-wide financial statements. Transfers are treated as simple internal transfers of cash.		
07/12/04	Computers	600,000	
	Cash		600,000
07/15/04	Office Supplies Expense	43,700	
	Voucher Payable		43,700
07/20/04	Receivables - Property Taxes	5,200,000	
	Revenues - Property Taxes		5,200,000
07/25/04	Cash	78,000	
	Receivables - Property Taxes		78,000
07/30/04	Cash	3,400,000	
	Revenues - Sales Taxes		3,400,000

Chapter 17

Accounting for State and Local Governments (Part II)

Chapter Outline

I.   State and Local Government Accounting – Additional Transactions

    A.   Capital Leases

        1.   Determination of whether a lease is a capital lease or an operating lease is made by referring to the four criteria established in FASB No. 13

            a.   Does the lease transfer ownership of the property to the lessee by the end of the lease term?

            b.   Does the lease contain an option to purchase the leased property at a bargain price?

            c.   Is the lease term equal to or greater than 75% of the estimated economic life of the leased property?

            d.   Is the present value of the rental or other minimum lease payments equal or exceed 90% of the fair value of the leased property less any investment tax credit retained by the lessor?

        2.   For Government-Wide Financial Statements

            a.   Debit the asset account and credit the *Capital Lease Obligation* account

            b.   Subsequent lease payments are recorded and broken down into *Interest Expense* and reduction of *Capital Lease Obligation* components.

        3.   For Fund-Based Financial Statements

            a.   Generally, do not record the signing of the lease agreement.

            b.   Subsequent lease payments are recorded as Expenditures.

    B.   Solid Waste Landfills

        1.   The very nature of landfills results in necessary efforts to alleviate environmental contamination at the time the landfill is closed. Those costs must be estimated at the time the landfill is opened.

2.   For Government-Wide Financial Statements

    a.   At the end of each period, an expense is recorded (along with a corresponding liability) to accrue a portion of the expected future cost of closing the landfill based on the percentage of the landfill that was filled during the current period.

    b.   Any cash payments made in relation to liability are recorded and charged against the liability

3.   For Fund-Based Financial Statements

    a.   No entry is recorded to accrue the liability related to the expected future cost of closing the landfill.

    b.   Any current cash payments related to the future closing of the landfill are recorded as expenditures in the current period.

C.   Compensated Absences

1.   Employees earn, along with their periodic salaries, the right to take paid vacations and paid sick leave.

2.   For Government-Wide Financial Statements

    a.   Record an expense in the period that the compensated absences are accrued and a corresponding liability.

    b.   When the employees take the vacation or sick leave, reduce the liability and record the payment.

3.   For Fund-Based Financial Statements

    a.   Record an entry in Expenditures and a corresponding liability only for the compensated absences that are likely to be used by employees during the next period and that will be paid out of available resources.

    b.   When the employees take the vacation or sick leave, reduce the liability and record the payment.

D.   Works of Art and Historical Treasures

1.   State and local governments sometimes acquire works of art and historical treasures. Those items are often used for display or research, rather than to generate revenue for the governmental unit.

2.   GASB No. 34 states that "governments should capitalize works of art, historical treasures, and similar assets at their historical cost or fair value at the date of donation."

3. For Government-Wide Financial Statements

 a. If the asset is purchased, record the asset at its cost.

 b. If the asset is donated, then record the asset at its fair value and increase *Revenue from Donations*.

 c. When three conditions are met, the governmental unit can opt to forego depreciation on the asset. Those criteria are:

  i. The asset must be held for public exhibition, education, or research in furtherance of public service, rather than financial gain.

  ii. The asset must be protected, kept unencumbered, cared for, and preserved.

  iii. The asset must be subject to an organizational policy that requires the proceeds from sales of collection items to be used to acquire other items for collections.

4. For Fund-Based Financial Statements

 a. If the asset is purchased, then record the acquisition as an *Expenditure*.

 b. If the asset is donated, no entry is made because current financial resources are unchanged.

II. Management's Discussion and Analysis (MD&A)

A. GASB No. 34 requires state and local governments to include in their published financial statements, a Management Discussion and Analysis document similar to what would be found in the financial statements of publicly traded companies.

B. A governmental unit's MD&A should include:

1. A brief discussion of the basic financial statements.

2. Condensed financial information derived from government-wide financial statements comparing the current year to the prior year.

3. An analysis of overall financial position and results of operations to aid assessment of whether financial position has improved or deteriorated.

4. An analysis of balances and transactions of individual funds explaining the reasons for significant changes in fund balances or net assets as well as any significant restrictions.

5. An analysis of significant variations between original and final budget amounts along with variations between final budget amounts and actual results for the General Fund.

6. A description of significant capital asset and long-term debt activity during the year.

7. If the modified approach is used for some or all infrastructure assets, information should be provided about its application.

8. A description of currently known facts, decisions, or conditions that are expected to have a significant effect on financial position or results of operations.

III. Comprehensive Annual Financial Report (CAFR)

    A. General Purpose Financial Statements

        1. Government-Wide Financial Statements

           a. Statement of Net Assets

           b. Statement of Activities

        2. Fund-Based Financial Statements

           a. Governmental Funds

               i. Balance Sheet

               ii. Statement of Revenues, Expenditures, and Changes in Fund Balances

           b. Proprietary Funds

               i. Statement of Net Assets

               ii. Statement of Revenues, Expenses, and Changes in Fund Net Assets

               iii. Statement of Cash Flows

                   (1) Cash Flows from Operating Activities

                   (2) Cash Flows from Noncapital Financing Activities

                   (3) Cash Flows from Capital and Related Financing Activities

              (4)   Cash Flows from Investing Activities

        c.   Fiduciary Funds – Statement of Changes in Fiduciary Net Assets

  B.   Combining Statements by Fund Type

  C.   Individual Fund and Account Group Statements

  D.   Schedules and Statistical Tables

IV.   Primary Government and Component Units

  A.   For reporting purposes, the primary government unit must be identified. The following criteria must be met:

      1.   The governmental unit must have a separately elected governing body.

      2.   The governmental unit must be legally independent, which can be demonstrated by having corporate powers such as the right to sue and be sued in its own name as well as the right to buy, sell, and lease property in its own name.

      3.   The governmental unit must be fiscally independent of other state and local governments.

  B.   Within the primary governmental unit, separately identifiable and reportable components can be identified by applying two criteria.

      1.   The separate organization is fiscally dependent of the primary organization.

      2.   Officials of the primary government must appoint a voting majority of the governing board of the separate organization, and the primary government must be able to impose its will on the board of the separate organization.

V.   Reporting Public Colleges and Universities

  A.   Financial Reporting guided by GASB No. 35

  B.   Must include:

      1.   A Management's Discussion and Analysis section

      2.   Both a government-wide *Statement of Net Assets* and a *Statement of Activities* must be produced for both governmental funds and business-type funds (if any).

Multiple Choice Questions

1. When a city signs a capital lease, which of the following entries would be made?

    A. For government-wide financial statements, debit *Encumbrances*.
    B. For fund-based financial statements, debit *Encumbrances*.
    C. For fund-based financial statements, credit *Capital Lease Obligation*.
    D. For government-wide financial statements, credit *Capital Lease Obligation*.
    E. For fund-based financial statements, debit an *Asset* account.

2. When a city establishes a new landfill, which of the following entries would be made?

    A. At the time of establishing the landfill, for government-wide financial statements, credit a *Liability* for the cost of closing the landfill.
    B. At the end of each period , for government-wide financial statements, credit a *Liability* for a pro-rata share of the cost of closing the landfill.
    C. At the time of establishing the landfill, for fund-based financial statements, credit a *Liability* for the cost of closing the landfill.
    D. At the end of each period , for fund-based financial statements, credit a *Liability* for a pro-rata share of the cost of closing the landfill.
    E. For government-wide financial statements, no entry is ever made until the cost is actually paid.

3. If Dayglow, a midwestern town, receives a priceless Van Gogh painting for display in the town hall, how should the gift be recorded?

    A. For government-wide financial statements, a credit is made to a fiduciary trust fund.
    B. For fund-based financial statements, a credit is made to a fiduciary trust fund.
    C. For government-wide financial statements, a credit is made to a *Revenue* account.
    D. For fund-based financial statements, a credit is made to a *Revenue* account.
    E. Such a donation is never recorded, because it is not considered as an available financial resource.

4. For public colleges and universities, which statement is true?

    A. For comparison purposes, the financial statements of public colleges and universities should look just like the financial statements of private colleges and universities.
    B. Public colleges and universities must prepare and publish, as part of their financial statements, a Management Discussion and Analysis.
    C. Public colleges and universities are not required to prepare a Management Discussion and Analysis.
    D. Public colleges and universities prepare only fund-based financial statements.
    E. Government-Wide Statement of Revenues, Expenditures and Changes in Fund Balance.

5.   Which of the following is **not** a CAFR requirement related to government-wide financial statements and fund-based financial statements?

A.   Statement of Net Assets
B.   Statement of Revenues, Expenditures, and Changes in Fund Balance.
C.   Statement of Activities
D.   Statement of Cash Flows
E.   Statement of Revenues, Expenditures and Changes in Fund Balance.

6.   Which item below is one of the criteria used to define a primary governmental unit?

A.   The unit must be fiscally dependent on a separate governmental unit.
B.   The unit must derive the majority of its revenues from its own local tax base.
C.   The unit must be fiscally independent of other state and local governments.
D.   The unit must not manage and fiduciary funds.
E.   The unit must qualify for the modified approach to accounting for depreciation.

7.   Which of the following is **not** required in the CAFR?

A.   Auditor's Report stating the GAAP was followed in the preparation of the governmental units financial statements
B.   General Purpose Financial Statements
C.   Combining Statements by Fund Type
D.   Individual Fund and Account Group Statements
E.   Schedules and Statistical Tables

8.   Which of the following is **not** a section that is included in the Statement of Cash Flows for Proprietary Funds?

A.   Cash flows from Operating Activities
B.   Cash flows from Noncapital Financing Activities
C.   Cash flows from Investing Activities
D.   Cash flows from Capital and Related Financing Activities
E.   Cash flows from External Sources

9.   Which of the following items is **not** required as part of a city's Management Discussion and Analysis?

A.   A brief discussion of the basic financial statements.
B.   An analysis of balances and transactions of individual funds explaining the reasons for significant changes in fund balances or net assets as well as any significant restrictions.
C.   A description of significant capital asset and long-term debt activity during the year.
D.   An analysis of the adequacy of the current facilities and a listing of all expected costs of replacement over the succeeding 5 years.
E.   An analysis of significant variations between original and final budget amounts along with variations between final budget amounts and actual results for the General Fund.

Brief Essay Questions

1.   What circumstances give rise to the accounting issues related to the future costs associated with closing a landfill?

2.   Under what conditions can a governmental unit forego depreciation on an acquired asset?

3.   Does GASB 34 "require" governments to capitalize works of art or historical treasures at cost or fair value at the date of donation?

Answers to Multiple Choice Questions

1.   D
2.   B
3.   C
4.   B
5.   D
6.   C
7.   A
8.   E
9.   D

Answers to Brief Essay Questions

1.   The government's environmental agencies impose very strict procedures related to any facility that handles hazardous waste materials. Those closing and clean-up costs are very large and the future nature of these costs dictates that, for the purpose of government-wide financial statements, the expense for closing the landfill must be accrued on a "as you go" basis.

2.   A governmental unit can elect to forego recording depreciation on a work of art or historical treasure if three conditions are met:

   A.   The asset must be held for public exhibition, education, or research in furtherance of public service, rather than financial gain.
   B.   The asset must be protected, kept unencumbered, care for, and preserved.
   C.   the asset must be subject to an organizational policy that requires the proceeds from sales of collection items to be used to acquire other items for collections.

3.   GASB No. 34 only says that the governmental unit "should" capitalize a work of art or historical treasure, but doesn't require it. In the event the asset is capitalized, it should be recorded at either its cost or the fair value at the date of donation.

Chapter 18

Accounting and Reporting for Private Not-for-Profit Organizations

Chapter Outline

I.   Financial Reporting

    A.   The framework for the FASB's standards for not-for-profit organizations include the following basic ideas:

        1.   The financial statements should focus on the entity as a whole.

        2.   Requirements for not-for-profit organizations should be similar to for-profit business entities unless there are critical differences in the information needs of financial statement users.

    B.   SFAS 117 requires three financial statements for not-for-profit organizations, while a fourth statement is required of voluntary health and welfare organizations:

        1.   The **statement of financial position** – reports the assets, liabilities, and net assets (rather than equity accounts) or fund balance.

        2.   The **statement of activities and changes in net assets** – reports revenues, expenses, gains, and losses for the period.

            a.   Revenues and expenses are determined using the accrual basis of accounting, including depreciation of fixed assets.

            b.   The statement presents the change in net assets for the period and reconciles to net assets appearing in the statement of financial position.

        3.   The **statement of cash flows** – uses the standard FASB classifications

            a.   Cash flows from Operating Activities – can be prepared either direct or indirect.

            b.   Cash flows from Investing Activities

            c.   Cash flows from Financing Activities

        4.   The **statement of function expense** – provides a detailed schedule of expenses by function and by object.

            a.   Only required for voluntary health and welfare organizations.

b.   Joint costs expended for fund-raising containing educational literature have traditionally been divided between fund-raising programs and program services costs. This practice is curtailed by SOP 98-2.

II.   Accounting for Contributions

    A.   SFAS 116 defines contributions as *unconditional transfers of cash or other resources to an entity in a voluntary nonreciprocal transaction.*

        1.   Recognized as revenue in the period received. Amount is based on the fair market value of the resources contributed.

        2.   If the pledge statements allow the donors to change their minds about their intention to give, the revenue is not recognized until the resource is received.

        3.   Contributions that won't be fully collected within the fiscal period are carried at their present value.

    B.   Conditional Promises to Give are not recognized as revenue until the conditions have been met.

    C.   Donated services and supplies (in-kind donations)

        1.   Donated services are recognized only if specific criteria are met.

            a.   The service must create or enhance a nonfinancial asset, or

            b.   The service requires a specialized skill possessed by the contributor and would have to be purchased if not donated.

        2.   Donated supplies and other materials are recognized as revenue and recorded at fair market value.

III.   Holding Contributions for Others

    A.   Some organizations receive donations that by agreement are to be distributed to other parties (for example The United Way that collects money to be redistributed to needy organizations with the local community)

    B.   If the beneficiary is identified, then a liability called *Liability to [Beneficiary]* is created to that specific beneficiary.

    C.   If the donor has the right to revoke or redirect the gift, then a liability called *Refundable Advance to Donor* is recorded.

IV.   Donations of Works of Art and Historical Treasures are not recorded when three conditions are met

   A.   If the items are added to a collection for public exhibition, education, or research; and

   B.   The items are protected and preserved; and

   C.   They are subject to a condition that, if they are ever sold, any receipts will be used to acquire other collection items.

V.   Accounting for Health Care Organizations

   A.   The most unique aspect to accounting for health care organizations are the existence of third-party payors, such as insurance companies.

      1.   In most businesses, the customer pays for the goods or services received, but in most health care organizations, the patient receives the service, while the insurance company (or some other third party payor) pays the bill.

      2.   Examples of third party payors include Blue Cross/Blue Shield, Medicare, and Medicaid.

   B.   The AICPA audit and accounting guide, Health Care Organizations, provides accounting standards and identifies three classes of health care providers:

      1.   Investor-Owned Health Care Enterprises

         a.   Owned by investors or medical practitioners and are operated for the purpose of making a profit.

         b.   FASB rules govern the accounting for these organizations.

      2.   Not-for-Profit Organizations

         a.   Not owned by investors or governments.

         b.   Contributions are received, but are mostly self-sustaining from the fees charged for goods and services.

         c.   FASB rules (including FASB 116 and 117) govern the accounting for these organizations.

      3.   Governmental Health Care Organizations

         a.   Either controlled by governments, or meet the definition of a governmental entity.

         b.   GASB rules govern the accounting for these organizations.

C. The AICPA audit and accounting guide requires four basic financial statements for all health care providers:

    1. Balance Sheet (or Statement of Financial Position)

    2. Statement of Operations

    3. Statement of Changes in Equity (or Net Assets/Fund Balance)

    4. Statement of Cash Flows

D. Patient revenues are recorded and receivables are recorded from the third-party payors for their portion, and from the patients for their portion.

E. To account for the fact that health care entities often receive less than the total amount normally charged for patient services, *Bad Debt Expense* and *Allowance for Doubtful Accounts* must be recorded at the end of the period.

F. Occasionally there is a difference between the amount of revenue recorded and the amount that the third party payor will pay (based on a prior negotiated agreement). This amount is written off as a *Contractual Adjustment*.

G. Verbal commitments or pledges from donors

    1. If the pledge or commitment is an *unconditional promise*, SFAS 116 requires that a receivable be immediately recorded to reflect the pledge.

    2. For unconditional pledge promises, an appropriate amount must be recorded in the *Provision for Doubtful Accounts*.

    3. If the pledge refers to a future period, the amount should be recorded as a *Deferred Revenue*.

    4. Unrestricted pledges are reported in the financial statements of the General Fund when the pledge is made as a nonoperating gain.

    5. If the pledge is restricted, the receivable should be recorded in an appropriate restricted fund category.

Multiple Choice Questions

1. A hospital has the following account balances:

Amount charged to patients	$500,000
Revenue from newsstand	15,000
Undesignated gifts	40,000
Contractual adjustments	70,000
Interest income	12,000
Salaries expense - nurses	120,000
Bad debts	8,000

    What is the hospital's net patient service revenue?

    A. $422,000
    B. $430,000
    C. $500,000
    D. $540,000
    E. $473,000

2. Which one of the following is **not** a required financial statement for a voluntary health and welfare organization?

    A. Statement of Financial Position
    B. Statement of Activities and Changes in Net Assets
    C. Statement of Fund Balance
    D. Statement of Cash Flows
    E. Statement of Functional Expense

3. Wakefield Hospital's accounting records disclosed the following information:

Cost of property and equipment net of accumulated depreciation	$9,500,000
Board designated funds	1,300,000
Grant proceeds that must be used to study treatment of burn victims	1,500,000
Investments reported in endowment funds	500,000

    What amount should be included as part of the General Funds?

    A. $12,800,000
    B. $12,300,000
    C. $ 9,500,000
    D. $10,800,000
    E. $11,400,000

4. Southside Medical Center, a not-for-profit hospital, provides its patients with services that would normally be charged at $600,000. However, a $70,000 reduction is estimated because of contractual adjustments. Another $30,000 reduction is expected because of bad debts. Finally, $100,000 will not be collected because the amounts are deemed to be charity care. Which of the following are correct?

	Patient Service Revenues	Net Patient Service Revenues
A.	$500,000	$430,000
B.	$600,000	$500,000
C.	$530,000	$400,000
D.	$500,000	$470,000
E.	$530,000	$450,000

5. In 2004, a not-for-profit hospital received an unrestricted gift of common stock with a fair market value of $100,000. The donor had paid $45,000 for the stock in 1991. The hospital should record the gift as a

A. Memorandum entry only.
B. Nonoperating gain of $ 45,000.
C. Nonoperating gain of $ 55,000.
D. Nonoperating gain of $ 65,000.
E. Nonoperating gain of $100,000.

6. According to the AICPA audit and accounting guide, which one of the following is **not** a required financial statement for a healthcare organization?

A. Statement of Operations
B. Balance Sheet
C. Statement of Changes in Equity
D. Statement of Functional Expense
E. Statement of Cash Flows

7. Ashley Shaw took a leave of absence from her job to work full-time for a voluntary health and welfare organization for three months. Ashley filled the position of program coordinator, a position that normally paid $24,000 per year. Ashley accepted no remuneration for her work. These donated services be recorded as

A. Revenue of $6,000 and an expense of $6,000.
B. A contribution of $6,000 and an expense of $6,000.
C. Revenue of $6,000 and a contribution of $6,000.
D. A contribution of $6,000 and public support of $6,000.
E. Public Support of $6,000 and an expense of $6,000.

8. A local voluntary health and welfare organization had the following expenditures:

Administrative Salaries	$ 20,000
Work to help elderly citizens	60,000
Fund-raising costs	5,000
Child care services provided for indigent familites	40,000

How should these items be reported by the organization?

	Program Service Expenses	Supporting Service Expenses
A.	$120,000	$ 5,000
B.	$100,000	$ 25,000
C.	$105,000	$ 20,000
D.	$ 80,000	$ 45,000
E.	$ 95,000	$ 30,000

9. A voluntary health and welfare organization received a pledge in 2003 from a donor specifying that the amount pledged be used in 2005. The donor paid the pledge with cash in 2004. The pledge should be accounted for as

A. Support in 2004 with no deferred credit in the balance sheet at the end of 2005.
B. Support in 2005.
C. Deferred support in the balance sheet at the end of 2003 and 2004, and support in 2005.
D. Deferred support in the balance sheet at the end of 2003, and support in 2004.
E. Deferred support in the balance sheet at the end of 2004, and support in 2005.

10. A voluntary health and welfare organization had the following asset inflows:

Cash gifts	$ 40,000
Membership dues	8,000
Dividend income	5,000
Interest income	3,000
Donated supplies	2,000

How should these items be reported?

	Revenues	Public Support
A.	$ 16,000	$ 42,000
B.	$ 8,000	$ 50,000
C.	$ 56,000	$ 2,000
D.	$ 10,000	$ 48,000
E.	$ 20,000	$ 38,000

Brief Essay Questions

1.   What are the two major ideas mentioned in the text that form the framework for the FASB's standards for not-for-profit organizations? Why are these ideas important?

2.   One of the major factors influencing the accounting practices of health care entities is the presence of third-party payors. What is a third-party payor, and how does the presence of third-party payors affect the financial accounting of a health care entity?

3.   The accounting process used for health care entities separates all financial resources into funds. Identify the types of funds found in health care accounting. Describe the purposes of these funds.

Problems

1.   A not-for-profit hospital, Barnes Hospital, had the following transactions:

    A.   Patients were charged $360,000 for services. Of this amount, $60,000 was actually charged to the patients. Hospital officials anticipate that $14,000 will be uncollectible. The remaining $300,000 was billed to insurance companies and other third-party payors. Officials believe that these companies will only pay $264,000 after determining reasonable costs for the procedures.

    B.   Insurance companies and other third-party payors paid $224,000 to cover 80% of the charges in A. The remaining invoices are under investiagtion.

    C.   An unrestricted pledge for $48,000 was received from a wealthy individual but the money cannot be spent for several years.

    D.   A local volunteer contributed services to the hospital to replace a retired worker. The value of these services was $11,000.

Required:

Prepare journal entries for the above transactions.

2.   A voluntary health and welfare organization has the following events and transactions:

    A.   A commitment was made to acquire a new vehicle for the charity.

    B.   A cash gift of $24,000 was received that must be used to acquire new equipment.

    C.   A cash gift of $16,000 was received that was completely unrestricted.

    D.   A cash dividend of $6,000 was received on investments being held to serve as funding for the acquisition of new equipment.

    E.   The money in B and D was used to buy equipment.

    F.   A cash gift of $15,000 was received that must be used for disaster relief.

    G.   Salary expense of $4,000 was paid to the administrative officers of the charity.

Required:

Prepare journal entries for the above events and transactions. For each entry, indicate the fund category in which the entry would be recorded.

3. During 2004, a voluntary health and welfare organization received unrestricted pledges of $120,000. 40% were payable in 2004 with the remainder payable in 2005 (for use in 2005). Officials estimate that 10% of these pledges will be uncollectible. In addition, a local medical technician earning $10 per hour working for a hospital, contributed 320 hours of time to the charitable organization. If not for these donated services, and additional staff person would have been hired by the organization.

Required:

A.   How much should the organization report as net public support for 2004?

B.   How should the organization record the contributed services?

Solutions to Multiple Choice Questions

1. **B**   Amount charged to patients .... $ 500,000
            Contractual adjustments .... (70,000)
            Net patient service revenue .... $ 430,000

2. **C**

3. **D**   Cost of property and equipment net of
                 accumulated depreciation .... $ 9,500,000
            Board designated funds 1,300,000
            Total amount included in General Funds .. $10,800,000

4. **A**   Fair market value of patient services ... $ 600,000
            Uncollectible charity care amount .... (100,000)
            Patient service revenues .... $ 500,000
            Contractual adjustments .... (70,000)
            Net patient service revenues .... $ 430,000

5. **E**

6. **D**

7. **E**   Normal annual amount of services .... $ 24,000
            Fraction of year .... × 3/12
                                                     $ 6,000

8. **B**   Program service expenses:
                 Work to help elderly citizens ...... $ 60,000
                 Child care services provided for indigent families .. 40,000
                 Total .... $ 100,000

            Supporting service expenses:
                 Administrative salaries .... $ 20,000
                 Fund-raising costs 5,000
                 Total .... $ 25,000

9.   C

10.   A   Revenues:
             Membership dues $ 8,000
             Dividend income   5,000
             Interest income   3,000
             Total $ 16,000

             Public support:
             Cash gifts $ 40,000
             Donated supplies   2,000
             Total $ 42,000

Answers to Brief Essay Questions

1.   The two ideas are:

      A.   The financial statements should focus on the entity as a whole. This idea is
            important because the organization's financial statements should not be centered
            around the funds that are used for internal record-keeping.

      B.   Requirements for not-for-profit organizations should be similar to business
            entities unless there are critical differences in the information needs of financial
            statement users. This idea is important because not-for-profit entities should use
            most of the same accrual accounting techniques used by business firms for
            recording and reporting transactions.

2.   A third-party payor is any outside party who assumes responsibility for all or part of a
      patient's medical charges. The most commonly encountered third-party payors are
      insurance companies, Medicare, Medicaid, and Blue Cross/Blue Shield. Because these
      third parties bear such a significant portion of the medical costs in this country, they
      require extensive and accurate financial information. Health care entities must, therefore,
      develop and maintain accounting systems that provide this data.

3.   Only two fund types are found in health care accounting:

      (1)   *General Funds* which account for all transactions as well as financial resources
            that have not been externally restricted and

      (2)   *Donor-Rrestricted Funds* which monitor assets given by outside donors for a
            designated purpose. When the money is spent for the designated purpose, the
            revenues and expenditures are reported in the *General Funds*.

Solutions to Problems

1.   Entries for Barnes Hospital

Entry	Accounts	Debit	Credit
A	Accounts Receivable - Patients	60,000	
	Bad Debt Expense	14,000	
	Patient Service Revenues		60,000
	Allowance for Uncollectible Accounts		14,000
	Accounts Receivable - Third-Party Payors	300,000	
	Bad Debt Expense	36,000	
	Patient Service Revenues		300,000
	Allowance for Reduced Accounts		36,000
B	Cash	224,000	
	Allowance for Reduced Accounts	16,000	
	Accounts Receivable - Third-Party Payors		240,000
C	Pledges Receivable	48,000	
	Contributed Support - Temporarily Restricted		
	Net Assets		48,000
D	Salaries Expense	11,000	
	Contributed Support (or Nonoperating Gain)		
	- Unrestricted Net Assets		11,000

2.   Entries for a Voluntary Health and Welfare Organization

Entry	Accounts	Debit	Credit
A	Commitments of this type are not recorded by a voluntary health and welfare organization.		
B	**Land, Building, and Equipment Fund**		
	Cash	24,000	
	Public Support - Gift		24,000
C	**Current Unrestricted Funds**		
	Cash	16,000	
	Public Support - Gift		16,000
D	**Land, Building, and Equipment Fund**		
	Cash	6,000	
	Revenued - Dividend Income		6,000
E	**Land, Building, and Equipment Fund**		
	Equipment	30,000	
	Cash		30,000
F	**Current Restricted Funds**		
	Cash	15,000	
	Public Support - Gift		15,000
G	**Current Unrestricted Funds**		
	Supporting Service Expenses - Salaries	4,000	
	Cash		4,000

3.   A.   Net Public Support

Pledges	$	120,000
Uncollectible (10%)		(12,000)
Net Pledges	$	108,000
Usable in 2004		40%
Net Pledges - 2004 Support	$	43,200
Donated servcies (320 hours x $10 per hour)		3,200
Net public support for 2004	$	46,400

       B.   The contributed services are recorded as public support of $3,200 and as an expenses of $3,200.

Chapter 19

Accounting for Estates and Trusts

Chapter Outline

I.   Accounting for an Estate

    A.   Estate accounting encompasses the recording and reporting of events that occur from the time of a person's death until distribution of all property.

    B.   Wills and probate laws.

        1.   An individual who dies with a legal will, dies *testate*.

        2.   An individual who dies without a legal will, dies *intestate*.

        3.   State probate laws govern will and estates, and have three goals:

            a.   Gather and preserve all of the decedent's property.

            b.   Carry out an orderly and fair settlement of all debts.

            c.   Discover the decedent's intent for the remaining property held at death and then follow those wishes.

        4.   Where no will exists, the laws of descent (for real property) and the laws of distribution (for personal property) are applicable.

    C.   A will should name an executor of the estate to oversee the conveyance of property.

        1.   If an executor is not named or is not able to serve, the court will appoint an administrator.

        2.   The executor is normally responsible for fulfilling several tasks:

            a.   Taking possession of all the decedent's assets and completing an inventory of this property.

            b.   discovering all of the claims against the decedent and settling these obligations.

            c.   Filing estate income tax returns, federal estate tax returns, and state inheritance or estate tax returns.

            d.   Distributing property according to the provisions of the will, or according to state laws if a valid will is not available.

e. making a full accounting to the probate court to demonstrate that the executor has properly fulfilled the fiduciary responsibility.

D. Claims against the estate must be paid in a specific order of priority.

1. Expenses of administering the estate. Without this preferential treatment, the appointment of an acceptable executor and the hiring of lawyers, accountants, and/or appraisers could become a difficult task in estates with limited funds.

2. Funeral expenses and the medical expenses of any last illness.

3. Debts and taxes given preference under federal and state laws.

4. All other claims.

E. A legacy may take one of several forms; the identification of the type of legacy becomes especially important if the estate has insufficient resources to meet the specifications of the will.

1. A **specific legacy** is a gift of personal property that is directly identified.

2. A **demonstrative legacy** is a cash gift made from a particular source.

3. A **general legacy** is a cash gift with the source being undesignated.

4. A **residual legacy** is a gift of any remaining estate property.

F. The federal estate tax is an excise tax assessed on the right to convey property tax.

1. The fair market value of estate property is taxed after reduction for several items:

a. Funeral expenses.

b. Estate administration expenses.

c. Liabilities.

d. Casualties and thefts during the administration of the estate.

e. Charitable bequests.

f. Marital deduction for property conveyed to the spouse.

2. For 2002, the remaining figure is taxed 50%, after an exclusion of $1 million. The tax rate is gradually reduced to 45% by 2009, and the estate tax is repealed in 2010. The estate tax returns in 2011, unless additional legislation is passed to extend the repeal.

3.   Until 2009, the value of the estate is reduced by an exemption that gradually increases over the years from $1 million in 2002 to $3.5 million in 2009.

4.   To lessen the estate tax, individuals have often made gifts to potential heirs prior to death. These gifts were tax-free as long as they did not exceed $10,000 per hear per recipient. The federal gift tax will not be eliminated completely, but an individual will be allowed a $1 million lifetime exclusion. Eventually, the gift tax will be essentially the same as the maximum individual income tax rate.

G.   State inheritance taxes are assessed on the right to receive property with the levy and all other regulations varying, based on state laws.

H.   Estate income taxes are based on the income earned by the estate property.

I.   Several features of estate accounting should be noted:

1.   All estate assets are recorded at fair market value to indicate the amount of the executor's accountability.

2.   Debts, taxes, or other obligations are only recorded at the date of payment.

3.   Income and principal have their balances and transactions separately identified; two cash balances are often maintained to assist in this process.

4.   The executor periodically files reports, known as charge and discharge statements, with the probate court to disclose the progress being made in settling the estate. The statement should indicate:

a.   The assets under the control of the executor.

b.   Disbursements made to date.

c.   Any property still remaining.

II.   Accounting for a Trust

A.   A *trust* is created by the conveyance of assets to a fiduciary (or trustee) who manages the assets that will ultimately be distributed to one or more beneficiaries.

B.   Trusts ensure that the distribution of a person's assets are as intended.

1.   An *inter vivos trust* is one started by a living individual.

2.   A *testamentary trust* is created by a will.

C.   In recent years, the revocable living trust has become popular as well as controversial.

D.   Common types of other trusts include:

1.   **Credit Shelter Trust** – is designed for couples, and each spouse agrees to transfer at death an amount up to $675,000 to a trust fund for the benefit of the other; also known as a *Bypass Trust* or *Family Trust*.

2.   **Qualified Terminable Interest Property Trust** – is frequently created to serve as a credit shelter trust. Property is conveyed to the trust with the income, and possible a portion of the principal, being paid to the surviving spouse (or other beneficiary). It is also known as a *QTIP Trust*.

3.   **Charitable Remainder Trust** – all income is paid to one or more beneficiaries identified by the trustor. After a period of time (or at the death of the beneficiaries), the principal is given to a stated charity.

4.   **Charitable Lead Trust** – is the reverse of a charitable remainder trust. Income from the trust fund goes to benefit a charity for a specified time with the remaining principal then given to a different beneficiary.

5.   **Grantor Retained Annuity Trust** – the trustor maintains the right to collect fixed payments from the trust fund with the principal being given to a beneficiary after a stated time or at the death of the trustor. It is known as a *GRAT*.

6.   **Minor's Section 2503(c) Trust** – is usually designed to receive a tax-free gift of up to $10,000 each year ($20,000 if the transfer is made by a couple). Over a period of time, especially if enough beneficiaries are available, a significant amount of assets can be removed from a person's estate.

7.   **Spendthrift Trust** – is established so that the beneficiary cannot transfer or assign any unreceived payments, and are usually established in hopes of preventing the beneficiary from squandering the assets being held by the fund.

8.   **Irrevocable Life Insurance Trust** – money is contributed to the trust to buy life insurance on the donor. If a couple is creating the trust, the life insurance policy is usually designed so that proceeds are paid only after the second spouse dies.

9.   **Qualified Personal Resident Trust** – the donor's home is given to the trust but the donor retains the right to live in the house for a period of time rent free, thus removing what is often an individual's most valuable asset from the estate.

E. Trust accounting is quite similar to the procedures previously described for an estate.

   1. Income and principal have their transactions and balances separately identified.

   2. In the same manner as an estate, the trust agreement should specify the distinction between transactions to be recorded as income and those to be recorded as principal.

      a. If the agreement is silent or if a transaction is incurred that is not covered by the agreement, state laws are applicable.

      b. GAAP are usually not considered appropriate.

   3. Adjustments to the trust's principal include:

      a. Investing costs and commissions.

      b. Income taxes on gains added to the principal.

      c. Costs of preparing property for rent or sale.

      d. Extraordinary repairs (improvements).

   4. Adjustments to the trust's income include:

      a. Rent expense.

      b. Lease cancellation fees.

      c. Interest expense.

      d. Insurance expense.

      e. Income taxes on trust income.

      f. Property taxes.

Multiple Choice Questions

1. The following statement appeared in Steven Jackson's will: "I leave $20,000 cash to my niece, Sally Martin." Such a gift is a

   A. Specific legacy.
   B. Demonstrative legacy.
   C. General legacy.
   D. Residual legacy.
   E. Major legacy.

2. Jay Jones believes that each individual should make his or her own way in life upon graduation from college. To help his children accomplish this goal, he created a trust which will distribute income to his children until they graduate from college, at which time the principal of the trust will go to the American Red Cross. For this type of trust, the American Red Cross is the

   A. Legatee.
   B. Remainderman.
   C. Grantor.
   D. Inheritor.
   E. Trustee.

3. If an estate has insufficient funds after paying administrative expenses to satisfy all gifts, a person who is to receive a demonstrative legacy would receive that gift ahead of individuals that are assigned to receive

	Residual Legacy	Specific Legacy	General Legacy
A.	No	No	Yes
B.	Yes	Yes	No
C.	No	Yes	No
D.	Yes	Yes	Yes
E.	Yes	No	Yes

4. Which one of the following expenses of an estate would normally **not** be charged against income?

   A. Brokerage fees for the sale of investments.
   B. Ordinary repair expenses.
   C. Insurance expenses.
   D. Property taxes.
   E. Utility expenses.

5. Which one of the following is **not** a valid reason for creating a trust?

   A. To save on estate taxes.
   B. To provide management expertise.
   C. To provide for the education of minor children.
   D. To reduce income taxes since trusts are not taxable entities.
   E. To prevent the beneficiary from squandering the protected assets.

Advanced Accounting – 7/e

6.   Which one of the following statements is correct?

        A.   If an individual dies without leaving a will, the property will be distributed
                according to federal laws.
        B.   An executor is named in a person's will whereas an administrator is appointed.
        C.   Because of the many accounting responsibilities involved such as filing federal
                income tax returns and federal estate tax returns, the administrator must be an
                accountant.
        D.   If real property is distributed according to the provision of a will, it is called a
                legacy.
        E.   The executor named in a person's will must be an attorney.

7.   Which one of the following statements is correct?

        A.   Real property transferred under state law without being subject to probate is
                excluded from the gross estate on the federal estate tax return.
        B.   If a trust document is silent regarding the appropriate accounting treatment for
                some type of transaction, the trustee is bound to follow generally accepted
                accounting principles.
        C.   The executor must file periodic reports called charge and discharge statements
                with the heirs of an estate.
        D.   An individual may make tax-free, lifetime gifts totalling $1 million to as many
                different individuals as they like.
        E.   Trust accounting is quite different from estate accounting.

8.   Catherine Miller died on March 1, 2003. All of her property was conveyed to several
        relatives on November 18, 2003. For federal estate tax purposes, the executor chose the
        alternative valuation date. On which one of the following dates was the value of the
        property determined?

        A.   November 18, 2003.
        B.   May 18, 2003.
        C.   September 1, 2003.
        D.   December 31, 2003.
        E.   May 18, 2003.

9.   The executor of an estate is filing an income tax return for the current period. Revenues
        of $36,000 have been earned. Which one of the following is a deduction allowed in
        calculating taxable income?

        A.   Funeral expense
        B.   Administrative expense
        C.   Accounting fees
        D.   Executor's fee for managing the estate's assets
        E.   Personal exemption

10. Which one of the following is designed for married couples and is known as *a bypass trust?*

   A. Credit shelter trust
   B. Charitable lead trust
   C. Charitable remainder trust
   D. Spendthrift trust
   E. Grantor retained annuity trust

Brief Essay Questions

1. Probate laws are usually designed to achieve what three goals?

2. What are the four types of legacies covered in the text?

Problems

1. The estate of Albert Johnstone reported the following:

Value of estate assets	$1,600,000
Conveyed to spouse	800,000
Conveyed to children	325,000
Conveyed to charities	300,000
Funeral expenses	10,000
Administrative expenses	15,000
Debts	150,000

Required:

Assuming that Albert made no taxable gifts during his lifetime, what is the taxable estate value?

2. An estate had the following income:

Rental income	$ 20,000
Interest income	10,000
Dividend income	12,000

The interest income was immediately conveyed to the appropriate beneficiary. 75% of the dividends were given to charity as per the decedent's will.

Required:

What is the taxable income of the estate?

Advanced Accounting – 7/e

Solutions to Multiple Choice Questions

1. **C**   When a cash gift is made without the source being designated, a general legacy is created.

2. **B**   the recipient of the principal of a trust is known at a specified point in time as the *remainderman.*

3. **E**   if the estate has insufficient available resources to satisfy all claims, the process of abatement is used. Each of the following categories is completely exhausted to pay all debts and expenses before money is taken from the next: (1) residual legacies, (2) general legacies, (3) demonstrative legacies, and (4) specific legacies and devises.

4. **A**   Investment expenses are normally charged against the principal of an estate.

5. **D**   Trusts normally pay income taxes unless all income has been distributed; in which case, the recipient of the income pays the tax. However, the trust is required to file annually.

6. **B**

7. **D**

8. **C**

9. **E**

10. **A**

Answers to Brief Essay Questions

1. Probate laws are usually designed to achieve the following three goals:

    A.   Gather and preserve all of the decedent's property.

    B.   Carry out an orderly and fair settlement of all debts.

    C.   Discover the decedent's intent for the remaining property held at death and then follow those wishes.

2. The four types of legacies are:

    A.   A specific legacy
    B.   A demonstrative legacy
    C.   A general legacy
    D.   A residual legacy

Solutions to Problems

1. Albert Johnson's taxable estate value:

Gross estate (fair market value)		$1,600,000
Funeral expenses	$10,000	
Administrative expenses	15,000	
Debts	150,000	
Charity bequests	300,000	
Marital deduction	800,000	(1,275,000)
Taxable estate		$ 325,000

2. The estate's taxable income:

Rental income	$20,000
Interest income	10,000
Dividend income	12,000
Total revenue	42,000
Personal exemption	(600)
Gift to charity ($12,000 x 75%)	(9,000)
Distributed to beneficiary	(10,000)
Taxable income	$22,400

Advanced Accounting – 7/e

Working Papers

Problem 1-11

Problem 1-12

Problem 1-13

Name _____

Journal Entries	Debit			Credit		

Problem 1-14

Journal Entries	Debit	Credit

Problem 1-15

Journal Entry to Defer Unrealized Gain:	Debit	Credit

a.

b.

c.

Working Papers

a.

b.

c.

d.

e.

f.

g.

h.

I.

a.

b.

c.

d.

e.

f.

g.

a.

b.

c.

d.

a.

b.

Name _____

Part a			
Part b			
Part c			

Journal Entries for Retroactive Adjustments:	Debit		Credit	

Name _____

Part a

Part b

Problem 1-23 (cont.)   **Name** _____

Part c

Problem 1-24

a.

a.

Part b

Problem 1-25

Journal Entries	Debit	Credit

Name _____

Journal Entries	Debit	Credit

Name _____

Computations								

Working Papers

a.

b.

Problem 1-28

Journal Entries	Debit			Credit		

Name _____

Journal Entries	Debit	Credit

Problem 2-18

Name _____

a.

b.

Problem 2-19

a.

b.

c.

d.

e.

f.

g.

h.

i.

j.

Problem 2-20

a.

b.

c.

d.

Problem 2-21

a.

b.

c.

d.

Name _____

a.

b.

c.

d.

e.

Problem 2-23

Journal Entries	Debit	Credit

Consolidated Balances			
Revenues			
Expenses			
Net Income			
Retained Earnings, 1/1/04			
Dividends			
Retained Earnings, 12/31/04			
Cash			
Receivables			
Inventory			
Buildings & Equipment			
Customer List			
Investment in Laredo			
Goodwill			
Total Assets			
Current Liabilities			
Long-term Liabilities			
Common Stock			
Additional Paid-in Capital			
Total Liabilities and Stockholders' Equity			

Problem 2-24

Consolidated Balances			
a. Inventory			
Land			
Buildings			
Goodwill			
Revenuew			
Additional Paid-in Capital			
Expenses			
Retained Earnings, 1/1/04			
b. Inventory			
and			
Buildings			
Goodwill			
Revenues			
Additional Paid-in Capital			
Expenses			
Retained Earnings, 1/1/04			

Problem 2-25

Name _____

Consolidated Balances						
Net Income						
Retained Earnings, 1/1						
Patented Technology						
Goodwill						
Liabiltiies						
Common Stock Additional Paid-in Capital						

Problem 2-26

Journal Entries	Debit			Credit		
a.						

Working Papers

Accounts	Debits		Credits		Consolidated Balances	
Cash						
Receivables						
Inventory						
Investment in Harriss						
Land						
Buildings						
Equipment						
Patent						
Goodwill						
Total Assets						
Accounts Payable						
Long-term Liabilities						
Common Stock						
Additional Paid-in Capital						
Retained Earnings						
Total Liabilities and Equity						

Name _____

Consolidated Balances				
Cash				
Receivables				
nventory				
Land				
Buildings				
Equipment				
Goodwill				
Total Assets				
Accounts Payable				
Long-term Liabilities				
Common Stock				
Additional Paid-in Capital				
Retained Earnings				
Total Liabilities and Equity				

Accounts	Debits		Credits		Consolidated Balances
Cash					
Receivables					
Inventory					
Land					
Buildings (net)					
Equipment (net)					
Investment in Grant					
Total Assets					
Accounts Payable					
Long-term Liabilities					
Common Stock					
Additional Paid-in Capital					
Retained Earnings, 1/1/04					
Total Liabilities and Equities					

Pratt Company and Subsidiary Spider, Inc.
Consolidated Balance Sheet
31-Dec-04

ASSETS			
Total Assets			
LIABILITIES			
Total Liabilities			
EQUITY			
Total Equity			
Total Liabilities and Equity			

POOLING QUESTIONS

Problem 2-35

Name _____

a.

b.

c.

Problem 2-36

a.

b.

Problem 2-36 (cont.)

Name _____

c.	Journal Entry				

d.	Journal Entry				

e.	Journal Entry				

f.

g.

h.

a.			
b.			
c.			
d.			

Problem 2-38

Consolidated Balances			
a.	Inventory		
	Land		
	Buildings		
	Goodwill		
	Revenues		
	Additional Paid-in Capital		
	Expenses		
	Retained Earnings, 1/1		
b.	Inventory		
	Land		
	Buildings		
	Goodwill		
	Revenues		
	Additional Paid-in Capital		
	Expenses		
	Retained Earnings, 1/1		

Consolidated Balances			
c. Inventory			
Land			
Buildings			
Goodwill			
Revenues			
Additional Paid-in Capital			
Expenses			
Retained Earnings, 1/1			

Problem 2-39

Consolidated Balances			
Revenues			
Expenses			
Net Income			
Retained Earnings, 1/1			
Dividends Paid			
Retained Earnings, 12/31			
Cash			
Receivables and Inventory			
Buildings			
Equipment			
Total Assets			
Liabilities			
Common Stock			
Additional Paid-in Capital			
Retained Earnings, 12/31 (from above)			
Total Liabilities and Stockholders' Equity			

a. Consolidated Balances			
Revenues			
Expenses			
Retained Earnings, 1/1			
Dividends Paid			
Retained Earnings, 12/31			
Cash			
Receivables			
Inventory			
Land			
Buildings			
Equipment			
Total Assets			
Accounts Payable			
Notes Payable			
Common Stock			
Additional Paid-in Capital			
Retained Earnings, 12/31 (from above)			
Total Liabilities and Stockholders' Equity			

Accounts		Debits	Credits	Consolidated Balances
Revenues				
Expenses				
Net Income				
Retained Earnings, 1/1				
Net Income				
Dividends Paid				
Retained Earnings, 12/31				
Cash				
Receivables				
Inventory				
Investment in Swathmore				
Land				
Buildings (net)				
Equipment (net)				
Total Assets				
Accounts Payable				
Notes Payable				
Common Stock				
Additional Paid-in Capital				
Retained Earnings 12/31				
Total Liabilities and Equities				

Accounts			Debits		Credits		Consolidated Balances
Revenues							
Expenses							
Net Income							
Retained Earnings, 1/1							
Net Income							
Dividends Paid							
Retained Earnings, 12/31							
Cash							
Receivables							
Inventory							
Investment in Atlanta							
Land							
Buildings (net)							
Equipment (net)							
Total Assets							
Accounts Payable							
Long-term Liabilities							
Common Stock							
Additional Paid-in Capital							
Retained Earnings 12/31							
Total Liabilities and Equities							

Accounts			Debits	Credits	Consolidated Balances
Revenues					
Expenses					
Net Income					
Retained Earnings, 1/1					
Net Income					
Dividends Paid					
Retained Earnings, 12/31					
Cash					
Receivables					
Inventory					
Investment in Atlanta					
Land					
Buildings (net)					
Equipment (net)					
Goodwill					
Total Assets					
Accounts Payable					
Long-term Liabilities					
Common Stock					
Additional Paid-in Capital					
Retained Earnings 12/31					
Total Liabilities and Equities					

a.	Consolidated Retained Earnings - Equity Method			
	Consolidated Retained Earnings - Partial Equity Method			
	Consolidated Retained Earnings - Cost Method			
b.	Investment in Rambis - Equity Method			
	Investment in Rambis - Partial Equity Method			
	Investment in Rambis - Cost Method			

Problem 3-12 (cont.)

Name _____

c.	Entry *C						
	Equity Method						
	Partial Equity Method						
	Cost Method						

Problem 3-13

Name _____

a.				
b.				
c.				

d.

Problem 3-14

Part A - Goodwill Impairment			
Part B - Goodwill Impairment			

Name _____

a. Goodwill Impairment Test - Step 1			
b. Goodwill Impairment Test - Step 2			
c.			

Working Papers

Problem 3-16

Name _____

a.

b.

c.

d.

Consolidation Journal Entries	Debit	Credit
ENTRIES FOR 12/31/04		

Consolidation Journal Entries	Debit	Credit
ENTRIES for 12/31/05		

Name _____

Consolidation Journal Entries	Debit	Credit
ENTRIES for 12/31/04		
ENTRIES for 12/31/05		

Problem 3-18 (Cont.)

Name _____

Consolidation Journal Entries	Debit	Credit

Problem 3-19

Name _____

Consolidation Journal Entries	Debit	Credit
ENTRIES for 12/31/04		

Consolidation Journal Entries	Debit	Credit
ENTRIES for 12/31/05		

Name _____

Consolidation Journal Entries	Debit	Credit
ENTRIES for 12/31/04		
ENTRIES for 12/31/05		

Consolidation Journal Entries	Debit	Credit

Problem 3-21

a. Equity Method		
Partial Equity Method		
Cost Method		

b.

c.

d. Equity Method

Partial Equity Method

Cost Method

Consolidation Journal Entries	Debit	Credit
e. Equity Method Entry		
Partial Equity Method		
Cost Method		
f.		
g.		

Name _____

a.

b.

c.

d.

a.	**Consolidated Balances**			
	Depreciation Expense			
	Dividends Paid			
	Revenues			
	Equipment			
	Buildings			
	Goodwill			
	Common Stock			

b.

c.

d.

e.   Cost Method R/E - 1/1/04

Partial Equity Method R/E - 1/1/04

Equity Method R/E - 1/1/04

a.

b.	**Consolidated Balances**			
	Revenues			
	Cost of Goods Sold			
	Depreciation Expense			
	Income of Little			
	Net Income			
	Retained Earnings, 1/1/04			
	Dividends Paid			
	Retained Earnings, 12/31/04			
	Cash			
	Receivables			
	Inventory			
	Investment in Little			
	Land			
	Buildings			
	Equipment			
	Goodwill			
	Total Assets			
	Liabilities			
	Common Stock			
	Retained Earnings, 12/31/04 (from above)			
	Total Liabilities and Equities			

Problem 3-24 c. WORKSHEET   Name _____

Accounts			Debits	Credits	Consolidated Balances
Revenues					
Cost of Goods Sold					
Depreciation Expense					
Income of Little					
Net Income					
Retained Earnings, 1/1/04					
Net Income					
Dividends					
Retained Earnings, 12/31/04					
Cash					
Receivables					
Inventory					
Investment in Little					
Land					
Buildings (net)					
Equipment (net)					
Goodwill					
Total Assets					
Liabilities					
Common Stock					
Retained earnings, 12/31/04					
Total Liabilities and equity					

Accounts		Debits	Credits	Consolidated Balances
Revenues				
Cost of Goods Sold				
Depreciation Expense				
Amortization Expense				
Dividend Income				
Net Income				
Retained Earnings, 1/1/04				
Net Income				
Dividends				
Retained Earnings, 12/31/04				
Cash				
Receivables				
Inventory				
Investment in Andrews Co.				
Land				
Buildings and Equipment				
Trademark				
Total Assets				
Liabilities				
Preferred Stock				
Common Stock				
Additional Paid-in Capital				
Retained Earnings, 12/31/04				
Total Liabilities and equity				

b.

c.

d.

Problem 3-26   Name _____

a.

b.	Consolidated Balances			
	Revenues			
	Cost of Goods Sold			
	Depreciation Expense			
	Equity in Income of Small			
	Net Income			
	Retained Earnings, 1/1/06			
	Dividends Paid			
	Retained Earnings, 12/31/06			
	Current Assets			
	Investment in Small			
	Land			
	Buildings Equipment			
	Goodwill			
	Total Assets			
	Liabilities			
	Common Stock			
	Retained Earnings, 12/31/06 (from above)			
	Total Liabilities and Equity			
c.	See Worksheet form on the next page			

d.		Debits		Credit	

Accounts	Debits	Credits	Consolidated Balances
Revenues			
Cost of Goods Sold			
Depreciation Expense			
Equity Income of Small			
Net Income			
Retained Earnings, 1/1/06			
Net Income			
Dividends			
Retained Earnings, 12/31/06			
Current Assets			
Investment in Small			
Land			
Buildings (net)			
Equipment (net)			
Goodwill			
Total Assets			
Liabilities			
Common Stock			
Retained Earnings, 12/31/04			
Total Liabilities and equity			

a.	Revenues			
	Cost of Goods Sold			
	Depreciation Expense			
	Amortization Expense			
	Buildings (net)			
	Equipment (net)			
	Customer List			
	Common Stock			
	Additional Paid-In Capital			

b.

c.	Debits		Credits	

c.	Debits			Credits		

Problem 3-28

CONSOLIDATED BALANCES			
Revenue			
Cost of Goods Sold			
Depreciation Expense			
Amortization Expense			
Investment Income			
Net Income			
Retained Earnings, 1/1/06			
Dividends Paid			
Retained Earnings, 12/31/06			
Current Assets			
Investment in Zeidner			
Land			
Building			
Equipment			
Goodwill			
Liabilities			
Common Stock			

Problem 3-29

Name _____

CONSOLIDATED BALANCES			
Accounts Receivable			
Buildings			
Cash			
Dividends Paid			
Equipment			
Expenses			
Inventory			
Investment in Juliet Company			
Land			
TOTAL OF DEBIT BALANCES			
Additional Paid-in Capital			
Common Stock			
Investment Income from Juliet Company			
Liabilities			
Retained Earnings, 1/1/03			
Revenues			
TOTAL OF CREDIT BALANCES			

Problem 3-30

a.	Debits		Credits	

Name _____

a. (cont.)	Debits			Credits		
b.						

Working Papers

a.

b.   See Worksheet on next page

c.

Accounts	Debits		Credits		Consolidated Balances
Revenues					
Cost of Goods Sold					
Depreciation Expense					
Amortization Expense					
Equity in Subsidiary Earnings					
Net Income					
Retained Earnings, 1/1/04					
Net Income					
Dividends					
Retained Earnings, 12/31/04					
Current Assets					
Investment in Storm Co.					
Land					
Buildings and Equipment					
Formula					
Total Assets					
Current Liabilities					
Long-term Liabilities					
Common Stock					
Additional Paid-in Capital					
Retained Earnings, 12/31/04					
Total Liabilities and equity					

a.

b.

c.

d.

e.				
f.				
g.				
h.				

a.	CONSOLIDATED BALANCES			
	Revenues			
	Expenses			
	Equity in Subsidiary Earnings			
	Net Income			
	Retained Earnings, 1/1/04			
	Dividends Paid			
	Retained Earnings, 12/31/04			
	Current Assets			
	Investment in Drexel			
	Buildings			
	Equipment			
	Total Assets			
	Liabilities			
	Common Stock			
	Additional Paid-in Capital			
	Total Liabilities and Equity			

Accounts			Debits		Credits		Consolidated Balances
Revenues							
Expenses							
Equity Income of Small							
Net Income							
Retained Earnings, 1/1/04							
Net Income							
Dividends							
Retained Earnings, 12/31/04							
Current Assets							
Investment in Drexel, inc.							
Buildings (net)							
Equipment (net)							
Total Assets							
Liabilities							
Common Stock							
Additional Paid-in Capital							
Retained Earnings, 12/31/04							
Total Liabilities and equity							

a.

b.   A worksheet for Part b is included on the next page.

c.

Accounts			Debits	Credits	Consolidated Balances
Revenues					
Cost of Goods Sold					
Depreciation Expense					
Subsidiary Income					
Net Income					
Retained Earnings, 1/1/04					
Net Income					
Dividends					
Retained Earnings, 12/31/04					
Cash					
Accounts Receivable					
Inventory					
Investment in Salsa					
Land					
Equipment (net)					
Total Assets					
Accounts Payable					
Long-term Debt					
Common Stock - Picante					
Common Stock - Salsa					
Retained Earnings, 12/31/04					
Total Liabilities and equity					

Problem 3-35

c.

d.

e.

Name _____

Accounts			Debits	Credits	Consolidated Balances
Revenues					
Expenses					
Equity in Lydia Earnings					
Impairment Loss					
Net Income					
Retained Earnings, 1/1/04					
Net Income					
Dividends					
Retained Earnings, 12/31/04					
Cash					
Receivables (net)					
Investment in Lydia, Co.					
Broadcast Licenses					
Movie Library					
Equipment (net)					
Goodwill					
Total Assets					
Current Liabilities					
Long-term Debt					
Common Stock					
Retained Earnings, 12/31/04					
Total Liabilities and equity					

Problem 4-20

Name _____

a.

b.

Problem 4-21

a. Revenues				
Expenses				
Noncontrolling Interest in Subsidiary's Net Income				
Net Income				
b. Revenues				
Expenses				
Noncontrolling Interest in Subsidiary's Net Income				
Preacquisition Income				
Net Income				

Working Papers

Problem 4-23

a.

b.

Problem 4-24

a.

b.

c.

Irwin/McGraw-Hill
Advanced Accounting, 7/e

a.

b.

c.

Working Papers

a.

b.

c.

d.

e.

a.

b.

c.

d.

e.

Problem 4-27 (cont.)

Name _____

f.

Problem 4-28

a.

	Debits	Credits

a. (continued)	Debits			Credits		
b.						
c.						
d.						

a.

b.

c.

d.   (1) Equity Method

(2) Partial Equity Method

(3) Cost Method

e.   (1) Equity Method

(2) Partial Equity Method

(3) Cost Method

f.

g.

h.

I.

Problem 4-30

Problem 4-31

a.

b.

c.

d.

e.

f.

g.

h.

Accounts			Debits	Credits	Noncontrolling Interest	Consolidated Balances

Name _____

Accounts			Debits	Credits	Noncontrolling Interest	Consolidated Balances

a.

Accounts			Debits	Credits	Noncontrolling Interest	Consolidated Balances

Accounts			Debits	Credits	Noncontrolling Interest	Consolidated Balances

a.

b. | CONSOLIDATED BALANCES | | | |
| --- | --- | --- | --- |
| Goodwill | | | |
| Equipment | | | |
| Common Stock | | | |
| Buildings Dividends Paid | | | |

a.	CONSOLIDATED BALANCES			
	Opearting Expenses			
	Noncontrolling Interest in Creedmoor's Net Income			
	Revenues			
	Retained Earnings, 1/1/05			
	Net Income			
	Dividends Paid			
	Land			
	Equipment			
	Liabilities			
	Common Stock			
	Retained Earnings, 12/31/05			
	Noncontrolling Interest in Creedmore			
b.		Debits		Credits

Accounts			Debits	Credits	Noncontrolling Interest	Consolidated Balances

Name _____

b.

Name _____

a.

b.

c.

d.

e.

f.

g.

h.

Accounts			Debits	Credits	Noncontrolling Interest	Consolidated Balances

a.

b.

c.

d.

e.

f.

Accounts			Debits	Credits	Noncontrolling Interest	Consolidated Balances

Accounts	Debits	Credits	Noncontrolling Interest	Consolidated Balances

Financial Statements

Accounts	Debits	Credits	Noncontrolling Interest	Consolidated Balances

Financial Statements

Problem 5-16

Name _____

Problem 5-17

a.

b.	Journal Entries	Debit		Credit	

Problem 5-18

a.

b.

c.

d.

e.

f.

g.

h.

	Debits	Credits

Problem 5-19

a.

	Debits	Credits
b.		

Problem 5-20

a.

b.

c.

a.

b. Income Statement

Problem 5-22

Name _____

a.

b.

	Debits			Credits		

Working Papers

Problem 5-23

Name _____

Journal Entries	Debit		Credit	

Problem 5-24

a.			
b.			
c.			
d.			

CONSOLIDATED BALANCES			
Sales			
Cost of Goods Sold			
Operating Expenses			
Investment Income			
Inventory			
Equipment (net)			
Buildings (net)			

Problem 5-26

a. Consolidation Entries	Debit		Credit	

Name _____

a.	(continued)	Debit				Credit			
b.	Computation of Noncontrolling Interest								

a.

b.

c.

d.

e.

f.

g.

h.				
I.				
j.				
k.				

I.	CONSOLIDATED BALANCES			
	Sales Revenue			
	Cost of Goods Sold			
	Expenses			
	Investment Income - Little			
	Noncontrolling Interest in Subsidiary's Net Income			
	Net Income			
	Retained Earnings, 1/1/04			
	Cash and Receivables			
	Inventory			
	Investment in Little			
	Land, Buildings, and Equipment			
	Patented Technology			
	Total Assets			
	Liabilities			
	Noncontrolling Interest in Little			
	Common Stock			
	Retained Earnings, 12/31/04			
	Total Liabilities and Stockholders' Equity			

Problem 5-28

CONSOLIDATED BALANCES			
Sales			
Cost of Goods Sold			
Operating Expenses			
Dividend Income			
Noncontrolling Interest in Consolidated Income			
Inventory			
Noncontrolling Interest in Subsidiary, 12/31/04			

CONSOLIDATED BALANCES			
Sales			
Cost of Goods Sold			
Operating Expenses			
Dividend Income			
Noncontrolling Interest in Consolidated Income			
Inventory			
Noncontrolling Interest in Subsidiary			

Accounts								Debits			Credits		Noncontrolling Interest		Consolidated Balances	

a.	Cost of Goods Sold				
b.	Operating Expenses				
c.	Net Income				
d.	Retained Earnings, 1/1/04				

e.	Inventory			
f.	Buildings (net)			
g.	Patents (net)			
h.	Common Stock			
I.	Noncontrolling Interest in Smith, 12/31/04			

a.

	Debits	Credits

b. CONSOLIDATION ENTRIES

CONSOLIDATION ENTRIES	Debits			Credits		

b.	CONSOLIDATION ENTRIES	Debits	Credits

Accounts				Debits			Credits		Noncontrolling Interest		Consolidated Balances

Consolidation Journal Entries	Debit			Credit		

Consolidation Journal Entries	Debit	Credit

Consolidation Journal Entries	Debit			Credit		

Working Papers

Consolidation Journal Entries	Debit		Credit	

Accounts					Debits	Credits	Noncontrolling Interest	Consolidated Balances

Name _____

Consolidation Journal Entries	Debit	Credit

Accounts					Debits	Credits	Noncontrolling Interest	Consolidated Balances

JOURNAL ENTRIES	Debit		Credit	
a.				
b.				
c.				

Problem 6-23

a.

b.

Problem 6-24

JOURNAL ENTRIES	Debit			Credit		
a.						
b.						
c.						

Name _____

CONSOLIDATED BALANCES			
Revenues and Interest Income			
Operating and Interest Expense			
Other Gains and Losses			
Extraordinary Loss on Retirement of Debt			
Net Income			

Problem 6-26

a.		Debits		Credits	
b.					

Problem 6-27

a.			
b.			
c.			

Problem 6-28

Name _____

Problem 6-29

Name _____

a.

b.

c.

Working Papers

a.

b.

c.

	Debits			Credits		

	Debits			Credits		

Name _____

Name _____

Working Papers

Problem 6-39

		Debit	Credit
a.			
b			
c.			

JOURNAL ENTRIES	Debit	Credit
a.		
b.		

Accounts					Debits	Credits	Consolidated Balances

Problem 6-42

Name _____

JOURNAL ENTRIES	Debit			Credit		
a.						

JOURNAL ENTRIES	Debit	Credit
a.		
b.		

c.	Debits	Credits

JOURNAL ENTRIES	Debit	Credit
a.		
b.		
c.		
d.		

	JOURNAL ENTRIES	Debit			Credit		
d.							

Accounts			Debits	Credits	Consolidated Balances

a.

b.

c.

d.

e.

f.

a.

b.

c.

d.

a.

b.

c.

a.

b.

Problem 7-20

CONSOLIDATED BALANCES			
Sales			
Cost of Goods Sold			
Expenses			
Dividend Income			
Noncontrolling Interests in Subsidiaries' Income			
Net Income			

Name _____

a.	CONSOLIDATED BALANCES			
	Sales			
	Cost of Goods Sold			
	Expenses			
	Dividend Income			
	Noncontrolling Interest in Wonderland's Income			
	Net Income			
b.	CONSOLIDATED BALANCES			
	Common Stock			
	Treasury Stock			

Problem 7-22

a.	CONSOLIDATED BALANCES			
	Sales			
	Cost of Goods Sold			
	Operating Expenses			
	Dividend Income			
	Noncontrolling Interst in Down's Income			
	Net Income			
b.				

a.

b.

c.

d.

e.

a.

b.

Working Papers

a.

b.

c.

d.

Problem 7-26

Name _____

a.					
b.					
c.					
d.					

Problem 7-27

Working Papers

Accounts			Debits		Credits		Noncontrolling Interest	Consolidated Balances

Accounts			Debits	Credits	Noncontrolling Interest	Consolidated Balances

JOURNAL ENTRIES	Debits			Credits		
a.						

Problem 7-29 (cont.)

Name _____

JOURNAL ENTRIES	Debits	Credits
b.		

Working Papers

JOURNAL ENTRIES	Debits			Credits		
c.						

Accounts									Debits		Credits		Noncontrolling Interest		Consolidated Balances	

b.

c.

	Debits			Credits		
d.						

Accounts			Debits	Credits	Noncontrolling Interest	Consolidated Balances

a.

b.

c.

d.

e.

f.

g.

h.

l.

j.

	Debits			Credits		

k.

Working Papers

JOURNAL ENTRIES	Debits			Credits		

JOURNAL ENTRIES	Debits	Credits

Name _____

Segments	Revenues from Outsiders			Intersegment Transfers			Operating Expenses			Profit			Loss		

Revenue Test

Segments	Revenues			Percent			Reportable? Yes/No

Profit or Loss Test

Segments	Revenues			Expenses			Profit (Loss)			Reportable? Yes/No

Asset Test

Segments	Assets			Percent			Reportable? Yes/No

a.

b.

c.

d.

Revenue Test

Segments	Revenues			Percent			Reportable? Yes/No

Profit or Loss Test

Segments	Revenues			Expenses			Profit (Loss)			Reportable? Yes/No

Asset Test

Segments	Assets			Percent			Reportable? Yes/No

Problem 8-36

Revenue Test (sales to unaffiliated parties)

Segments	Sales to Outsiders			Percent			Material? Yes/No

Long-lived Asset Test

Segments	Balance			Percent			Material? Yes/No

Name _____

a. Determination of Income Tax by Quarter - Estimated Annual Tax Rate 40%

Account	1st Quarter			2nd Quarter			3rd Quarter			4th Quarter		

b. Determination of Income by Quarter - Change in Estimated Annual Tax Rate

	1st Quarter			2nd Quarter			3rd Quarter			4th Quarter		

a. Determination of After-tax Effect of Change in Depreciation

	Straight Line Depr.			Accelerated Depr.			Difference			After-tax Difference		

	3-Months Ended June 30				6-Months Ended June 30			
	2000		2001		2000		2001	

b. restatement of 1st Quarter 2001 Income and Earnings per Share

	Debits	Credits
Journal Entries		

Problem 9-23

Problem 9-24

Problem 9-25

JOURNAL ENTRIES		Debit			Credit		

JOURNAL ENTRIES	Debit		Credit	

Problem 9-27

Working Papers

JOURNAL ENTRIES	Debit	Credit

a.

b.

c.

JOURNAL ENTRIES	Debit	Credit

JOURNAL ENTRIES	Debit			Credit		
b.						

JOURNAL ENTRIES	Debit			Credit		
a.	CASH FLOW HEDGE						

JOURNAL ENTRIES	Debit	Credit
b. FAIR VALUE HEDGE		

	JOURNAL ENTRIES	Debit			Credit		
a.	CASH FLOW HEDGE						

JOURNAL ENTRIES	Debit	Credit
b. FAIR VALUE HEDGE		

	JOURNAL ENTRIES	Debit			Credit		
a.	CASH FLOW HEDGE						

JOURNAL ENTRIES	Debit	Credit
b. FAIR VALUE HEDGE		

	JOURNAL ENTRIES	Debit			Credit		
a.	CASH FLOW HEDGE						

JOURNAL ENTRIES	Debit	Credit
b. FAIR VALUE HEDGE		

JOURNAL ENTRIES	Debit		Credit	

JOURNAL ENTRIES	Debit	Credit

JOURNAL ENTRIES	Debit			Credit		
a. FOREIGN CURRENCY RECEIVABLE						

JOURNAL ENTRIES	Debit			Credit		
b. FOREIGN CURRENCY FIRM SALES COMMITMENT						

Problem 9-38

Name _____

JOURNAL ENTRIES	Debit	Credit

JOURNAL ENTRIES	Debit	Credit
a.		
b.		
c.		

JOURNAL ENTRIES	Debit			Credit		
a.						

JOURNAL ENTRIES	Debit	Credit
b.		

JOURNAL ENTRIES	Debit			Credit		
a.						
b.						

JOURNAL ENTRIES	Debit	Credit
a.		
b.		

JOURNAL ENTRIES	Debit	Credit
c.		

JOURNAL ENTRIES	Debit	Credit
d.		

JOURNAL ENTRIES	Debit	Credit
e.		

a. Rent Expense
b. Dividends Paid
c. Equipment
d. Notes Payable
e. Sales
f. Depreciation Expense
g. Cash
h. Accumulated Depreciation
I. Common Stock

Problem 10-22

		Translation			Remeasurement		
	Accounts Payable						
	Accounts Receivable						
	Accumulated Depreciation						
	Advertising Expense						
	Amortization Expense						
	Buildings						
	Cash						
	Common Stock						
	Depreciation Expense						
	Dividends Paid						
	Notes Payable						
	Patents (net)						
	Salary Expense						
	Sales						

Account	Swiss Francs	Translation Rate	US $	Remeasurement Rate	US $

	Sfr	Rate	US $

a.

b.

	LCU		RATE		US$	

	LCU		RATE		US $	

	LCU		RATE		US $	

Problem 10-26

Name _____

		LCU			RATE			US$		

Problem 10-27

		LCU			RATE			US$		
a.										

b.	LCU		RATE		US$	

Problem 10-28

	LCU		RATE		US$	
a.						
b.						
c.						

Problem 10-29

Name _____

Account	(a) Translation			(b) Remeasurement		
Sales						
Inventory						
Equipment						
Rent Expense						
Dividends						
Notes Receivable						
Accumulated Depreciation - Equipment						
Salary Payable						
Depreciation Expense						

Problem 10-30

Name _____

		Kites			RATE			US$		
a.										

		Debit			Credit		
b.							

		KQ			RATE			US$		
a.	Cash									
	Accounts Receivable									
	Equipment									
	Accumulated Depreciation									
	Land									
	Accounts Payable									
	Notes Payable									
	Common Stock									
	Dividends Paid									
	Sales									
	Salary Expense									
	Depreciation Expense									
	Miscellaneous Expense									
b.	Cash									
	Accounts Receivable									
	Equipment									
	Accumulated Depreciation									
	Land									
	Accounts Payable									
	Notes Payable									
	Common Stock									
	Dividends Paid									
	Sales									
	Salary Expense									
	Depreciation Expense									
	Miscellaneous Expense									

Problem 10-32 Name ______________________________

		Goghs	RATE	US$

		Goghs	RATE	US $

		Goghs	RATE	US $

		KR			RATE			US$		
a.										
b.										

Name _____

a.		Francs			RATE			US$		

		(b) DM			RATE			(c) US $		

		(b) DM			RATE			(c) US $		

		(b) DM			RATE			(c) US $		

Problem 10-35

Name _____

Translation Worksheet										
Accounts		Pounds			RATE			US $		

Consolidation Worksheet

Accounts	Cayce (US $)		Simbel (US $)		Debits		Credits		Consolidated Balances	

JOURNAL ENTRIES	Debit		Credit	

PART I (a)

Accounts	KCS	RATE	US $

Problem 10-36 (cont.)

Name _____

PART I (b)				
Accounts	KCS	RATE	US $	

PART I (c)

Accounts	KCS			RATE			US $		

PART II

a.

b.

Problem 11-29

Name _____

Problem 11-30

Name _____

Name _____

Name _____

Working Papers

a.   **Blue Sky Laws**

b.   **S-1 Statement**

c.   **Letter of Deficiencies**

d.   **Public Company Accounting Oversight Board**

e.   **Prospectus**

Name _____

Problem 12-22

Problem 12-24

Form S-1

Form S-2

Form S-3

Form S-4

Form SB-1

Form SB-2

Form F-3

Problem 12-25

Problem 12-26

a.　　**Staff Accounting Bulletins**

b.　　**Wrap Around Filing**

c.　　**Incorporation by Reference**

d.　　**Division of Corporate Finance**

e.　　**Integrated Disclosure System**

f.　　**Management's Discussion and Analysis**

g.　　**Chief Accountant of the SEC**

Problem 13-23

Problem 13-24

Problem 13-25

Name _____

Problem 13-26

Problem 13-27   Name _____

a.

b.

Problem 13-28

Problem 13-29

Problem 13-31

Problem 13-32

		Debit			Credit		

a.

b.

c.

Name _____

JOURNAL ENTRIES	Debit			Credit		

JOURNAL ENTRIES	Debit			Credit		

Working Papers

a.

b.

Book Value				Available for Unsecured Creditors		

a.

b.

	JOURNAL ENTRIES	Debit			Credit		

c.

Accounts	Cash	Noncash Assets	Liabilities with Priority	Fully Secured Liabilities	Partially Secured Creditors	Unsecured Nonpriority Liabilities	Stockholders' Equity

JOURNAL ENTRIES	Debit			Credit		

Working Papers

a.

Book Value				Available for Unsecured Creditors		

b.

c.

d.

Book Value					Available for Unsecured Creditors		

Accounts	Cash	Noncash Assets	Liabilities with Priority	Fully Secured Liabilities	Partially Secured Creditors	Unsecured Nonpriority Liabilities	Stockholders' Equity

a.	Goodwill Method			
b.	Bonus Method			

Name _____

	JOURNAL ENTRIES	Debit			Credit		
a.							
b.							
c.							

Problem 14-17

a.	Capital Balances:			
	Nixon			
	Hoover			
	Polk			
	Grant			
b.	Capital Balances:			
	Nixon			
	Hoover			
	Polk			
	Grant			

Problem 14-18

Name _____

		Debit		Credit	
a.					

b.		Com		Pack		Hal		Total	

Problem 14-19

		Jones		King		Lane		Total	

ALLOCATION OF INCOME	Purkerson			Smith			Traynor			Total		

STATEMENT OF PARTNERS' CAPITAL												
	Purkerson			Smith			Traynor			Total		

INCOME ALLOCATION - 2001	Left	Center	Right	Total

STATEMENT OF PARTNERS' CAPITAL - December 31, 2001				
	Left	Center	Right	Total

INCOME ALLOCATION - 2002	Left	Center	Right	Total

STATEMENT OF PARTNERS' CAPITAL - December 31, 2002				
	Left	Center	Right	Total

INCOME ALLOCATION - 2003	Left	Center	Right	Total

STATEMENT OF PARTNERS' CAPITAL - December 31, 2003				
	Left	Center	Right	Total

Problem 14-22

Name _____

a.

Partner	Capital Balances After Withdrawal			
	Original Balance	Goodwill Allocation	Withdrawal	Final Balance
Lennon				
McCartney				
Harrison				
Starr				

b.

Problem 14-23

a.

b.

Journal Entries	Debit	Credit
c.		

Journal Entries	Debit			Credit		
c.						
d.						

a.

Individual Capital Balances Following E's Investment of $36,000, Goodwill

b.

	A	B	C	D	E
Balance					

Individual Capital Balances Following E's Investment of $42,000, Goodwill

c.

	A	B	C	D	E
Balance					

Individual Capital Balances Following E's Investment of $55,000, Bonus

d.

	A	B	C	D	E
Balance					

Individual Capital Balances Following C's Retirement

e.

	A	B	C	D
Balance				

ALLOCATION OF INCOME - 2004	Boswell		Johnson		Total	
Total Allocation						

STATEMENT OF PARTNERS' CAPITAL - December 31, 2004	Boswell		Johnson		Total	

WALPOLE INVESTMENT - January 1, 2005

ALLOCATION OF INCOME - 2005	Boswell		Johnson		Walpole		Total	
Total Allocation								

STATEMENT OF PARTNERS' CAPITAL - December 31, 2005	Boswell		Johnson		Walpole		Total	

POPE INVESTMENT - January 1, 2006										

ALLOCATION OF INCOME - 2006															
	Boswell			Johnson			Walpole			Pope			Total		

STATEMENT OF PARTNERS' CAPITAL - December 31, 2006															
	Boswell			Johnson			Walpole			Pope			Total		

ALLOCATION OF INCOME - 2004	Gray		Stone		Lawson		Total	
a.								

CAPITAL ACCOUNT BALANCES 12/31/04	Gray		Stone		Lawson		Total	

ALLOCATION OF INCOME - 2005		Gray		Stone		Lawson		Monet		Total	

CAPITAL ACCOUNT BALANCES 12/31/05		Gray		Stone		Lawson		Monet		Total	

		ALLOCATION OF INCOME - 2006								
		Gray		Stone		Lawson		Monet		Total

		CAPITAL ACCOUNT BALANCES 12/31/06								
		Gray		Stone		Lawson		Monet		Total

b.

		Gray		Stone		Lawson		Totals	

	JOURNAL ENTRIES	Debit			Credit		
a.							
b.							
c.							
d.							
e.							
f.							

JOURNAL ENTRIES	Debit		Credit	
a.				

JOURNAL ENTRIES	Debit			Credit		
a. (continued)						
b.						

JOURNAL ENTRIES	Debit	Credit
b. (continued)		

Problem 15-13

		Nixon		Cleveland		Pierce	

Problem 15-14

a.	Land is sold for $25,000	Brown		Fish		Stone	
b.	Land is sold for $15,000						
c.	Land is sold for $5,000						

Problem 15-15

Name _____

		ALLOCATION OF RASPUTIN'S CASH										
		Atkinson		Kaporale		Dennsmore		Rasputin	

Problem 15-16

		PRELIMINARY CASH DISTRIBUTION										
		Ace		Ball		Eaton		Lake	

Problem 15-17

		PRELIMINARY CASH DISTRIBUTION											
		Cash		Other Assets		Accounts Payable		Hardwick, Loan & Capital		Saunders, Capital		Ferris, Loan & Capital	

Problem 15-18

Problem 15-19

Partner	Share of Loss	New Balance		

Problem 15-21

a.

Partner	Share of Loss	New Balance		

b.

Partner	Share of Loss	New Balance		

c.

Partner	Share of Loss	New Balance

d.

	Adams	Baker	Carvil	Dobbs

Assumed Loss Schedules

Partner	Loss Allocation	Max. Loss that can be absorbed

d.

	Adams			Baker			Carvil			Dobbs		

	Assumed Loss Schedules		
Partner	**Loss Allocation**	**Max. Loss that can be absorbed**	

a.   Predistritution Plan

		Able		Moon		Yerkl	

b.

Problem 15-24

		Simpson			Hart			Bobb			Reidl		

Predistritution Plan

Problem 15-25

a.

b.

Problem 15-26

JOURNAL ENTRIES	Debit		Credit	
a.				
b.				
c.				
d.				

JOURNAL ENTRIES	Debit		Credit	
e.				
f.				
g.				
h.				
I				

Problem 15-27

Predistritution Plan								
		W		X		Y		Z

Problem 15-27 (cont.)

Predistritution Plan

Problem 15-28

		Van		Bakel		Cox		Total	
Van, Bakel, and Cox Partnership									
Safe Installment Payments to Partners									
January 31, 2004									

Van, Bakel, and Cox Partnership							
Safe Installment Payments fo Partners							
January 31, 2004							
	Van		Bakel		Cox		Total

Van, Bakel, and Cox Partnership							
Safe Installment Payments fo Partners							
February 28, 2004							
	Van		Bakel		Cox		Total

Van, Bakel, and Cox Partnership							
Safe Installment Payments fo Partners							
March 31, 2004							
	Van		Bakel		Cox		Total

Part A			Simon, Capital		Haynes, Loan and Capital		Jackson, Capital	

Part B			Hough, Loan & Capital		Luck, Loan & Capital		Cummings, Capital	

Part C			Hough, Loan & Capital		Luck, Loan & Capital		Cummings, Capital	

Part D			Hough, Loan & Capital		Luck, Loan & Capital		Cummings, Capital	

Accounts	Cash	Noncash Assets	Liabilities	Frick, Capital (60%)	Wilson, Capital (20%	Clarke, Capital (20%)

		Wingler, Capital			Norris, Capital			Rodgers, Loan & Capital			Guthrie, Capital		
Part A															
Predistribution Plan															
Supporting Schedules															

b. JOURNAL ENTRIES	Debit			Credit		

b. JOURNAL ENTRIES	Debit		Credit	

Capital Balances

		Wingler, Capital	Norris, Capital	Rodgers, Loan & Capital	Guthrie, Capital

Problem 16-29

Name _____

JOURNAL ENTRIES	Debit			Credit		
Beginning of Year - Recording of Budget						
End of Year - Removal of Budget						

Problem 16-30

JOURNAL ENTRIES	Debit			Credit		
Fund-Based Financial Statements - General Fund						
Government-Wide Financial Statements						

JOURNAL ENTRIES	Debit			Credit		
Government-Wide Financial Statements						
Fund-Based Financial Statement						
General Fund						
Capital Projects Fund						

JOURNAL ENTRIES	Debit	Credit
Fund-Based Financial Statements		
a.		
b.		
c.		
d.		
e.		
f.		
g.		
h.		

JOURNAL ENTRIES	Debit	Credit
Fund-Based Financial Statements		
l.		
j.		
Government-Wide Financial Statements		
a.		
b.		
c.		
d.		
e.		
f.		
g.		
h.		

Problem 16-32 (cont.)

Name _____

JOURNAL ENTRIES	Debit			Credit		
Government-Wide Financial Statements						
I.						
j.						

Problem 16-33

JOURNAL ENTRIES	Debit			Credit		
Fund-Based Financial Statements						
a.						
b.						
c.						
d.						
e.						

JOURNAL ENTRIES	Debit	Credit
Fund-Based Financial Statements		
f.		
g.		
h.		
Government-Wide Financial Statements		
a.		
b.		
c.		
d.		

JOURNAL ENTRIES	Debit			Credit		
Fund-Based Financial Statements						
e.						
f.						
g.						
h.						

Problem 16-34

Name _____

JOURNAL ENTRIES	Debit	Credit
Fund-Based Financial Statements		
a.		
b.		
c.		
d.		
e.		
f.		
g.		

Working Papers

Problem 16-34 (cont.)

Name _____

JOURNAL ENTRIES	Debit			Credit		
Government-Wide Financial Statements						
a.						
b.						
c.						
d.						
e.						
f.						
g.						

Name _____

a.

b.

c.

d.

e.

f.

g.

h.

I.

j.

a.

b.

c.

d.

	Debit	Credit

e.

f.		

g.		

h.	Debit	Credit

JOURNAL ENTRIES	Debit			Credit		
Fund-Based Financial Statements						
a.						
b.						
c.						
d.						
e.						
f.						
g.						

JOURNAL ENTRIES	Debit	Credit
Fund-Based Financial Statements		
h.		
I.		
Government-Wide Financial Statements		
a.		
b.		
c.		
d.		
e.		
f.		

JOURNAL ENTRIES	Debit	Credit
Government-Wide Financial Statements		
g.		
h.		
I.		

Problem 16-38

CITY OF JENNINGS		
GENERAL FUND		
Statement of Revenues, Expenditures, and Changes in Fund Balance		
(Condensed)		
Year Ending December 31, 2001		

CITY OF JENNINGS		
GENERAL FUND		
Balance Sheet (condensed)		
December 31, 2004		

JOURNAL ENTRIES	Debit			Credit		
a.						
b.						
c.						
d.						
e.						
f.						
g.						
h.						
l.						

City of Lost Angel		
GENERAL FUND		
Statement of Revenues, Expenditures, and Changes in Fund Balance		

JOURNAL ENTRIES	Debit			Credit		
a.						
b.						
c.						
d.						
e.						
f.						
g.						

Name _____

JOURNAL ENTRIES	Debit			Credit		
h.						
I.						

City of Lost Angel		
Government-Wide Financial Statements		
Statement of Net Assets		

Problem 16-42

a.

b.

c.

d.

e.

Problem 16-43

a.

b.

c.

d.

e.

a.

b.

c.

d.

Problem 16-45

a.

b.

c.

d.

e.

Problem 16-46

Name _____

a.

b.

Problem 16-47

Problem 16-48

Name _____

a.

b.

c.

Problem 16-49

a.

b.

a.

b.

Problem 16-51

a.

b.

Problem 16-52   **Name** _____

a.

b.

JOURNAL ENTRIES	Debit	Credit
Government-Wide Financial Statements		
a.		
b.		

JOURNAL ENTRIES	Debit			Credit		
a. *Government-Wide Financial Statements*						
b. *Fund-Based Financial Statements*						
c. *Fund-Based Financial Statements*						

JOURNAL ENTRIES	Debit	Credit
a. Government-Wide Financial Statements		
b. Fund-Based Financial Statements		
c. Fund-Based Financial Statements		
d. Fund-Based Financial Statements		

Problem 17-31

Name _____

JOURNAL ENTRIES	Debit			Credit		
a. Government-Wide Financial Statements						
b Fund-Based Financial Statements						

Problem 17-32

JOURNAL ENTRIES	Debit			Credit		
a. Government-Wide Financial Statements						
b Fund-Based Financial Statements						
c.						

Problem 17-33

Name _____

JOURNAL ENTRIES	Debit			Credit		
a. *Government-Wide Financial Statements*						
b.						
c.						

Problem 17-34

JOURNAL ENTRIES	Debit			Credit		
a. *Government-Wide Financial Statements*						
b. *Fund-Based Financial Statements*						

Problem 17-35

Name _____

JOURNAL ENTRIES	Debit			Credit		
Government-Wide Financial Statements						

Problem 17-36

Name _____

a.

b.

c.

d.

e.

f.

g.

h.

JOURNAL ENTRIES	Debit	Credit
Enterprise Fund		

JOURNAL ENTRIES	Debit			Credit		
Enterprise Fund						

WILLIAMSON						
STATEMENT OF ACTIVITIES						
For Year Ended December 31, 2004						
Functions/Programs	Expenses	Charges for Services	Operating Grants and Contributions	Capital Grants and Contributions	Governmental Activities	Business-Type Activities	Total

WILLIAMSON			
STATEMENT OF NET ASSETS			
December 31, 2004			
Primary Government			

WILLIAMSON			
STATEMENT OF REVENUES, EXPENDITURES, AND CHANGES IN FUND BALANCES			
Government Funds			
For Year Ended December 31, 2004			

WILLIAMSON			
Balance Sheet			
Government Funds			
December 31, 2004			

			CITY OF BERNARD			
			STATEMENT OF ACTIVITIES			
			For Year Ended December 31, 2004			
Functions/Programs	Expenses	Charges for Services	Grants and Contributions	Governmental Activities	Business-Type Activities	Total

BERNARD			
STATEMENT OF NET ASSETS			
December 31, 2004			
Primary Government			

BERNARD			
STATEMENT OF REVENUES, EXPENDITURES, AND CHANGES IN FUND BALANCES			
Government Funds			
For Year Ended December 31, 2004			

BERNARD			
Balance Sheet			
Government Funds			
December 31, 2004			

Working Papers

JOURNAL ENTRIES	Debit			Credit		
a.						
b.						
c .						
d.						
e.						
f.						
g.						
h.						

JOURNAL ENTRIES	Debit	Credit
h. (cont)		
l.		
j.		
k.		
l.		
m.		
n.		

JOURNAL ENTRIES	Debit	Credit
o.		
p.		
q.		
r.		
s.		
t.		
u.		

JOURNAL ENTRIES	Debit			Credit		
u. (cont)						

Working Papers

		City of Pfeiffer					
		STATEMENT OF ACTIVITIES					
		Government-Wide Financial Statements					
		For Year Ended December 31, 2004					
Functions/Programs	Expenses	Charges for Services	Grants and Contributions		Governmental Activities	Business-Type Activities	Total

City of Pfeiffer			
STATEMENT OF NET ASSETS			
Government-Wide Financial Statements			
December 31, 2004			

JOURNAL ENTRIES	Debit	Credit
a.		
b.		
c.		
d.		
e.		
f.		
g.		

JOURNAL ENTRIES	Debit	Credit
h.		
l.		
j.		
k.		
l.		
m.		

JOURNAL ENTRIES	Debit	Credit
n.		
o.		
p.		
q.		
r.		
s.		
t.		

JOURNAL ENTRIES	Debit	Credit
u.		

City of Pfeiffer				
STATEMENT OF REVENUES, EXPENDITURES, AND CHANGES IN FUND BALANCES				
Fund-Based Financial Statements - Governmental Funds				
For Year Ended December 31, 2004				

City of Pfeiffer				
Balance Sheet				
Fund-Based Financial Statements - Governmental Funds				
December 31, 2004				

City of Pfeiffer	
STATEMENT OF REVENUES, EXPENDITURES, AND CHANGES IN FUND BALANCES	
Fund-Based Financial Statements - Proprietary Funds	
December 31, 2004	

City of Pfeiffer	
STATEMENT OF NET ASSETS	
Fund-Based Financial Statements - Proprietary Funds	
December 31, 2004	

a.

b.

c.

d.

e.

f.

g.

h.

Problem 17-43

a.

b.

c.

Problem 17-44

a.

b.

Working Papers

Problem 17-45

Name _____

Problem 17-46

a.

b.

Problem 17-44

a.

b.

c.

Problem 17-48

Name _____

a.

b.

Problem 17-49

a.

b.

c.

d.

e.

f.

g.

h.

Problem 17-50

Name _____

a.

b.

c.

d.

e.

f.

Problem 17-51

a.

b.

c.

d.

Name _____

a.

b.

c.

d.

e.

f.

Problem 17-53

a.

b.

c.

d.

Working Papers

Problem 18-29

Name _____

Problem 18-30

a.

b.

c.

Problem 18-32

a. Statement of Activities									
	Unrestricted Net Assets			Temporarily Restricted Net Assets			Permanently Restricted Net Assets		

b. Statement of Financial Position										

Problem 18-34

JOURNAL ENTRIES	Debit			Credit		

JOURNAL ENTRIES	Debit		Credit	

	Unrestricted Net Assets		Temporarily Restricted Net Assets		Permanently Restricted Net Assets	

JOURNAL ENTRIES	Debit	Credit

University of Danville Statement of Activities	Unrestricted Net Assets			Temporarily Restricted Net Assets			Permanently Restricted Net Assets		

a.

b.

c.

d.

e.

f.

g.

a.

Community Association for Handicapped Children								
Statement of Activity								
Year Ended June 30, 2004								
	Unrestricted Net Assets			Temporarily Restricted Net Assets			Permanently Restricted Net Assets		

b.

Community Association for Handicapped Children									
Statement of Financial Position									
June 30, 2004									

JOURNAL ENTRIES	Debit	Credit

ENDING BALANCES	Unrestricted			Temporarily Restricted			Permanently Restricted		

Problem 18-39

JOURNAL ENTRIES	Debit			Credit		

JOURNAL ENTRIES	Debit	Credit

Watson Organization								
Statement of Activities								
	Unrestricted Net Assets			Temporarily Restricted Net Assets			Permanently Restricted Net Assets		

Watson Organization							
Statement of Financial Position							

Problem 18-40

a.

b.

Problem 18-41

Name _____

a.

b.

c.

Problem 18-42

a.

b.

c.

Problem 18-43

Problem 18-44

a.

b.

c.

Problem 18-45

a.

b.

Will

Estate

Intestate

Probate Laws

Trust

Inter vivos trust

Charitable Remainder Trust

Remainderman

Executor

Homestead Allowance

Problem 19-31 Name _____

Problem 19-32 Name _____

Problem 19-33

Name _____

a.

b.

Problem 19-34

Problem 19-35

a.

b.

Problem 19-36

Name _____

Problem 19-37

a. JOURNAL ENTRIES	Debit			Credit		

Working Papers

a. JOURNAL ENTRIES	Debit	Credit

b.

Estate of Wilbur Stone						
Charge and Discharge Statement						
As to Principal						
As to Income						

Problem 19-38

Name _____

Estate of James Cooper							
Charge and Discharge Statement							
As to Principal							

As to Income							

JOURNAL ENTRIES	Debit	Credit

a. JOURNAL ENTRIES	Debit			Credit		

a. JOURNAL ENTRIES	Debit			Credit		

b.

Estate of Lawrence Pope
Charge and Discharge Statement

JOURNAL ENTRIES	Debit	Credit

JOURNAL ENTRIES	Debit		Credit